MAKING ROMAN PLACES, PAST AND PRESENT

JOURNAL OF ROMAN ARCHAEOLOGY®

JRA® SUPPLEMENTARY SERIES NUMBER 89

General Editors: J. H. Humphrey and L. M. Anderson
Layout: D. L. Davis and C. Corey

ISBN 1-887829-89-X
ISBN-13: 978-1-887829-89-2   ISSN 1063-4304 (for the supplementary series)
Copyright © 2012 Journal of Roman Archaeology, L.L.C.   Printed by Thomson-Shore, Dexter, Michigan
JRA® and Journal of Roman Archaeology® are registered trademarks of Journal of Roman Archaeology, L.L.C.

This and other supplements to the *Journal of Roman Archaeology* may be ordered from:
JRA, 95 Peleg Road, Portsmouth, RI 02871, U.S.A.
Telephone (+USA) 401 683 1955   telefax (+USA) 401 683 1975   e-mail: jra@JournalofRomanArch.com
Web site: JournalofRomanArch.com

Reprints of all *JRA* works available at nominal cost by sending a message to jra@JournalofRomanArch.com
Permission to copy may be obtained only direct from *JRA*, by e-mail, letter, fax or phone.
Kindly note that the Copyright Clearance Center (USA), the Copyright Licensing Agency (UK), and other national Reproduction Rights Organizations are not permitted to authorize copying or to collect fees for doing so.

MAKING ROMAN PLACES, PAST AND PRESENT

Papers presented at the first Critical Roman Archaeology Conference
held at Stanford University in March, 2008

edited by
Darian Marie Totten and Kathryn Lafrenz Samuels

with contributions by

J. A. Baird, D. Booms, R. Collins, C. Feldman Weiss,
J. M. Gordon, R. Hingley, K. Lafrenz Samuels, C. Paludan-Müller,
B. M. Sekedat, D. M. Totten, & P. van Dommelen

PORTSMOUTH, RHODE ISLAND
2012

ADDRESSES OF CONTRIBUTORS

J. A. Baird — Department of History, Classics & Archaeology, Birkbeck College, University of London, 27 Russell Square WC1B 5DQ, England
j.baird@bbk.ac.uk

Dirk Booms — Institute of Archaeology, University of Oxford, 36 Beaumont Street, OX1 2PG, England
dirk.booms@arch.ox.ac.uk

Robert Collins — Great North Museum, Newcastle University, Barras Bridge, Newcastle upon Tyne NE2 4PT, England
robert.collins@ncl.ac.uk

Cecelia Feldman Weiss — Department of Classics, 524 Herter Hall, University of Massachusetts Amherst, Amherst, MA 01003
cfweiss@classics.umass.edu

Jody Michael Gordon — Department of Classics, University of Cincinnati, P.O. Box 210226, P.O. Box 210226, Cincinnati, OH 45221
jodymichaelgordon@gmail.com

Richard Hingley — Department of Archaeology, Durham University, South Road, Durham, DH1 3LE, England
richard.hingley@durham.ac.uk

Kathryn Lafrenz Samuels — North Dakota State University, Dept 2350, PO Box 6050, Fargo, ND 58108-6050
kathryn.lafrenz.samuels@ndsu.edu

David Mattingly — School of Archaeology and Ancient History, University of Leicester, University Road, Leicester, LE1 7RH, England
djm7@le.ac.uk

Carsten Paludan-Müller — General Director NIKU, The Norwegian Institute for Cultural Heritage Research, PO Box 736 Sentrum, NO-0105 Oslo, Norway
carsten.paludan-muller@niku.no

Bradley M. Sekedat — Joukowsky Institute for Archaeology and the Ancient World, Brown University, Box 1837 / 60 George St., Providence, RI 02912
bradley_sekedat@brown.edu

Darian Marie Totten — Davidson College, Box 7051, Davidson, NC 28035
darianmariearch@gmail.com

Peter von Dommelen — Department of Archaeology, University of Glasgow, Glasgow, G12 8QQ, Scotland
peter.vandommelen@glasgow.ac.uk

TABLE OF CONTENTS

Preface *David Mattingly*	7
1. Roman place-making: from archaeological interpretation to contemporary heritage contexts *Kathryn Lafrenz Samuels and Darian Marie Totten*	11

PLACE-MAKING IN THE ROMAN PAST

2. Constructing Dura-Europos, ancient and modern *J. A. Baird*	34
3. Bodies in motion: civic ritual and place-making in Roman Ephesus *Cecelia Feldman Weiss*	50
4. Social spaces at the end of the Empire: the *limitanei* of Hadrian's Wall *Rob Collins*	65
5. Carved in stone: long-term modification of the landscape as place-making practice at Fasıllar (Turkey) *Bradley M. Sekedat*	81
6. Problematising privacy at the imperial villas *Dirk Booms*	91
7. Commentary: Roman places in the making *Peter van Dommelen*	103

PLACE-MAKING THROUGH ROMAN HERITAGE

8. Making boundaries in modern Cyprus: Roman archaeology as 'touristic archaeology' in politically fractured landscapes *Jody Michael Gordon*	111
9. Tarquinia and Cerveteri, the best of Etruria: Etruscan heritage and place-making in contemporary Italy *Darian Marie Totten*	131
10. The imperial mirror: Rome as reference for empire *Carsten Paludan-Müller*	145
11. Roman archaeology and the making of heritage citizens in Tunisia *Kathryn Lafrenz Samuels*	159
12. Commentary: Inheriting Roman places *Richard Hingley*	171

Preface
David Mattingly

The meeting of the Critical Roman Archaeology Conference (CRAC) held at Stanford University in March 2008 was a welcome (and overdue) development. The organisers of the conference and editors of this volume are to be congratulated for their imaginative vision and hard work in bringing this to fruition. However, it is important that this is seen as simply the first step in a larger project. Classical Archaeology in the United States has many outstanding strengths, but engagement with current theoretical debates in archaeology and the social sciences is one not generally associated with it. This postgraduate-organised event represented a pioneering attempt to bridge that gap and to encourage more theoretical approaches to the study of Roman archaeology. The event was to some extent following in the footsteps of the UK-based Theoretical Roman Archaeology Conference (TRAC), now in its 22nd year, which has held annual conferences since 1991 and has mostly succeeded in publishing the proceedings. While initially shunned by most established academics and accused by some of academic faddism, there can now be no doubt about its impact on the subject as a whole or its largely beneficial effects — especially in re-invigorating debate, in helping to change research agendas, and in establishing new paradigms. Those of us who regularly attend both TRAC and its 'grown-up cousin' RAC (the Roman Archaeology Conference) have noted an increasing convergence in themes and audience for both events, reflecting how the TRAC agenda has become mainstream.

There are a number of reasons why it is important that US-based classical archaeologists should become more theoretically informed. Having taught Roman archaeology in both the US and the UK systems (at Michigan, Oxford and Leicester), I am well aware of the strengths and weaknesses of both and of the historical and structural circumstances that have influenced the rather different pattern of development on each side of the Atlantic. Roman archaeology is generally taught out of Classics departments in the US but within broad-based archaeology departments in the UK, which means that British academics and students are more immediately exposed to broader theoretical debates within archaeology. Nonetheless, UK-based Roman archaeology in the late 20th c. was still seen by many as somewhat out of step with the increasingly theory-driven archaeological discipline, remaining conservative and intellectually stale. That is now changed, in part due to TRAC. There has been considerable debate in the UK in the last 20 years about the future direction of Roman archaeology, stimulated by the 'pressure from below' that TRAC exemplifies. Some of this has been soul-searching and rather alarmist — based on some well-known centres of Roman studies encountering temporary crises because of falling postgraduate numbers or staff retirements not being followed with new hires. Yet, when one looks closely at the national picture, Roman archaeology in British universities seems as strong as it has ever been, and, measured according to a variety of yardsticks, on an upward trajectory. Whereas the 1980s were a period of limited development and non-replacement of retiring staff, the 1990s and 2000s have seen an expansion of the UK University system and an overall increase in the archaeological student body. The total number of staff in university posts teaching Roman archaeology has grown consistently across this period and the research interests of the group as a whole have also shifted. While study of Britain in the Roman empire remains a uniquely British academic fascination, it is by no means as dominant as it was, say, 20 years ago. Most university academics also work on some other area of the empire; some do so exclusively. Postgraduate numbers have also boomed — and here one can point to the 'TRAC effect' as highly significant in creating a student perception that Roman archaeology is a 'happening area' of the discipline, where old certainties can be challenged and there is an intellectual energy for them to feed off. Higher postgraduate recruitment in Roman archaeology to some degree has been at the expense of some other periods of archaeology that once attracted the best and brightest students in archaeology.

For the most part, the traditional strengths of Roman archaeology (e.g., art, architecture, and the Roman army) continue to be represented in the research expertise of university staff, but overall there has been a significant broadening of geographical, thematic and practical areas of research (e.g., much more emphasis on landscape archaeology, economic themes, material culture and identity). Moreover, the recruitment of researchers from other academic traditions has enriched the UK's scholarly community and increased its diversity (I can think of New Zealand, German, Dutch, Italian, Romanian, American, and Greek academics currently in post). However, this has not been at the expense of the TRAC generation, who have increasingly been making the transition from 'sceptical postgraduates' to established academics. For instance, 11 of the editors (to say nothing of the much larger number of authors) of the TRAC volumes published to date hold university posts, and many others are working in UK professional archaeology. Although the initial stages of the 'TRAC revolution' (as we might term it) were quite slow, the academic landscape of Roman archaeology has by now been largely transformed and revitalised.

S. Dyson's *Pursuit of ancient pasts* (2006) had some harsh things to say about the continuing relevance and contribution of US-based Roman archaeologists to the wider international discipline. It is not simply the demise of the 'big dig' that is to blame for a diminished impact of American scholarship within Europe. The question can be asked to what extent Roman archaeology in the US is agenda-setting and eye-catching. There are exceptions, but given the total numbers of practitioners and the excellent postgraduate training they receive, it is fair to say that the US system 'punches below its weight'. A degree of intellectual re-invigoration can only help. For this reason alone, the intellectual arguments in favour of Critical Roman Archaeology far outweigh the demerits. No doubt some will decry the introduction of 'theory-speak' and jargon as the harbingers of a wider decline in academic standards, and I would agree that theoretical debate is at its best when it is carried out in clear and comprehensible language; but it is equally apparent to me that linguistic purity does not guarantee critical integrity. Indeed, much established scholarship in the US remains remarkably unaware of the potential implications of post-colonial theory on discourse for the underlying principles of the discipline of classical studies. Understanding these debates is crucial for the future health of our subject.

There is an argument that the small classics department in a liberal arts college in the American Midwest cannot afford the luxury of employing a theoretically-informed Romanist, when there are so many of the 'old faithful' courses (Roman art and architecture, the Roman city, sport and daily life in Rome, and so forth) to be covered. What was very clear at the conference from which this publication derives is that the best of the CRAC generation will be able to offer both core strengths and new approaches. Courses on the Roman economy, Roman identities, Roman imperialism and its reception, and so on, can prove to be excellent student recruiters.

Others will provide commentary on the papers included in this volume. I shall finish by reflecting that the themes evoked for the conference and book are original and insightful. Place-making in the Roman world has important implications for our understanding of past behaviours and our engagement with modern perceptions of Rome. As I commented at the conference, more than half of the area of the Roman empire is occupied today by nation states that endured periods of modern colonial rule, and an even larger area has experienced some period of autocratic government in the past century. Small wonder then that the progressive and positivistic 'Western Civilisation' perception of the Roman empire is not the best fit for many who still live under its shadow. There are profound issues here relating to ethics and responsibilities that all classicists ought to be more aware of.

As CRAC develops in the future, we need to engage with a thorough deconstruction of concepts and terms — to help us better define things and to understand the underlying paradigms of our subject. Linked to this is the necessity for more profound historiographical study, to disentangle past biases and changing approaches. We can also gain insights from an analysis of the reception and re-invention of the Roman empire in contemporary society and the recent past. Classical studies could also benefit from a broadening of perspective, exploring multivocal and multifocal approaches, rather than simply the 'Western Civilisation' paradigm. This could be facilitated by extending our field of study away from great sites and élite material culture, to encompass a greater socio-economic range.

My personal vision of Roman research agendas includes the following themes: identity and material culture; power and its operation; imperial exploitation (of land, people and resources) and its effects; historiographical study (deconstructing historical discourse); bottom-up social histories; rural cultures and taskscapes; urban cultures and townscapes; economies of growth and exceptional characteristics; migration and diaspora; and regionality and landscape biography. All of these engage with established data sources, but encourage new lines of enquiry and analysis. Removed from my agenda is all reference to 'Romanisation', a tired concept that evokes all that is worst about the sterility of much recent debate.

In Britain and much of Europe the debate is moving on; this volume suggests that the US may still make a valuable theoretical contribution to the reshaping of agendas in Roman Archaeology in the 21st c.

Roman place-making:
from archaeological interpretation
to contemporary heritage contexts

Kathryn Lafrenz Samuels and Darian Marie Totten

Archaeology is a discipline intimately connected to the study of space. Each site, each survey scatter, each monument occupies a specific geographic location that allows it to be interpreted within spatial contexts of varying scales and dimensions. Such remains show that humans once lived in that particular place and context, working, worshipping, eating, sleeping, creating, discarding, and so on. The task of the archaeologist is to study these remains to decipher how human activity unfolded in space and how, at the same time, human practice made these places what they were. As an intellectual pursuit, Roman archaeology yields great insights into how Romans used, inhabited and related to the places in which they lived.[1]

Roman society left behind impressive and geographically extensive remains, attesting to its ability to construct and manipulate space on a scale and with an intensity never experienced before. The remains of this built environment are visible today in the multitude of buildings, roads, bridges and aqueducts scattered across the urban and rural landscapes of Europe, North Africa and Western Asia. Roman places live on, in other words. Their material substance shapes, and is shaped by, the experiences and practices of our contemporary society, all of which work to turn Roman spaces into places with modern significance. The material remains of the Roman past do not remain simply in the past, but continue to make places in the present.

On March 1-2, 2008, the Stanford Archaeology Center hosted the Critical Roman Archaeology Conference (CRAC).[2] Taking its cue from the success of the United Kingdom-based Theoretical Roman Archaeology Conference (TRAC), this two-day meeting was the first to be held in the United States aimed at advancing critical approaches to Roman archaeology. We devised the conference as a forum to discuss how Roman archaeology might contribute more productively to the wider discipline of archaeology by employing its rich data set and intellectual resources to propel the field to greater engagement with theory-making and paradigm development in the study of the past.

The "Roman world" offers a diverse range of archaeological evidence, as well as a myriad of written records that offer perspectives and commentaries on that world. The resulting complexity provides us with unique access to the intricacies of the Roman empire, but it also introduces difficulties in approaching, demonstrating, and claiming knowledge about

---

1   Throughout this chapter we understand 'Roman' as shorthand for the material remains of the Roman empire; it is not taken to signify an identification of 'Roman' made by individuals or groups in the past, nor does it assume an homogeneous totality, given the diversity of social actors and experiences involved in the creation of the material world we interpret as 'Roman'. Moreover, when we do refer to 'Romans' as a social group or culture, this diversity is understood.
2   The conference was organized by the two editors and authors of this chapter together with Corisander Fenwick, and was made possible by funding from the Stanford Archaeology Center, Department of Classics, Department of Anthropology, and the Dean of Humanities and Sciences.

the past. Explicit theorizing helps us make sense of this complexity by offering frameworks in which to order, organize and hypothesize about evidence from everyday life. From our discussions at the conference, it became clear that the ways in which places are made, the practices that fashion specific places — which here we call 'place-making' — provided a productive avenue for theorizing and integrating a broad array of research agendas within Roman archaeology and contributing to the discipline of archaeology more broadly.[3]

We have chosen to focus on 'place' and acts of 'place-making' in order to move debates beyond the sometimes abstract and dehumanizing perspectives of previous studies on space and the spatial world. We consider space to be a very specific and highly specialized mode or form of place. For example, space is fashioned by scientists, architects, geographers, cartographers as well as by archaeologists; it is a particularly western and rationalistic form of ordering the world, with its own Euclidean and Cartesian heritage.[4] Y.-F. Tuan writes that space is "more abstract" than place.[5] Although space and place are distinct in this sense, they must both be understood as socially constructed. Place-making highlights the human crafting of the worlds we inhabit, to which we ascribe meaning through experience. We therefore emphasize a practice-based and experiential understanding of place. This means untangling how people related to the places they inhabited, and how their activities informed the relationships between people and place.[6] In this way, place becomes an embodied routine, defined by the movements of the body, with place even inscribed onto or extending the body itself.[7]

Place-making foregrounds human practice as both experiential and habitual. Our aim is to turn attention to the human practices that actively 'make' place, so that all places are understood as the construction and product of individuals, families, social groups and whole societies. These places in turn shape practices and social relations, so that places are never completely 'made' but are constantly in a state of re-working and re-visioning. This perspective insists that we acknowledge the dynamism of places, which cannot be achieved without an investigation of the links between place and time. Indeed, much of the scholarship on space, place, landscape and social geography recognizes that understanding temporal relationships is integral to understanding spatial ones. Our approach here is an interrogation of how place-making is interwoven with time and our perception of time's progression.[8]

For this reason, one aim of the conference, and of this volume, is to connect archaeological knowledge of the past with discussions of the present-day inheritance from the Roman empire, thereby taking these spatial and temporal links seriously. We are interested in

---

3   In addition to this introductory chapter, this volume brings together 9 papers from the conference, along with additional invited papers and commentaries, all of which speak to the subject of Roman place-making.
4   In this way we could draw a similar parallel to the histories fashioned by archaeologists, as very specific, scientific, western, and rational forms of 'heritage-making', in a world with a great diversity of ways to engage with the past.
5   Tuan 1977, 6.
6   See Bourdieu 1979; De Certeau 1984; Gupta and Ferguson 1997; Gray 1999; and Crang 2000.
7   Tuan 1977; Bourdieu 1979; Lefebvre 1991; Butler 1993; and Casey 2001.
8   For example, time may be registered at different scales, and need not advance in a linear manner. The cyclical, often repetitive, nature of everyday life and habitual practice profoundly informs the experience of space and the construction of places as socially meaningful.

how Roman material is called upon to do particular kinds of work in modern society, and how Roman archaeological practice influences and affects this Roman heritage. 'Heritage', as we define it, understands that the study of the past is never simply about the past, but rather about the relationships formed between the past and present. Place-making offers us an effective lens for focusing theoretical discussion in Roman archaeology on the kind of tacking back and forth between past and present that we advocate here. We aim to inject some of the wider debates on heritage into theoretical approaches to the Roman world, and we consider place-making to be a particularly suitable vehicle for this endeavor. As a result, this volume has been organized in two parts: the first addresses place-making in the Roman past, while the second explores place-making in the present, through the heritage of the Roman world.

Place-making in the Roman past was fashioned across intersecting scales of experience and human practices. Whether highly localized within a single urban *domus* or at the scale of empire, place-making requires us to acknowledge that places generate meanings that extend beyond immediate spatial boundaries. Just as the relationships between town and country, movement along Roman roads, or fluctuations of a frontier zone can each be understood at the regional or empire-wide level, they still comprised the day-to-day, local reality of some group or individual. Each investigation into Roman place-making is fundamentally concerned with how Romans perceived their world and how their daily political, religious, social and economic activities *all* contributed to how places were fashioned and made significant for human actors. In each act of place-making there was a constant negotiation of behaviors, beliefs and values that influenced the manner in which places were made, sustained and transformed over time. For this reason, place-making should be studied as a highly contextualized process, but it can also be employed to speak to the wider realities of life in the city, province or empire.

Places are inhabited

A fitting beginning for our discussion is the Roman house, since domestic space is an intimate site, even the foundation, of place-making in any society. It is where the individual first experiences built and enclosed space, how it is used, and how to decipher its meaning. This is also the first space in which familial relationships are forged among members of the household, underscoring the importance social relationships can have for place-making practices.[9] Within an often discrete and delimited domestic place are enacted a complex web of connections, interactions, activities, perceptions and movements that would all have served to create a particular human experience of place for family members and visitors. How, then, do we interpret the architectural and material remains of houses to understand lived experience in the Roman past?

At the outset we must acknowledge that the study of place is a window into social interaction. For example, domestic places were central to the Roman *familia*, and an important site of self-representation for the *pater familias*. Any discussion of the domestic realm must

---

9 Y.-F. Tuan (1977, chapt. 4) discusses how infants, toddlers and children come to notice and apprehend space. It starts with the mother as their first 'place' in the world, and moves on to the confines of domestic space. See also Bourdieu 1979, whose discussion of Berber houses has done much to inform how social relationships are constituted and reinforced through the division of domestic space.

therefore confront issues of kinship and familial organization, as well as the transmission of the experiences of the house into a society's wider social relationships. The variable of human presence was fundamental to the place-making process: the making of a particular domestic place was strongly determined by who was present, during what times of day, and how activities brought individuals and family members together or set them apart.[10] It is not simply about *which* activities were performed there. Research on architecture has tended to overlook the dynamism and variety inherent in uses of domestic space. Since architectural plans do not translate into straightforward or unambiguous uses or functions, the study of artifact assemblages is important to achieve a fuller understanding of place-making.[11]

This extends to discussions of accessibility in the house by inhabitants and visitors. Through a close reading of architectural plans and room decoration, A. Wallace-Hadrill's seminal work offers a convincing model to explain the separation between public and private places in the houses of Pompeii and Herculaneum.[12] Scholars acknowledge that Roman concepts of 'public' and 'private' differed markedly from our modern ones.[13] A shifting spectrum of what constituted public and private spaces has emerged, one which has important consequences for our conception of domestic place-making practices in and beyond the walls of the house.[14] This is because the ordering of places in the minds of the Romans as 'public' and 'private' — or somewhere in between — did much to influence behavior and the nature of social interaction. Our own experiences with the mutability of what constitutes public and private life (not least in our increasingly technological world) should also encourage questions about the diversity of this experience for the Romans. The archaeology of multiple élite and non-élite Roman contexts has much to offer the study of domestic life. Here D. Booms studies the most élite of places, the imperial villas, because, as properties of the emperor, they were not constrained by the same logistical or spatial restrictions as was the *domus*. Although it was possible to manipulate space without limits at the imperial villas, his analysis underscores how the presence or absence of certain individuals (visitors, members of the imperial court, the emperor) affected place-making practices there. Even representations of people, as painted soldiers on a building façade, were given agency in limiting visitors' movements. This is not unlike what was encountered in more humble *domus*.

It is also necessary to balance the domestic scale with the scale of empire. Analyses of the Roman house have revealed the challenges of studying domestic space, including its varieties and differences, both within a single city and across the empire.[15] Long gone are the

---

10   The experience and structuring of time is important to the place-making of domestic spaces: cf. Laurence 1995; Nevett 1999; and Allison 2001. This includes everyday activities as well as more 'special occasion' events, such as weddings, births, funerals, and coming-of-age ceremonies. See also Clarke 1991; Flower 1996; and Hales 2003.
11   Berry 1997; Allison 1999 and 2004. For instance, the *atrium* had a variety of functions, from backdrop for the morning *salutatio* of the *paterfamilias* to presentation space for the family ancestors, to productive or storage space (Allison 2001 and 2004). Overall, the variety of practices calls into question the analytical value of focusing on use and utility. While function provides one perspective on the kinds of specifically utilitarian activities involved in making place, it cannot discern the multiplicity of practices that animate human experience and social relationships.
12   Wallace-Hadrill 1988 and 1994.
13   Id. 1994; Riggsby 1997.
14   Riggsby 1997.
15   Ellis 1991; Hales 2003.

days when the remains of Pompeii and Herculaneum could be viewed as representative of wider imperial realities. To be understood in a wider imperial context, the domestic world must be studied first as a local manifestation, where *mores* and culture played an integral rôle in the ways people constructed and inhabited these places. This extends to how we understand local variation between domestic structures. Each home offered its own unique site of place-making. Here J. Baird investigates domestic life in the frontier city of Dura-Europos, demonstrating the benefits of studying not only each individual housing unit as a single entity, but also their collective rôle in crafting an urban landscape. Place-making processes within the house informed, and were informed by, the wider urban fabric.

Out of the house and into the *urbs*

The Roman house, while set off architecturally from others in urban space, was not isolated or impermeable to the world beyond its confines. Wallace-Hadrill's picture of doors open wide, with free access to the atrium, invokes an élite-centered domestic place that was connected to a larger urban fabric through the comings and goings of residents and visitors, while offering a view of its interiors to passers-by.[16] However, the city was more than the sum of its domestic residences; principally it was a dynamic place for human interaction and movement. We must think about the city, then, in two interconnected ways, considering what it was meant to achieve politically, economically and religiously, *and* how this conditioned everyday experience.[17] Further, while the city and its organization had profound effects on the inhabitants, we must acknowledge that the urban plan was more dynamic than the perspective we gain by viewing it from above.[18]

We can move to a more place-oriented picture of urban experience in the Roman world by looking at the organization of cities and the placement of monuments, while also staying attuned to the differences found across sites. This requires integrating residential spaces with the monumental, to achieve a more holistic picture of urban life and experience, as well as acknowledging the centrality of the human element to making urban places.[19] De Certeau's picture of urban places insists that a city was created to be moved around in; it is thus incomplete without such movement. While a city can be planned and organized, it is ultimately transformed by those who live there.[20] The multiple iterations of movement

---

16 Wallace-Hadrill 1994.
17 The model of the "consumer" city (Weber 1930/2002; Finley 1973/1999; Hopkins 1980; Whittaker 1990; Morley 1996) created one picture of economic life that has been challenged by recent research on the productive spaces in cities (Wilson 2001; see also Parkins 1997). Political analyses (Patterson 2006) meanwhile portray the city as a forum for the political ambitions and activities of élites. Studies that focus on the monuments, living quarters, baths, aqueducts and roads have given us a good sense of the spatial organization of urban centers. Work has also been done on urban design and the potential of empire-wide similarities to 'Romanize' newly conquered peoples: MacDonald 1986; Woolf 1998; Fentress 2000; Zanker 2000; and Terrenato 2001a. G. Rogers' (1991) research on Ephesus, as well as that of D. Favro (1994) and M. Beard (2003) on the Roman triumph, have illuminated the religious and ritual aspects of Roman cities.
18 Favro 1996; Laurence 1997 and 2008. The social geographer D. Cosgrove (1984 and 1985) treated maps and other such representations of space as 'ways of seeing' that facilitated the exercise of power and reinforced property and its ownership.
19 Laurence 1995 and 1997.
20 De Certeau 1984.

possible within a single urban plan — the jaywalker is an apt example of an individual not fully constrained by roadways — demonstrates how the city can supply a multitude of spatial experiences to its residents as they move about and interact with it.

In the metropolis of Rome, boasting a population of one million by the 1st c. A.D., the hustle and bustle, the sea of people from all walks of life, and the ever-present violence vividly characterize the urban fabric.[21] Nonetheless, Rome was exceptional because of its size and the resources needed to sustain it. Despite the dangers of anachronism or of projecting our own values in any comparison of ancient and modern urban life,[22] we need to take account of certain shared human experiences present in the city.[23] Phenomenology has been used to explore the Roman city as it would have been experienced 'on the ground',[24] but phenomenological approaches have received much criticism for their tendency to neglect the rôle of social relationships and the difficulty they have in imagining a diversity of engagements with places in the past.[25] While it is not possible for us to walk about the city as a Roman would have, we can analyze the function of movement as a binding force. Although certain features in the city, such as streets, monuments or people, have often been studied singularly, cities were composed of all these features in interaction with one another. By looking to daily movements and routines, we can understand how the city would have been bound together as a cohesive site of human experience.

Below, C. Feldman Weiss gives a picture of the rôle of movement and embodiment in the urban landscape of imperial Ephesus. Her analysis emphasizes the rôle played by certain civic rituals, and human participation in them, for how the city was experienced and lived. She highlights the double duty of ritual activity, balancing continuity and change, in maintaining place through iterative embodied practice and in allowing a performative spontaneity.[26] Her chapter also brings us back to the theme of daily life as it was organized temporally and how the progression of time — the distinctions between day and night, holidays and work days — contributed to the making of urban places.[27]

---

21 Edwards and Woolf 2003.
22 Laurence 1997.
23 E.g., crowding would have had a great effect on how the urban fabric was experienced (Tuan 1977, chapt. 5). The face-to-face familiarity among most communities in the Roman world would have been replaced by a certain level of anonymity and the promotion of an 'imagined' community of Rome (cf. Anderson 1983), or it would have promoted community building at the neighborhood level. While perceptions of crowding are no doubt strongly influenced by cultural factors, understanding how this played into the Roman experience of cities brings us back to the ways that people, as both actors and objects, are part of making place.
24 See Favro 1996 and Witcher 1998 for Roman contexts; also Tilley 1994; Ingold 1993 and 2000. M. Merleau-Ponty (1945) insists that, while phenomenology can be a rigorous science, it should also give an account of space, time and the world as lived.
25 See in particular Myers 2002; also, M. Strathern's (1988) "partible persons" or "dividuals". Criticism of phenomenology has arisen because its vantage point can never truly be free of our own western biases and perception, which privilege a highly individualized, subject-oriented picture of experience.
26 We see this emphasis on performance as a promising avenue for future research in place-making, balancing the tendencies in current scholarship on space and place to focus on representation and symbolic orders. For 'non-representational' approaches in social geography, see Nash 2000 and Thrift 2008.
27 See Favro 1994 and Laurence 1995.

Rural places and (non-)spaces

Research on the city raises the question of where the city ends and rural landscapes begin. For Roman archaeologists this boundary is a tenuous one, mainly because the division is not clear-cut. If the city and country were as economically and politically connected as scholars have claimed, how do we gauge the limits of the urban experience?[28] Discussions on the relationship between city and country have often been contingent on their economic interaction, with the countryside providing the alimentary needs of urban residents and serving as a place for élite profit-making through the villa system. While analyses of the villa have emphasized its élite character, from the advances brought about by survey archaeology we know that the Roman countryside was much more complex. Survey has populated rural landscapes once thought 'empty' or ill-suited to archaeological analyses.[29] The rural spaces of the Roman world are provocative contexts for exploring place-making, due to the always complex interaction between the human-made and natural landscape. Added to this are the diverse groups who inhabited, worked and moved through rural places, navigating their human, material and natural components. For this reason, approaches to survey have been allied with theories of landscape, to investigate the rôle of human presence and experience in these contexts.[30] The landscape is no longer an inanimate background on which human activity unfolds, but instead a central social actor, constituting and constituted by human interaction.[31] Yet the engagement by ancient peoples with their landscapes was not necessarily predicated on values similar to our own. Therefore we must grapple with the theoretical underpinnings of this difference in perception.[32]

We must also strive to identify and analyze places that are not easily labeled urban or rural, sacred or profane, productive or for leisure, but lie somewhere in between. These places, often viewed as transitional from the point of view of a modern mindset, were integral to the continuum of city to countryside. B. Sekedat's contribution, which looks at the town of Fasıllar in modern Turkey and the quarries located nearby, asks us to re-orient

---

[28] Rich and Wallace-Hadrill 1991; Millett 1991; and Lomas 1997.

[29] Inspired by the work of F. Braudel and the *Annales* School of history, survey methodologies have also aimed to link the *longue durée* of environmental processes to the *conjonctures* of human activity and change over a mid-range timescale, an enterprise that is well suited to utilizing the fragmentary evidence available to archaeologists. See Barker and Lloyd 1991; Bintliff 1991; and Barker 1995.

[30] van Dommelen 1993; Given and Knapp 2003; Witcher 2006. In the Mediterranean region, survey archaeology is a means of archaeological exploration. Landscape theory is a different but related mode of enquiry that expands archaeological investigation from single sites to local landscapes, and tries to understand how people construct their worlds and experience their surroundings. For archaeological perspectives, see Bender 1992 and 1993; Ashmore and Knapp 1999; Canuto and Yaeger 2000; Alcock 2002; Ashmore 2004; Blake 2004; Launaro 2004; Leone 2005; Stone and Stirling 2007; and Johnson 2007. Criticisms of survey as merely creating 'dots on a map' go so far as to claim that survey reinforces environmentally or historically deterministic narratives: Blanton 2001; Witmore 2006; Witcher 2006; and Gibson 2007. These critiques make clear that, while survey has done much to uncover patterns of settlement in rural landscapes, work is still needed to turn these scatters into the remains of socially-engaged human actors.

[31] Thomas 2001, 174.

[32] For instance, while archaeologists may single out particular natural features as important markers in the landscape, often the inhabitants do not take them to be such. See Fitzjohn 2007.

how we think about places of production in rural contexts not necessarily associated with agriculture or located on once-inhabited sites. While 'in-between' places are not neatly bounded or definable as sites in the archaeological sense, roads, way-stations, extra-urban tombs, and so forth could hold social significance for those who interacted with and moved through them.[33] Sekedat demonstrates the ways in which long-term and multi-temporal practices were drawn together in making place at the quarries of Fasıllar. He underscores his thesis by walking the reader through the site today.

Natural elements in the landscape — e.g., rivers, forests, mountains — could also be conceived of as "non-places" because they are often found at the periphery of human settlement, serving as boundaries between landscapes that do not belong to one place or the other.[34] Mountains and forests have often been interpreted as a hindrance to movement, but such features should be studied on a case-by-case basis. We must be open to the rôle they played in enhancing movement and communication.[35] The same approach applies to rivers too. Baird explores the ways in which the Euphrates — at times the edge of empire for the Romans — was more than just a boundary for local inhabitants: instead of being a dividing line and an obstacle to movement, this 'boundary' served as an important point of contact and entry into Dura.

Liminal places?

How are we to conceive of the limits of the Roman empire? As Baird's and Collins' contributions highlight, debates on the frontiers of the Roman world offer interesting insights into place-making of Romans living on the frontiers, as well as Romans located firmly within the empire. In any study of Roman place-making, the frontiers, as the 'limits' of empire, epitomize the need continually to look at local places in the wider context of the imperial world. The frontiers challenge us to understand the ways space could be circumscribed and contained.[36] Yet they were perceived in one way by those distant from them, and in another by those living there. Tuan makes this distinction between space and place: the former being unknown because it has yet to be experienced, the latter being already apprehended through experience.[37] If we were to follow his line of thinking, the frontier existed in space, but only a subset of Romans experienced it as place. In this way the frontiers were abstract entities, not necessarily part of the everyday lives of many Romans.[38]

---

33 R. Witcher (1998) has noted that roads, while often viewed as complete tracks from start to finish, were not necessarily experienced this way by those who lived nearby or used them for local movements. However, the perspective of 'in-betweenness' is relative: some places perceived as liminal to one group were the local and central reality for others. Roads have a local life as well as serving as transitional places: in this vein, see B. Bender and M. Winer (2001) on transitional places in modern society. While Witcher (1998) and R. Laurence (1999) conclude that roads were an integral element to the dissemination of Roman imperial power, we must be willing to accept that this was not the only 'reading' of these places made by ancient audiences, and acknowledge the multiple meanings possible in daily engagements with place.
34 Augé 1995.
35 Horden and Purcell 2000.
36 In recent years, the frontiers have been increasingly characterized as a zone of overlapping institutions at the margins of empire (Elton 1996), and a dynamic place with 'ill-defined' limits (Whittaker 1994 and 2004). At the heart of these models is the rôle in defining place played by central institutions, the military, and contacts with groups living near the frontiers.
37 Tuan 1977, 54.
38 C. R. Whittaker (1994) argued that the empire was not conceived by the Romans to have limits,

The Roman frontiers were vast, extending across temperate Europe, Western Asia, and the deserts of North Africa. Their diverse ecologies and their indigenous inhabitants would have affected the experience of place.[39] Interactions with the Parthians were not the same as those with Germanic tribes or with Libyco-Punic peoples in the pre-desert. Of course, interaction on the frontiers between soldiers and locals is not a clear-cut matter.[40] Archaeology has done much to amplify our understanding of everyday life on the frontiers and to challenge models that view the frontiers as peripheral to an imperial core.[41] The frontiers can now be treated on their own terms, as places of cultural and social exchange between 'Roman' and 'non-Roman' communities (categories which defy proper definition) Although frontier garrisons, boundaries, and villages were constructed in landscapes that were by no means empty upon the arrival of the Romans, the effects of Roman building on sights and sounds in the landscape would have been profound.[42]

The perspectives and experiences of those within the frontiers and those on the frontiers differed. Not all frontier-dwellers had the same perception and experience of these places, a point made evident by comparing the contributions of J. Baird and R. Collins. The contrast is based not only on the difference between the eastern and western halves of the empire: it also highlights the experiences within towns and forts of communities and individuals who were negotiating their rôle both as members of a local society but also as part of the wider empire. Baird's view of Dura-Europos underlines how much the experience of this place was based not simply on its location along the eastern frontier but on the site's long history and the routines of daily life. In his picture of the later empire, Collins demonstrates the ways in which forts and garrisons on the Roman frontier, once intimately tied to the central administration, became more localized. This increasing localization made the experience of military life and military places distinct from places elsewhere on the frontiers.[43] Collins also highlights the ways in which structural changes to living quarters transformed social interaction in these places.

Roman place-making is not just the sum of architectural forms, urban plans, artifact scatters or artistic decoration. Rather, Roman place-making requires a more complex interpretation of how humans and their material worlds influenced and shaped one another. Place-making analyses contemplate the intersection of the built and natural environments and call for a greater account of the central rôle played by people — through their movements, presences and absences — in the experience of place. Individuals, families, groups, armies, *collegia*, the living and the dead, all made an impact on the perception and habitation of places. Roman archaeologists have noted the need for a peopled space, but much theorizing is necessary to make the human a meaningful variable in analyses of place.

---

since to do so would have constrained the potential of their power. This resonates with Tuan because space. being not yet experienced, was venture, freedom, openness — and, we would add, potential too — in the minds of Roman leaders, military officials and merchants.

39   For the European frontiers, see, e.g., Dyson 1985; Okun 1989; Elton 1996; Ellis 1998; Sommer 1999; and Gardner 2004. For the eastern frontiers, see, e.g., Isaac 1990; Elton 1996; and Kennedy 1996. For N Africa, see, e.g., Fentress 1979; Shaw 1983; Mattingly 1987; Barker 1996; and Cherry 1998 (citations here are merely the Anglophone scholarship).
40   Shaw 1983; Bowman 2003; and Wells 2005.
41   Lightfoot and Martinez 1995.
42   Goldsworthy and Haynes 1999; Wells 2005.
43   Gardner 2004.

Doing so, moreover, would encourage the study of the continued rôle and relevance of Roman places in our own societies.

Places are inherited

We can imagine a temporal depth to any of the places discussed thus far. Places are inscribed through daily practice, continually refashioned according to inherited strategies of innovation. Monuments are built with commemorative purposes in order to defy the ravages of decay and oblivion. Power is rooted in specific places through allusions to prior authorities, to name just a few examples where the temporal depth or 'heritage' of places matter. Place-making is therefore never a singular event or gesture, but rather an extensive layering of various (re)makings of place. Approaches that deal most directly with temporal depth include studies on memory and 'the past of the past', providing access to the ways people in the past viewed and interacted with their own history and its material heritage.[44] The question of temporal depth is also at the core of studies that, inspired by F. Braudel and the *Annales* school, consider the *longue durée* and juxtapose various temporalities, durations and cyclical rhythms.[45]

This temporal depth extends all the way to the present day, mobilizing the Roman past through acts of contemporary place-making, and extends also to our own work as archaeologists, operating within a discipline that enacts practices of place-making at every step of the research process. This volume argues that temporality constitutes place, and *vice versa*,[46] so that any discussion of place-making requires recognition of the ways heritage, tradition and historical processes aided in making specific places. Archaeology is particularly well suited to explaining the interconnectedness of place and time, and therefore has much to contribute to studies of place-making in other disciplines. Focusing on the temporality of Roman material culture likewise brings into sharp relief how it works in the present to construct contemporary places, through a myriad of strategies having their own social, political and economic effects. The papers in the second half of this volume provide a variety of contexts and practices to illustrate how Roman material heritage makes places in the present.

Thinking about the ways in which the work of archaeologists contributes to making place helps us to analyze the temporal depth of place-making. It also draws us to consider the wider contexts in which Roman archaeology is deployed by third parties, revealing the implications and effects of our work, and allows us to view the mobilization of Rome's material heritage as a part of larger social projects, for example in nation-building, fostering global citizenship, and tourism development. In these broader contexts, Roman material becomes one factor among many, but it becomes important because it situates specific social

---

44 Applied to Roman material by, amongst others, Alcock 1996, 2001 and 2002; Hope 2003; Eckardt and Williams 2003; Eckardt 2004; Grigoropoulos 2004; Meade 2004; and Williams 2004; and to other archaeological contexts by Bradley and Williams 1998; Bender 2002; Bradley 2002 and 2003; Blake 2003; Olivier 2003; Van Dyke and Alcock 2003; Williams 2003; and Mills and Walker 2008.
45 Braudel 1996. *Annales*-inspired approaches in archaeology include: Parker Pearson 1984; Hodder 1987; Skeates 1990; Barker 1991; Bintliff 1991; Snodgrass 1991; Knapp 1992; van Dommelen 1998; Horden and Purcell 2000; Shaw 2001 and Morris 2003.
46 This sentiment could be glossed as the production of 'timespace', following Soja 1989; Lefebvre 1991; and May and Thrift 2001, amongst others.

projects in a geographic location and within indexical properties of empire, western identity, profit generation, and so on. Present-day political endeavors and social struggles effectively 'map onto' Rome's material heritage in order to claim these properties. Therefore, the object of study for archaeologists shifts from a focus on the past to an interdisciplinary consideration of broader social contexts. Archaeologists find themselves having to become informed about politics, social geography, political economy, modern identities, social movements, and legal systems, for example. Although archaeology becomes just one (and a particularly western and scientific) practice or project among many, it is one that is equipped to inform and contribute to a wide range of contemporary issues.

Much of this kind of work has already begun: research on the historiography of Roman studies as well as on memory and "the past of the past" quickly come to mind. Historiographic work on the formation and development of Roman studies has shown how interactions with the material heritage of Rome's empire have shaped, and been shaped by, particular projects (social, political, economic, moral, and so on) throughout the course of modern history.[47] In these cases, the construction of knowledge about the past has worked in tandem with specific visions of place-making, especially ones relating to colonial empire — its construction, justification, appropriation of place, and subjugation of alternative place-makings.

Previous work has thus demonstrated the necessity of temporality for making Roman places, especially through a consideration of the ways that different historical contexts crafted distinct relationships to the Roman past and its study. Contributors to this volume apply the same impulse to the contemporary contexts of Roman material, asking how Roman places continue to be made in the present through archaeological research. There has been much work in political science and public policy on empire and the West's Roman heritage. Recent work also focuses on the casting of America as the new Rome.[48] Research both within and outside the discipline of Roman archaeology therefore offers great potential for intersecting analyses on the reception of Roman culture throughout history and into the present.[49]

The many contexts of Roman heritage: local, national and global

Research in archaeology illuminates the relevance of place-making to the heritage of the Roman empire. The issues involved in the antiquities trade and looting of archaeological sites are well known,[50] but the economics of the antiquities trade, from source to collec-

---

47 Historiography follows the same impulse as 'past of the past' studies, but with a specialized focus on modernity and its preferred forms of historical record. See Shaw 1980; Mattingly 1996; Webster and Cooper 1996; Dyson 1998, 2001 and 2006; Hingley 1999, 2002 and 2005; Laurence 2001; Munzi 2001; and Terrenato 2001b.
48 See, e.g., Hardt and Negri 2000; Ferguson 2004. Hardt and Negri argue that the United States military is the monarchy of the new world empire, with the economic wealth of the G7 and transnational corporations and organizations constituting the aristocracy, and the internet the democratic sphere.
49 On the reception of Roman culture, see Richard 1994; Edwards 1999; Payne, Kuttner, and Smick 2000; Whittaker 2000; Hingley 2001; Joshel, Malamud and McGuire 2001; Winterer 2002; Goff 2005; and Malamud 2009.
50 On the antiquities trade and looting, see Brooks 2005; Brodie *et al.* 2006; Merryman 2006; Vitelli and Colwell-Chanthaphonh 2006; and Rhodes 2007. For research on the collecting of classical

tor, is only one manifestation of broader trends in the commodification of Roman material heritage, for tourism and other purposes.[51] Much research on the contemporary uses of the material past refers uncritically to local, national, and transnational (or global) places. What is needed is an analysis of how these scales — local, national and global — are not *a priori* categories, but instead are places fashioned in part from the present-day activities surrounding historic remains. Here we turn briefly to 'unpack' these analytical scales, before proceeding to discuss the ways Roman places are made in the present within and through these scales.

In part, the focus on scale builds on earlier work on the influence of politics on the construction of knowledge about the past, which was focused on the nation-state and archaeology's legitimizing rôle for national authority.[52] The nation-state is also the most closely linked to a rubric of territories and boundaries for its authority. Attention to politics was also critical to the broadly defined set of concerns and issues that have since become known as 'heritage studies'. It was research on national politics that built an appreciation for the political uses of archaeology at both the local and global scale and, in turn, highlighted the diversity *between* contexts, both local and national, when compared across the world.[53] These differences include disparities in resources, the treatment of material heritage, and the connection of heritage to globalizing social projects.

Roman material heritage has proven especially relevant to projects 'making place' on the grand scale, such as the European Union, which cover wide spatial distances and imagine communities along global and regional dimensions. In many ways the heritage of the Roman empire better suits place-making at the global and regional scale rather than the national, which is one reason why Roman material bears increased relevance in today's globalizing society. Indeed, our current globalism shares many similarities to the Roman world; through a study of their similarities we can begin to tease out a more detailed account of their differences. Still, global processes are always intersecting with national ones. Roman material will continue to be used within place-making practices that promote national sovereignty because the Roman past offers nations and states a greater flexibility and diversity of strategies, to invoke either a national or international community, or both.[54] At the same time, local politics also matter. Communities residing near (and sometimes within) Roman sites might reinforce indigenous or provincial identity in opposition to, or within, global and national re-workings and re-interpretations of the Roman material.

---

antiquities, see Skeates 2000. More generally on the phenomenon of collecting, see Elsner and Cardinal 1994; Baudrillard 1994 and 1996; Belk 1995; Pearce 1995; and Messenger 1999. For discussions on cultural property, see Reid 2002, Brown 2003, Gibbon 2005 and Watkins 2005.

[51] As evident in the antiquities trade, the consumption of material heritage increasingly drives its production and circulation and necessitates the search for more diverse contexts and material resources for this commodification. See also AlSayyad 2001; Graburn 2001; Rowan and Baram 2004; and Layton and Wallace 2006.

[52] E.g., Anderson 1983; Ranger and Hobsbawm 1983; Trigger 1989; Diaz-Andreu and Champion 1996; Kohl and Fawcett 1996; Meskell 1998; and Chapman 2008.

[53] See Byrne 1991; Boniface and Fowler 1993; Appadurai 2001; Kane 2003; Smith 2004 and 2006; Omland 2006; Silverman and Ruggles 2007; Habu, Fawcett and Matsunaga 2008; McManamon, Stout and Barnes 2008; Meskell 2009; Lafrenz Samuels 2009 and 2010.

[54] See, e.g., Dietler 1994; Guidi 1996; and Terrenato 2001b. Or the opposite may happen, whereby national narratives consider the Roman past to be a negative heritage: see Meskell 2002 on negative heritage. C. Fabião (1996) paints a picture of ambivalence towards Roman remains in Portugal.

Economies of Roman heritage

One of the main themes of the conference was an examination of what we called the 'economies of heritage' in Roman archaeology. With this term we seek an approach that joins the political with the economic. Often issues of heritage are narrowly conceived as the overtly political effects of archaeological research, or in relation to issues of identity. With 'economies of heritage' we wanted to extend politics to include the rôle of economic practices in creating, reinforcing and understanding the heritage of the Roman empire. Through a broad-based approach to political economy, analysis focuses not just on the production or consumption of heritage to the exclusion of other economic practices; rather, all the economic practices that surround Roman material heritage are equally important for embedding it in a social context, and for making specific places in the present day.

Several papers in this volume examine the intersections between regional and global claims on the Roman material past. J. M. Gordon grapples with the way the two polities of divided Cyprus compete for legitimacy in the increasingly globalized tourist markets, and asks how our rôles as producers of archaeological data implicate us within that data's subsequent circulation and consumption in political projects — with potentially dangerous and damaging outcomes. D. M. Totten highlights how Etruscan heritage came to circulate beyond a local or national context, both in narratives of the European Union and in attempts to reclaim material lost to the antiquities market. For the region of North Africa, K. Lafrenz Samuels discusses the contemporary fashioning of Roman places through political allegiances to a global community increasingly defined by economic relations and the push for democratization. She argues that citizenship, and especially the notion of the global citizen, are constructed through Roman material within the market logic of neoliberalism. At the global scale, C. Paludan-Müller shows the ways that the political institution of empire is produced and circulated in contemporary times in reference to previous models of empire, with the Roman empire playing a pivotal rôle in this economy of political form and its symbolic manifestations. Taken together, the papers demonstrate the distinctive, particular and winding nature of the paths of 'economies of heritage' through the places created while producing, exchanging, circulating and consuming the Roman past.

Property and power

Evaluating how Roman places are made in the present requires attention to the legacy of Rome's empire within the rise of capitalism, and attention to present-day logistics of power. It is therefore helpful to turn to the production of space under capitalism, set forth by Marxist scholars, and to the centrality of power and governance, following M. Foucault, even though neither Marx nor Foucault had much to say on the subject of space.[55] H. Lefebvre's work is the most notable extension of Marxist approaches to space, and it is particularly relevant for our purposes because it offers a provocative analysis of Roman space and its relationship to modern spaces of capitalist accumulation.[56] Lefebvre argues

---

[55] E.g., Williams 1973; Soja 1989; Lefebvre 1991; Harvey 2001 and 2006; Scott 2005. Foucault's (1986) discussion of space was limited to brief and somewhat obtuse references to utopias and 'heterotopia'; see also discussions in Elden 2001 and Johnson 2006. See Hall and Bombardella 2005, Owens 2002, and Samuels 2010 for applications of Foucault's spatial concepts to archaeology and heritage.

[56] Lefebvre 1991. He uses the word 'space', so his usage will be retained here in our discussion of his work. Space for him is a decidedly social construct: "(social) space is a (social) product"

that every society has its own unique space, based on its mode of production:[57] Roman space was a "productive space", as well as "a space of power".[58] Power in the Roman world was based on landownership, so that space was produced and organized according to rights and laws, the most important of which covered property and patrimony. Lefebvre argues that it is through these rights to land that power came to define space under the Romans.[59] The usefulness of Lefebvre's work to the present volume resides in his argument that contemporary acts of place-making themselves have a Roman heritage. Therefore, extending his argument, our inheritance from the Roman empire includes its material remains but also, critically, how we spatially organize and relate to that material heritage — namely, under specific modes of ownership, where Roman places in the present are fashioned according to particular kinds of legalistic and rights-bearing relations.

Foucault, meanwhile, offers other approaches for Roman heritage. The making of places that embody power and resistance is particularly germane to the deployment of Roman material in present-day projects of empire. Yet we know there is no easy correspondence between past and present power-relations, no easy dichotomies between subjugators and subjugated. The case of England, at different times both the subject and the author of empire, highlights the complexity of imperial place-makings with Roman material.[60] Foucault also provides an approach that addresses the more subtle, diffuse and relational politics of heritage. Heritage studies often focus on the overtly hyper-politicized contexts where the material past comes into play, which, while important, overshadows how material heritage and archaeological practices are always situated within and actively make a political space.[61] The 'political' becomes everything: ways of life, culture, discourses and everyday practices. This point is all the more important for Roman heritage, which, being in some ways so familiar and uncontroversial (compared to the highly politicized focus of most heritage studies), would seem to preclude a need for making heritage an integral part of research programs in Roman archaeology.

Lafrenz Samuels argues otherwise, and traces some of these more subtle workings of power. The mobilization of Roman material heritage in North Africa directs governance inwards to an individual's self-discipline and self-monitoring, so that specific place-making relationships — particularly those invoking the international community and its

---

(ibid. 26). His argument focuses on the production of space, through the 'trialectic' of perceived, conceived and lived spaces. These three modes of engagement with space corresponded to spatial practice, representations of space, and representational space, respectively. Spatial practice (perceived) is the relationship of the body to the environment, representations of space (conceived) are symbols and cognitive conceptions of space, whereas representational space (lived) is the realm of social relations and historical action.

57 Ibid. 31. His argument is that every mode of production has its own unique space, in which the balance and articulation between these three modes (perceived, conceived and lived) shifts. He traces the development, through changes in modes of production, of the modern-day space of capitalistic accumulation from Greek, Etruscan and Roman roots. Unlike the empty space of the Greeks, in which form and function were joined, Roman space, as exemplified by the Forum, was "a place occupied and filled by objects and things" (ibid. 237).
58 Ibid. 239 and 243-45.
59 The decline of the city, with power gradually becoming rooted in the villa, he also described as having "durably defined a *place* as an establishment bound to the soil" (Lefebvre 1991, 253; original emphasis).
60 Hingley 2002 and 2005.
61 Akin to H. R. Hurst's (2007, 75) "small politics".

western pedigree — are mediated through the construction of the 'heritage citizen'. Further, we can see in the chapters by Totten and Gordon how these subtle forms of power are implicated recursively in heritage studies. Both authors highlight that acts of preserving are themselves a form of heritage — i.e., inherited from the Romans and foundational to heritage management today. In the daily business of heritage and its management, power is de-centered, situated in a web of social relations; although seemingly subtle in practice, it becomes insidious in its effects. These two points together — that all practices in heritage are political, and that these practices are a heritage in themselves, part and parcel of our inheritance from the classical past — suggest that the making of Roman places in the present (through scholarship, preservation, tourism, and so on) are steeped in a history of power relations. In short, the 'politics' of Roman archaeology and heritage seems apolitical precisely because it structures our entire way of relating to and managing heritage.

Conclusion

This volume would not be complete without the two perspectives presented here: place-making in the Roman past, and place-making in the Roman present.[62] To concentrate only on place-making in the past ignores the epistemological question of how we know what we know, and how our knowledge about place-making in the Roman past is produced.[63] More importantly, it obscures the fact that such knowledge is produced within a specific place and social context, and that this knowledge has its own ramifications and reverberations in that specific place as well as more broadly, with consequences, to other contexts. It also diminishes our understanding of the ways we engage with the places fashioned in the Roman past. Meanwhile, to focus only on place-making in the present ignores the products of archaeological research — interpretations and reconstructions of the Roman past — which are, in part, the 'stuff' from which heritage is fashioned. This focus would lack a familiarity with and grounding in the aims, goals, ideals and values of Roman archaeology and, more significantly, with their realization. It would also advance the impression that places of the past have no empirical effect on places in the present, that the lives and activities of people in the Roman past have no bearing on, or contribution to, our world today, thereby creating and reifying an artificial division between 'the past', as over and done with, and 'the present'.

Approaches to space and place, as well as to Roman archaeology in general, benefit from greater interdisciplinary engagements, helping to pull multiple lines of evidence together and to better situate our work and Roman heritage more generally. Roman archaeologists are confronted with a variety of contexts within a geographically heterogeneous empire of the past, and various configurations of present-day localities, nation-states, communities, and regions. The evidence that we draw upon and the methodologies that we employ are diverse too. However, such interdisciplinary engagements are not easily made. Merely calling for interdisciplinary or multidisciplinary dialogue will not advance the study of Roman place-making; we must first acknowledge that each approach comes to the table with its own set of theoretical and historical assumptions about the evidence. To advance

---

62 We use the phrase "the Roman present" to highlight how Roman material lives on and continues to make places in the present.
63 These issues concern research questions and design, field methodologies, material analysis, historical interpretation, narratization, publication, and the circulation and citation of works, to name just a few modes of knowledge production in Roman archaeology.

place-making approaches, the goal should not be simply to synthesize multiple kinds of evidence, but also to examine critically the potential, as well as the pitfalls, that each brings to any analysis. To disregard interdisciplinarity no longer seems a viable option; the study of heritage asks us to take seriously the present-day contexts of the material past, and the mobilization of our research within projects and agendas with real social consequences.

Archaeological research represents one very specific kind of engagement with the Roman material past. There are many others. Here we take the stance that any phenomenon, any object of research, is best approached and understood through a multiplicity of perspectives: while each is partial in orientation, when joined together they form a more objective accounting.[64] Both the multitude of perspectives in the Roman past and the many perspectives in the heritage present apply here. Therefore, applying modern concepts, and asking about the present-day relevance, as well as the socio-political and economic contexts, of Roman material are not to be avoided. We wish to counter the assumption that 'anachronistic' analytical frameworks and concerns are automatically problematic. When taken alone, they can be problematic (as are archaeological interpretations devoid of responsibilities to the present), but not when it is recognized that a richer account is formed by adding together multiple perspectives.

The use of modern concepts also forces us to ask why we are interested in applying them to the past: what is it about our present situation, and our relationship to the Roman past, that offers this as an interesting or productive line of inquiry? This self-reflexive questioning is important because it explains some of the heritage issues raised in this volume. Not only do we want to know how Romans thought about and engaged with their places; we also want to convey, as fundamental to the discipline of archaeology, why it is important *to us* to understand how Romans engaged with their places and for us to think about those places. All these questions represent different perspectives on place-making in the Roman world. When joined in all their contradictions and similarities, they provide a richer account of past and present places.

Bibliography

AlSayyad, N. (ed.) 2001. *Consuming tradition, manufacturing heritage: global norms and urban forms in the age of tourism* (New York).
Alcock, S. E. 1996. *Graecia capta: the landscapes of Roman Greece* (Cambridge).
Alcock, S. E. 2001. "The reconfiguration of memory in the eastern Roman Empire," in ead., T. N. D'Altroy, K. D. Morrison and C. M. Sinopoli (edd.), *Empires: perspectives from archaeology and history* (Cambridge) 323-50.
Alcock, S. E. 2002. *Archaeologies of the Greek past: landscape, monuments, and memories* (Cambridge).
Allison, P. M. (ed.) 1999. *The archaeology of household activities* (London).
Allison, P. M. 2001. "Using the material and written sources: turn of the millennium approaches to Roman domestic space," *AJA* 105, 181-208.
Allison, P. M. 2004. *Pompeian households: an analysis of the material culture* (Cotsen Institute of Archaeology Monog. 42; Los Angeles, CA).
Anderson, B. 1983. *Imagined communities: reflections on the origin and spread of nationalism* (London).
Appadurai, A. 2001. "The globalization of archaeology and heritage: a discussion with Arjun Appadurai," *J. Social Archaeology* 1, 35-49.

---

64   E.g., see D. Haraway's (1991, especially chapt. 9) feminist re-definition of objectivity as "limited location and situated knowledge" (190), composed of multiple perspectives, each perspective being from a particular location by a particular body. Situated knowledge embraces bias and foregrounds accountability. We regard Haraway's approach to objectivity as particularly appropriate to studies of place-making, situatedness, and heritage.

Ashmore, W. 2004. "Social archaeologies of landscape," in Meskell and Preucel 2004, 255-71.
Ashmore, W. and A. B. Knapp (edd.) 1999. *Archaeologies of landscape: contemporary perspectives* (London).
Augé, M. 1995. *Non-places: introduction to an anthropology of supermodernity* (London).
Barker, G. 1991. "Two Italys, one valley: an *Annaliste* perspective," in Bintliff 1991, 34-56.
Barker, G. (ed.) 1995. *A Mediterranean valley: landscape archaeology and* Annales *history in the Biferno Valley* (London).
Barker, G. (ed.) 1996. *Farming the desert. The UNESCO Libyan Valleys Archaeological Survey,* 1: *synthesis* (UNESCO, Paris).
Barker, G. and J. Lloyd (edd.) 1991. *Roman landscapes: archaeological survey in the Mediterranean region* (British School at Rome Monog. 2).
Baudrillard, J. 1994. "The system of collecting," in J. Elsner and R. Cardinal (edd.), *The cultures of collecting* (Cambridge, MA) 7-24.
Baudrillard, J. 1968/1996. *The system of objects* (transl. J. Benedict; London).
Beard, M. 2003. "The triumph of the absurd: Roman street theatre," in Edwards and Woolf 2003, 21-43.
Belk, R. W. 1995. *Collecting in a consumer society* (London).
Bender, B. 1992. "Theorising landscapes, and the prehistoric landscapes of Stonehenge," *Man* 27.4, 735-55.
Bender, B. 1993. "Landscape — meaning and action," in ead. (ed.), *Landscape: politics and perspectives* (Oxford) 1-17.
Bender, B. 2002. "Time and landscape," in *Repertoires of timekeeping in anthropology* (*CurrAnthr* 43, no. S4) S103-S112.
Bender, B. and M. Winer 2001. *Contested landscapes: movement, exile and place* (Oxford).
Berry, J. 1997. "Household artefacts: towards a re-interpretation of Roman domestic space," in Laurence and Wallace-Hadrill 1997, 183-95.
Bintliff, J. (ed.) 1991 *The* Annales *School and archaeology* (Leicester).
Blake, E. 2003. "The familiar honeycomb: Byzantine era reuse of Sicily's prehistoric rock-cut tombs," in Van Dyke and Alcock 2003, 203-20.
Blake, E. 2004. "Space, spatiality, and archaeology," in Meskell and Preucel 2004, 230-54.
Blanton, R. E. 2001. "Mediterranean myopia," *Antiquity* 75, 627-29.
Boniface, P. and P. J. Fowler (edd.) 1993. *Heritage and tourism in "the global village"* (London).
Bourdieu, P. 1977. *Outline of a theory of practice* (transl. R. Nice; Cambridge).
Bourdieu, P. 1979. "The Kabyle house or the world reversed," in id., *Algeria 1960* (Cambridge) 133-54.
Bowman, A. K. 2003. *Life and letters on the Roman frontier: Vindolanda and its people* (London).
Bradley, R. 2002. *The past in prehistoric societies* (London).
Bradley, R. 2003. "The translation of time," in Van Dyke and Alcock 2003, 221-27.
Bradley, R. and H. Williams (edd.) 1998. *The past in the past: re-use of ancient monuments = World Arch* 30.1.
Braudel, F. 1996. *The Mediterranean and the Mediterranean world in the age of Philip II* (Berkeley, CA).
Brodie, N. *et al.* (edd.) 2006. *Archaeology, cultural heritage, and the antiquities trade* (Gainesville, FL).
Brooks, N. 2005. "Cultural heritage and conflict: the threatened archaeology of Western Sahara," *J. North African Studies* 10, 413-39.
Brown, M. F. 2003. *Who owns native culture?* (Cambridge, MA).
Butler, J. 1993. *Bodies that matter* (London).
Byrne, D. 1991. "Western hegemony in archaeological heritage management," *History and Anthropology* 5, 269-76.
Canuto, M. A. and J. Yaeger 2000. *The archaeology of communities: a new world perspective* (New York).
Casey, E. S. 2001. "Body, self and landscape: a geophilosophical inquiry into the place-world," in P. Adams, S. Hoelscher and K. Till (edd.), *Textures of place: exploring humanist geographies* (Minneapolis, MN) 403-26.
Chapman, R. 2008. "Alternative states," in Habu, Fawcett and Matsunaga 2008, 144-65.
Cherry, D. 1998. *Frontier and society in Roman North Africa* (Oxford).
Clarke, J. 1991. *The houses of Roman Italy 100 B.C.–A.D. 250: ritual, space and decoration* (Berkeley, CA).
Cosgrove, D. E. 1984. *Social formation and symbolic landscape* (London).
Cosgrove, D. E. 1985. "Prospect perspective and the evolution of the landscape idea," *Trans. Inst. British Geographers* 10, 45-62.

Crang, M. 2000. "Relics, places and unwritten geographies in the work of Michel de Certeau (1925-86)," in M. Crang and N. Thrift (edd.), *Thinking space* (London) 136-53.
de Certeau, M. 1984. *The practice of everyday life* (Berkeley, CA)
Diaz-Andreu, M. and T. Champion (edd.) 1996. *Nationalism and archaeology in Europe* (London).
Dietler, M. 1994. "'Our ancestors the Gauls': archaeology, ethnic nationalism, and the manipulation of Celtic identity in modern Europe," *American Anthropologist* 96, 584-605.
Dyson, S. 1985. *The creation of the Roman frontier* (Princeton, NJ).
Dyson, S. L. 1998. *Ancient marbles to American shores: classical archaeology in the United States* (Philadelphia, PA).
Dyson, S. L. 2001. "Roman archaeologists in the 19th and 20th c.," *JRA* 14, 710-14.
Dyson, S. L. 2006. *In pursuit of ancient pasts: a history of classical archaeology in the nineteenth and twentieth centuries* (New Haven, CT).
Eckardt, H. 2004. "Remembering and forgetting in the provinces," in *TRAC 2003* (Oxford) 36-50.
Eckardt, H. and H. Williams 2003. "Objects without a past? The use of Roman objects in Early Anglo-Saxon graves," in Williams 2003, 141-70.
Edwards, C. (ed.) 1999. *Roman presences: receptions of Rome in European culture, 1798-1945* (Cambridge).
Edwards, C. and G. Woolf (edd.) 2003. *Rome the cosmopolis* (Cambridge).
Elden, S. 2001. *Mapping the present: Heidegger, Foucault and the project of a spatial history* (London).
Ellis, L. 1998. "'Terra deserta': population, politics, and the (de)colonization of Dacia," *World Arch.* 30, 220-37.
Ellis, S. P. 1991. "Power, architecture and décor: how the Late Roman aristocrat appeared to his guests," in E. K. Gazda (ed.), *Roman art in the private sphere* (Ann Arbor, MI) 117-34.
Elsner, J. and R. Cardinal (edd.) 1994. *The cultures of collecting* (Cambridge).
Elton, H. 1996. *Frontiers of the Roman empire* (London).
Fabião, C. 1996. "Archaeology and nationalism: the Portuguese case," in Diaz-Andreu and Champion 1996, 90-107.
Favro, D. 1994. "The street triumphant: the urban impact of Roman triumphal parades," in Z. Celik, D. Favro and R. Ingersoll (edd.), *Streets: critical perspectives on public space* (Berkeley, CA) 151-64.
Favro, D. 1996. *The urban image of Augustan Rome* (Cambridge).
Fentress, E. W. B. 1979. *Numidia and the Roman army: social, military, and economic aspects of the frontier zone* (BAR S53; Oxford).
Fentress, E. (ed.) 2000. *Romanization and the city* (JRA Suppl. 38).
Ferguson, N. 2004. *Colossus: the rise and fall of the American empire* (New York).
Finley, M. I. 1973/1999. *The ancient economy* (with an introduction by I. Morris; Berkeley, CA).
Fitzjohn, M. 2007. "Viewing places: GIS applications for examining the perception of space in the mountains of Sicily," *World Arch.* 39, 36-50.
Flower, H. 1996. *Ancestor masks and aristocratic power in Roman culture* (Oxford).
Foucault, M. 1986. "Of other spaces," *Diacritics* 16, 22-27.
Gardner, A. 2004. "Agency and community in 4th century Britain: developing the structurationist project," in id. (ed.), *Agency uncovered: archaeological perspectives on social agency, power, and being human* (London) 33-50.
Gibbon, K. F. 2005. *Who owns the past? Cultural policy, cultural property, and the law* (Piscataway, NJ).
Gibson, E. 2007. "The archaeology of movement in a Mediterranean landscape," *JMedArch* 20, 61-87.
Given, M. and A. B. Knapp 2003. *The Sydney Cyprus Survey Project: social approaches to regional archaeological survey* (Monumenta Archaeologica 21).
Goff, B. (ed.) 2005. *Classics and colonialism* (London).
Goldsworthy, A. and I. Haynes (edd.) 1999. *The Roman army as a community* (JRA Suppl. 34).
Graburn, N. 2001. "Learning to consume: what is heritage and when is it traditional?," in AlSayyad 2001, 68-89.
Gray, J. 1999. "Open spaces and dwelling places: being at home on hill farms in the Scottish borderlands," *American Ethnologist* 26.2, 440-60.
Grigoropoulos, D. 2004. "Tomb robbing and the transformation of social memory in Roman Knossos," in *TRAC 2003* (Oxford) 62-77.
Guidi, A. 1996. "Nationalism without a nation: the Italian case," in Diaz-Andreu and Champion 1996, 108-18.
Gupta, A. and J. Ferguson 1997. "Culture, power, place: ethnography at the end of an era," in iid. (edd.), *Culture, power, place: explorations in critical anthropology* (Durham, NC) 1-32.

Habu, J., C Fawcett and J. Matsunaga (edd.) 2008. *Evaluating multiple narratives: beyond nationalist, colonialist, imperialist archaeologies* (New York).
Hales, S. 2003. *The Roman house and social identity* (Cambridge).
Hall, M. and P. Bombardella 2005. "Las Vegas in Africa," *J. Social Archaeology* 5, 5-24.
Haraway, D. 1991. *Simians, cyborgs, and women: the reinvention of nature* (London).
Hardt, M. and A. Negri 2000. *Empire* (London).
Harvey, D. 2001. "Cosmopolitanism and the banality of geographical evils," in J. Comaroff and J. L. Comaroff (edd.), *Millennial capitalism and the culture of neoliberalism* (Durham, NC) 529-64.
Harvey, D. 2006. *Spaces of global capitalism: towards a theory of uneven geographical development* (London).
Hingley, R. 1999. "The imperial context of Romano-British studies and proposals for a new understanding of social change," in P. Funari, M. Hall and S. Jones (edd.), *Back from the edge: archaeology in history* (London) 137-50.
Hingley, R. (ed.) 2001. *Images of Rome: perceptions of ancient Rome in Europe and the United States in the modern age* (JRA Suppl. 44).
Hingley, R. 2002. *Roman officers and English gentlemen: the imperial origins of Roman archaeology* (London).
Hingley, R. 2005. *Globalizing Roman culture: unity, diversity and empire* (London).
Hodder, I. 1987. "The contribution of the long term," in id. (ed.), *Archaeology as long-term history* (Cambridge) 1-8.
Hope, V. 2003. "Remembering Rome," in Williams 2003, 113-40.
Hopkins, K. 1980. "Taxes and trade in the Roman empire (200 B.C.–A.D. 400)," *JRS* 70, 101-25.
Horden, P. and N. Purcell 2000. *The corrupting sea: a study of Mediterranean history* (Malden, MA).
Hurst, H. R. 2007. "Doing archaeology in classical lands: the Roman world," in S. E. Alcock and R. Osborne (edd.), *Classical archaeology* (Malden, MA) 69-88.
Ingold, T. 1993. "The temporality of the landscape," *World Arch.* 25.2, 152-74.
Ingold, T. 2000. *The perception of the environment: essays of livelihood, dwelling and skill* (London).
Isaac, B. 1990. *The limits of empire: the Roman army in the East* (Oxford).
Johnson, M. 2007. *Ideas of landscape* (Malden, MA).
Johnson, P. 2006. "Unraveling Foucault's 'different spaces'," *History of the Human Sciences* 19, 75-90.
Joshel, S. R., M. Malamud and D. T. McGuire, Jr. (edd.) 2001. *Imperial projections: ancient Rome in modern popular culture* (Baltimore, MD).
Kane, S. (ed.) 2003. *The politics of archaeology and identity in a global context* (Boston, MA).
Keay, S. and N. Terrenato (edd.) 2001. *Italy and the West: comparative issues in Romanization* (Oxford).
Kennedy, D. L. (ed.) 1996. *The Roman army in the East* (JRA Suppl. 18).
Knapp, A. B. (ed.) 1992. *Archaeology, annales, and ethnohistory* (Cambridge).
Kohl, P. and C. Fawcett (edd.) 1996. *Nationalism, politics, and the practice of archaeology* (Cambridge).
Lafrenz Samuels, K. 2009. "Trajectories of development: international heritage management of archaeology in the Middle East and North Africa," *Archaeologies: Journal of the World Archaeological Congress* 5, 68-91.
Lafrenz Samuels, K. 2010. "Heritage management and poverty reduction," in S. Labadi and C. Long (edd.), *Cultural heritage and globalisation* (London) 200-15.
Launaro, A. 2004. "Experienced landscapes from intentional sources," in *TRAC 2003* (Oxford) 111-22.
Laurence, R. 1995. *Roman Pompeii: space and society* (London).
Laurence, R. 1997. "Space and text," in id. and Wallace-Hadrill 1997, 7-14.
Laurence, R. 1999. *The roads of Roman Italy: mobility and cultural change* (London).
Laurence, R. 2001. "Roman narratives: the writing of archaeological discourse — a view from Britain," *Archaeological Dialogues* 8, 90-101.
Laurence, R. 2008. "City traffic and the archaeology of Roman streets from Pompeii to Rome: the nature of traffic in the ancient city," in D. Mertens (ed.), *Stadtverkehr in der antiken Welt* (Palilia 18; Wiesbaden)
Laurence, R. and A. Wallace-Hadrill (edd.) 1997. *Domestic space in the Roman world: Pompeii and beyond* (JRA Suppl. 22).
Layton, R. and G. Wallace 2006. "Is culture a commodity?" in Scarre and Scarre 2006, 46-68.
Lefebvre, H. 1991. *The production of space* (Oxford).
Leone, M. P. 2005. *The archaeology of liberty in an American capital: excavations in Annapolis* (Berkeley, CA).
Lightfoot, K. G. and A. Martinez 1995. "Frontiers and boundaries in archaeological perspective," *Annual Review of Anthropology* 24, 471-92.

Lomas, K. 1997. "The idea of the city: élite ideology and the evolution of urban form in Italy 200 BC –100 AD," in Parkins 1997, 21-41.
MacDonald, W. L. 1986. *The architecture of the Roman empire* (New Haven, CT).
Malamud, M. 2009. *Ancient Roman and modern America* (Malden, MA).
Mattingly, D. J. 1987. "Libyans and the '*limes*': culture and society in Roman Tripolitania," *AntAfr* 23, 71-94.
Mattingly, D. J. 1996. "From one colonialism to another: imperialism in the Maghreb," in Webster and Cooper 1996, 49-69.
May, J. and N. Thrift (edd.) 2001. *Timespace: geographies of temporality* (London).
McManamon, F., A. Stout and J. Barnes (edd.) 2008. *Managing archaeological resources: global context, national programs, local actions* (Walnut Creek, CA).
Meade, J. 2004. "Prehistoric landscapes of the Ouse valley and their use in the Late Iron Age and Romano-British period," in *TRAC 2003* (Oxford) 78-89.
Merleau-Ponty, M. 1945. *Phenomenology of perception* (transl. C. Smith; London 2002).
Merryman, J. H. 2006. *Imperialism, art and restitution* (Cambridge).
Meskell, L. M. (ed.) 1998. *Archaeology under fire: nationalism, politics and heritage in the eastern Mediterranean and Middle East* (London).
Meskell, L. M. 2002. "Negative heritage and past mastering in archaeology," *Anthropological Quarterly* 75.3, 557-74.
Meskell, L. M. (ed.) 2009. *Cosmopolitan archaeologies* (Durham, NC).
Meskell, L. M. and R. W. Preucel (edd.) 2004. *A companion to social archaeology* (London).
Messenger, P. 1999. *The ethics of collecting cultural property* (Albuquerque, NM).
Millett, M. 1991. "Roman towns and their territories: an archaeological perspective," in Rich and Wallace-Hadrill 1991, 169-89.
Mills, B. J. and W. H. Walker (edd.) 2008. *Memory work: archaeologies of material practices* (Santa Fe, NM).
Morley, N. 1996. *Metropolis and hinterland: the city of Rome and the Italian economy, 200 B.C–A.D. 200* (Cambridge).
Morris, I. 2003. "Mediterraneanization," *Medit. Hist. Rev.* 18, 30-55.
Munzi, M. 2001. *L'epica del ritorno: archeologia e politica nella Tripolitania italiana* (Rome).
Myers, F. 2002. "Ways of place-making," *La Ricerca Folklorica* 45, 101-19.
Nash, C. 2000. "Performativity in practice: some recent work in cultural geography," *Progress in Human Geography* 24, 653-64.
Nevett, L. C. 1999. *House and society in the ancient Greek world* (Cambridge).
Okun, M. L. 1989. "An example of the process of acculturation in the Early Roman frontier," *OJA* 8, 41-54.
Olivier, L. 2003. "The past of the present: archaeological memory and time," *Archaeological Dialogues* 10, 204-13.
Omland, A. 2006. "The ethics of the World Heritage concept," in Scarre and Scarre 2006, 242-59.
Owens, B. M. 2002. "Monumentality, identity, and the state: local practice, World Heritage, and heterotopia at Swayambhu, Nepal," *Anthropological Quarterly* 75, 269-316.
Parker Pearson, M. 1984. "Economic and ideological change: cyclical growth in the pre-state societies of Jutland," in D. Miller and C. Tilley (edd.), *Ideology, power and prehistory* (Cambridge) 69-92.
Parkins, H. (ed.) 1997. *Roman urbanism: beyond the consumer city* (New York).
Patterson, J. 2006. *Landscapes and cities: rural settlement and civic transformation in Early Imperial Italy* (Cambridge).
Payne, A., A. Kuttner and R. Smick (edd.) 2000. *Antiquity and its interpreters* (Cambridge).
Pearce, S. M. 1995. *On collecting: an investigation into collecting* (London).
Ranger, T. and E. Hobsbawm 1983. *The invention of tradition* (Cambridge).
Reid, D. M. 2002. *Whose pharaohs? Archaeology, museums, and Egyptian national identity from Napoleon to World War I* (Berkeley, CA).
Rhodes, R. F. (ed.) 2007. *The acquisition and exhibition of classical antiquities: professional, legal, and ethical perspectives* (Notre Dame, IN).
Rich, J. and A. Wallace-Hadrill (edd.) 1991. *City and country in the ancient world* (London).
Richard, C. J. 1994. *The founders and the classics: Greece, Rome, and the American Enlightenment* (Cambridge, MA).
Riggsby, A. M. 1997. "'Public' and 'private' in Roman culture: the case of the *cubiculum*," *JRA* 10, 36-56.

Rogers, G. 1991. *The sacred identity of Ephesos* (London).
Rowan, Y. and U. Baram (edd.) 2004. *Marketing heritage: archaeology and the consumption of the past* (Walnut Creek, CA).
Samuels, J. 2010. "Of other scapes: archaeology, landscape, and heterotopia in Fascist Sicily," *Archaeologies* 6.1, 62-81.
Scarre, C. and G. Scarre (edd.) 2006. *The ethics of archaeology: philosophical perspectives on archaeological practice* (Cambridge).
Scott, J. C. 2005. "Afterword to 'Moral economies, state spaces, and categorical violence'," *American Anthropologist* 107, 395-402.
Shaw, B. D. 1980. "Archaeology and knowledge: the history of the African provinces of the Roman empire," *Florilegium* 2, 28-60.
Shaw, B. 1983. "Soldiers and society: the army in Numidia," *Opus* 2.1, 133-57.
Shaw, B. D. 2001. "Challenging Braudel: a new vision of the Mediterranean," *JRA* 14, 419-53.
Silverman, H. and D. F. Ruggles (edd.) 2007. *Cultural heritage and human rights* (New York).
Skeates, R. 1990. "What can the *Annaliste* approach offer the archaeologist?" *Papers from the Institute of Archaeology* 1, 56-61.
Skeates, R. 2000. *The collecting of origins: collectors and collections of Italian prehistory and the cultural transformation of value (1550-1999)* (BAR S868; Oxford).
Smith, L. 2004. *Archaeological theory and the politics of cultural heritage* (London).
Smith, L. 2006. *The uses of heritage* (New York).
Snodgrass, A. 1991. "Structural history and classical archaeology," in Bintliff 1991, 57-72.
Soja, E. W. 1989. *Postmodern geographies: the reassertion of space in critical social theory* (London).
Sommer, C. S. 1999. "From conquered territory to Roman province: recent discoveries and debate on the Roman occupation of SW Germany," in R. J. A. Wilson and J. D. Creighton (edd.), *Roman Germany: studies in cultural interaction* (JRA Suppl. 32) 160-98.
Stone, D. L. and L. M. Stirling (edd.) 2007. *Mortuary landscapes of North Africa* (Toronto).
Strathern, M. 1988. *The gender of the gift: problems with women and problems with society in Melanesia* (Studies in Melanesian Anthropology 6; Berkeley, CA).
Terrenato, N. 2001a. "A tale of three cities: the Romanization of northern coastal Etruria," in Keay and Terrenato 2001, 54-67.
Terrenato, N. 2001b. "The perception of Rome in modern Italian culture," in Hingley 2001, 71-89.
Thomas, J. 2001. "Archaeologies of place and landscape," in I. Hodder (ed.), *Archaeological theory today* (New York) 166-83.
Thrift, N. 2008. *Non-representational theory: space, politics, affect* (New York).
Tilley, C. 1994. *A phenomenology of landscape* (Oxford).
Trigger, B. G. 1989. *A history of archaeological thought* (Cambridge).
Tuan, Y-F. 1977. *Space and place: the perspective of experience* (Minneapolis, MN).
van Dommelen, P. 1993. "Roman peasants and rural organization in central Italy: an archaeological perspective," in E. Scott (ed.), *Theoretical Roman Archaeology: first conference proceedings* (Aldershot) 167-86.
van Dommelen, P. 1998. *On colonial grounds: a comparative study of colonialism and rural settlement in the first millennium BC West Central Sardinia* (Leiden Univ. Archaeological Studies 2).
Van Dyke, R. and S. Alcock (edd.) 2003. *Archaeologies of memory* (Malden, MA).
Vitelli, K. D. and C. Colwell-Chanthaphonh (edd.) 2006. *Archaeological ethics* (Walnut Creek, CA).
Wallace-Hadrill, A. 1988. "The social structure of the Roman house," *PBSR* 56, 43-97.
Wallace-Hadrill, A. 1994. *Housing and society in Pompeii and Herculaneum* (Princeton, NJ).
Watkins, J. 2005. "Cultural nationalists, internationalists, and 'intra-nationalists': who's right and whose right?" *Int. J. Cultural Property* 12, 78-94.
Weber, M. 1930/2002. *The Protestant ethic and the spirit of capitalism* (New York).
Webster, J. and N. Cooper (edd.) 1996. *Roman imperialism: post-colonial perspectives* (Leicester Arch. Monog. 3).
Wells, P. 2005. "Creating an imperial frontier: archaeology of the formation of Rome's Danube borderland," *Journal of Archaeological Research* 13.1, 49-88.
Whittaker, C. R. 1990. "The consumer city revisited: the vicus and the city," *JRA* 3, 110-18.
Whittaker, C. R. 1994. *Frontiers of the Roman empire: a social and economic study* (Baltimore, MD).
Whittaker, C. R. 2000. "Roman frontiers and European perceptions," *J. Hist. Sociology* 13, 462-82.
Whittaker, C. R. 2004. *Rome and its frontiers* (London).
Williams, H. (ed.) 2003. *Archaeologies of remembrance: death and memory in past societies* (New York).

Williams, H. 2004. "Ephemeral monuments and social memory in Roman Britain," in *TRAC 2003* (Oxford) 51-61.

Williams, R. 1973. *The country and the city* (Oxford).

Wilson, A. 2001. "Urban production in the Roman world: the view from North Africa," *PBSR* 70, 231-73.

Winterer, C. 2002. *The culture of classicism: ancient Greece and Rome in American intellectual life, 1780-1910* (Baltimore, MD).

Witcher, R. 1998. "Roman roads: phenomenological perspectives on roads in the landscape," in *TRAC 97* (Oxford) 60-70.

Witcher, R. 2006. "Broken pots and meaningless dots? Surveying the rural landscapes of Roman Italy," *PBSR* 74, 39-72.

Witmore, C. 2006. "Vision, media, noise and the percolation of time: symmetrical approaches to the material world," *J. Material Culture* 11, 267-92.

Woolf, G. 1998. *Becoming Roman: the origins of provincial civilization in Gaul* (Cambridge).

Zanker, P. 2000. "The city as symbol: Rome and the creation of an urban image," in Fentress 2000, 26-41.

PLACE-MAKING IN THE ROMAN PAST

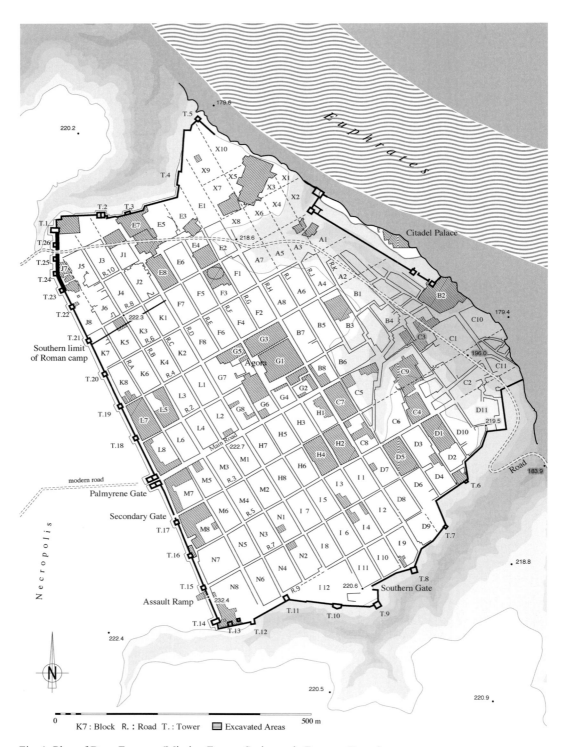

Fig. 1. Plan of Dura-Europos (Mission Franco-Syrienne de Europos-Doura).

Constructing Dura-Europos, ancient and modern

J. A. Baird

The middle Euphrates and the site of Dura, which, as Isidore tells us, the Greeks called *Europos*, is in many ways an ideal case-study for the topic of place-making and boundaries in the ancient world.[1] Not only did the bounds of the Roman and 'Persian' empires overlap here, but the site also lay directly on the Euphrates, which at several points in Roman history was the perceived boundary between Rome and Parthia.[2]

The archaeological evidence tells a story of urban transformation at Dura, and a way of being Roman, that is in some ways at odds with the perception of the frontier from the core. An examination of previous understandings of the site demonstrates some of the ways in which the conception of place held by the Yale University and the *Académie des Inscriptions et Belles-Lettres* excavators in the first half of the 20th c. has been interpolated onto the understanding of the place as it existed in the Roman period.

A Hellenistic foundation of the late 4th c. B.C., Dura was under Parthian rule from the late 2nd c. B.C. until the early 2nd c. A.D. (fig. 1). It was held, briefly, by the Romans under Trajan, and captured again in the campaigns of the 160s, when it was incorporated into the province of Syria.[3] Through its lifespan of less than 600 years, the town was in a zone of constantly shifting control. It manifested itself differently in different periods: sometimes a regional capital, sometimes under direct rule, Dura constantly had to renegotiate its place in the world — be that world Seleucid, Arsacid or Roman. The past several decades have transformed our view of frontiers; while these are now generally thought of as zones rather than distinct geographical boundaries, our understanding of cultural interaction in frontier regions remains ill-defined.[4] Scales of space and time are necessarily dynamic in our reading of the material from Dura, as control of the town changed hands several times. It is necessary to study both the short-term daily practices, where change occurs, and the long-term, where changes manifest themselves on a level that is visible historically. At Dura there is not only the tension of its location between the great empires of the east and west in the broad historical narrative, but also the riparian outlook created by its position. It is often asserted that rivers are connectors as much as boundaries; the current of the Euphrates made it both.[5] What function did the river itself have in creating sense of place?[6]

Our understanding of Dura is shaped by an excavation that occurred between the two World Wars in a colonial Middle East, yet the relationship between the interpretation of the archaeological material and the context of its recovery, grounded as they were in that time and place, has been little explored. The study of such sites therefore necessarily involves

---

1 Isidore of Charax, *Parthian Stations* 1.3-4. For Roman historians, at least, the river had important symbolic significance as a boundary. The name Dura-Europos is a modern compound.
2 The Parthians, according to Plutach, had requested the use of the river as the boundary between the empires, and Gaius met the Parthian king Phraates IV on an island in the middle of the river: Plut., *Pomp*. 33.6; Vell. Pat. 2.101.
3 A recent re-examination of the historical sequence at Dura is given by Edwell 2008.
4 For changing views of Roman frontiers, see particularly Whittaker 1994 and 2004.
5 Whittaker 1994, 78 and 99; id. 2004, 6-9.
6 For a study of the significance of water in the Roman Near East, see Kemash 2008.

a historiographic element.[7] The typologies constructed, the nomenclature used, and the photographic record are all indicative of how place was made at Dura: in describing its past, as a city at the edge of the Roman empire, and in describing its present, as a Western-run archaeological project in the Middle East.

> It cannot be stressed too strongly that, for all its distinctive regional architecture and art-forms — partially paralleled in both Palmyra and Osrhoene — as a community Dura always remained a Greek, or in the end a Graeco-Roman, city. The traces there of the use of Semitic languages ... do not serve to refute this position (Millar 1993, 469-70).

The legacy of Hellenism in what became Rome's eastern provinces has led to an understanding of this region in the Roman period predicated on the relationship between Rome and captured Greece. A closer reading of the material and textual sources, however, can show that some interpretations of the Near East under Roman rule are more informed by modern constructions of the notion of Hellenism than by the evidence.[8]

Constructing modern Dura

> "The tragedy of a buried city told by its ruins" (Hopkins 1934).
>
> "Thus Dura experienced in the short space of a half-century the whole tragedy of the Roman empire, which, while endeavoring to combine civilization with security, succeeded in losing both" (Welles 1951, 274).
>
> "On the civil side [at Dura] the dream of Hellenizing the Orient had faded rapidly" (Ward-Perkins 1974, 20).

Like other sites excavated in the early 20th c., Dura was not just an archaeological site but also an avatar for anxieties of the time. Both C. Hopkins, one of the field directors of Dura, and C. B. Welles, one of the contributors to the published reports and editors of the preliminary and final reports series, endowed Dura with the tragic qualities of lost empire. Later, J. B. Ward-Perkins, in his oft-cited volume on town planning, described the lack of enduring "Greek-style public buildings" as a longed-for but lost dream. The expedition's colonial framework pervaded not only the practice of the excavation (through the presence of the team in Syria, their connections to the military, and their use of a large local workforce) but also their interpretations.[9]

Hundreds of preserved parchments and papyri found at the site have been used to write its history and the history of the Roman East more generally.[10] However, this has encouraged a periodization of the site into Hellenistic, Parthian and Roman phases, which masks much of the lived experience on the ground. The large proportion of documentary evidence from the site in Greek has also led to the characterization of the site and its people as 'Greek'.[11] This primacy given to the textual sources was formative in the

---

7   On the cultural production of the archaeological record, see the work of Y. Hamilakis, including id. 1999.
8   On this perception amongst the editors of Dura's excavation, see, e.g., Welles 1959, 27-28: "They [the people of Dura] might not have been very intellectual ... [b]ut they learned their Greek correctly".
9   On the history of the excavations, see Velud 1988, Gelin 1997 and Yon 1997.
10 The main publication of these documents was in Welles, Fink and Gilliam 1959.
11 For instance, as has been pointed out by T. Kaizer (amongst others), the names assigned to the sanctuaries by the excavators have been tenacious, despite the epigraphic evidence that

interpretation of Dura, where the search for new texts was a prime motivator of the expedition.[12] Once the first papyri were uncovered, the search for more became an obsession for the excavators. This was not simply a case of using archaeology as an illustrated guide to the written sources:[13] it was using archaeology to *provide* written sources.[14] This attitude has shaped the relationship between classical archaeology and texts in such a way that the texts are seen as primary and the classical languages are privileged as indicators of cultural identity;[15] there is a presumed correlation between the use of written Greek and the presence of Greek culture.

The historical periodization of the site and the implicit equation of language with culture disguise aspects both of continuity and of change that vary amongst different parts of the population. This is not to sideline the rich textual evidence of Dura in our understanding of the site, nor to deny the place of documentary evidence in Roman archaeology more generally. However, the troubled relationship between archaeology and text and, more crucially in this instance, the way the texts have been understood hamper our ability to engage with past lived experience.[16] I have discussed elsewhere how the view of the excavators of their contemporary eastern setting affected the nomenclature used at the site, where areas were labelled with tags such as *bazaar* and rooms as *harems* and *diwans*.[17] The perceived importance of Hellenism in modern scholarship has also had ramifications for the study of Dura: the study of town planning, domestic architecture and artefacts can be shown to have been shaped by this paradigm. Take, for instance, the description of Dura by the historian F. Millar quoted above. What does it mean to be 'Greek' (a term itself interesting in a colony founded by Macedonians) if the population is Greek despite its architecture, despite its art, and despite the presence of other languages? Is this being Greek or simply writing Greek?[18]

If we turn to the series of reports published by the excavators, we can see that, just as the ancient and modern textual sources have emphasised the Hellenic elements of Dura, affinity towards the Hellenic also affected the way archaeological material was categorised. The typologies constructed of the lamps and ceramics show the interests of the excavators: the dozens of 'Mesopotamian' lamps are placed under a single type, whereas the 'Hellenistic' lamps, due to their perceived importance and place in the canon of classical objects, have

---

contradicts or complicates these names — e.g., the designation of the temple adjacent to tower 16 as that of Zeus Kyrios, when the Palmyrenean part of this bilingual inscription gives the name of the deity as Baal Shamin. For this and other examples, see Kaizer 2009b, 158-59.

12 A letter in the Dura archive of Yale University Art Gallery, dated December 28 (no year given), from H. T. Rowell to A. R. Bellinger repeatedly calls the excavation a "papyrus hunt", and one that cost lives and caused physical injury, after the partial collapse of one of the city towers killed three workers. On the relationship between classical archaeology and philology, see Dyson 1995. On the search for texts in early excavations, see Moreland 2003, 18.
13 As has been discussed by Allison 2001.
14 The other central motivator of the expedition was, of course, the search for wall-paintings. It was the chance discovery of paintings that had led to the site's excavation (Breasted 1924).
15 Allison 1997, 19.
16 On the relationship between archaeology and text, see Andrén 1998 and papers in Sauer 2004.
17 Baird 2007.
18 I use Millar's excellent study as an example because he is so often followed by others. For instance, when J. Elsner (2001, 275) writes that Dura's "basic culture was Greek", he cites Millar, as do L. Dirven (1999, 11) and Kaizer (2009a, 238).

three typological groups for a total of just three lamps.[19] The privileging of Greek forms with regard to the lamps is shown vividly in correspondence dated February 21, 1930 (Dura archive) between H. T. Rowell (then at Dura) and M. I. Rostovtzeff (at Yale), when Rowell wrote:

> ... we found 43 (forty-three) Roman lamps in one of the houses. With your permission I shall attempt to exchange a few of them in Beirut for earlier models. In sha Allah, the houses will yield us some good pottery and perhaps papyri.

The way objects were classified stemmed from implicit assumptions of cultural hierarchy, and from the desire to collect particular material for museums. The letter seems to indicate (no reply is preserved) that there was at least a desire to exchange the later material for 'good' artefacts, and to the excavators 'Greek' artefacts were 'good' artefacts.

Green-glazed pottery is known at Dura from at least the 1st c. B.C. down to the end of the city, with many of the identified types showing continuity not only in their glaze but also in their shape for the entirety of that period. This was a continuation of a local Mesopotamian ceramic technique.[20] While the green-glazed pottery is second only to the common ware in frequency, it is not possible to quantify their relative proportions in any meaningful terms. The excavators for the most part collected only complete or noteworthy ceramics (i.e., those that were decorated, inscribed or otherwise remarkable in terms of rarity or date, so that early wares, including Greek imports, are over-represented). This is also the case for the so-called Greek and Roman wares. Although they cannot be quantified in a modern sense due to the method of collection, their occurrence is very rare. Only a few sherds of the earliest ware — those with black glaze — parallel the tiny number of early lamps, which, although they are rare, are categorized in a way that suggests that they are more important than the more ubiquitous forms.[21] Problems of nomenclature also enter the descriptions of ceramics: large *dolia* found in houses are, in the published and unpublished Dura reports, referred to as "Ali Baba jars"; indeed, in unpublished photographs taken at Dura, workmen are posed so as to appear to be inside these large ceramics, in a visual construction of this orientalist *topos* (fig. 2).[22]

---

[19] P. V. C. Baur (1947) classified the lamps in a total of 11 types, most of which were further subdivided. Types 4 and 5 make up the largest portion, numbering in the hundreds, and both were apparently local (moulds are known from the site, but are not considered to be 'Roman'). Type 8 is the 'Mesopotamian' type, of which there were more than 50 recorded examples. Type 9 is the 'Roman' type, of which there are only three examples. The corpus is treated chronologically, but with the 'local' types the chronological approach largely breaks down, as if lamps ceased to be made or used in the Roman period. The reality is that local types continued in production and use (and are thus chronologically 'Roman') alongside those that are categorised as 'Roman' by comparison with other sites. If the corpus of lamps is considered in terms of the lamps used contemporaneously, then it seems that local, 'Mesopotamian' and 'Roman' types were used in the same periods. There is a problem, at sites like Dura, of a false distinction between 'Roman' and 'Roman period' objects.

[20] Toll 1943, 5-6 and 72.

[21] Cox 1949. The study of the ceramics excavated by the current Franco-Syrian expedition reveals that the vast majority of the Hellenistic ceramics are indeed local. The focus, however, remains on earlier Hellenistic material at the expense of that of later periods. See, e.g., Alabe 1992 and 2005. The work done on ceramics at Dura is important but at odds with the sophistication of work on ceramics elsewhere in the region; see, e.g., the study of ceramics at Tel Anafa in Herbert 1997.

[22] E.g., Rostovtzeff *et al.* 1936, 117. This description was not, however, used by S. Dyson (1968), who later published the common and brittle wares from the site. See Baird 2011.

Fig. 2. Dura Archive, neg. FIV83, taken during 1932-33 field season (reproduced by kind permission of Yale University Art Gallery).

This is relevant to modern studies of the region, for Dura remains a type site for the Roman East, particularly with regard to objects such as glass vessels, ceramics, lamps and bronzes. If archaeologists are to offer a critical understanding of sites such as Dura, then we must re-assess the very periods and typologies we use to categorise and interpret the material, because they are themselves historically shaped. This is all the more problematic in that archaeologists relied on a series of textually-derived monolithic identities in the very part of the empire where, it might be argued, it is most crucial to deal with diversity and negotiate co-presence.[23]

In the interpretation of the houses at Dura, the excavators used pseudo-ethnographic comparisons; for instance, one room in house C3D is proposed as a women's room because of its high, narrow, windows, which "[t]he Armenian foreman tells ... can be paralleled today in houses in Meyadin and Deir-ez-Zor ... in the walls between the men's and women's quarters".[24] This understanding is then interpolated onto the social structure of the household inhabiting the space in the Roman period. The room adjacent to that, when compared to the contemporary women's quarters, is thought to have been "the master's room".[25] Rooms and structures were named and interpreted by means of contemporary housing in the Middle East, as understood by the excavators. Such functional labels (for both architecture and material culture) as were applied at Dura have been tenacious in modern scholarship. P. M. Allison has noted a similar phenomenon at Pompeii.[26]

The tendency to examine the archaeological evidence closely for Hellenic or Roman 'types' of artefacts[27] has masked another phenomenon, that of continuity in many elements

---

23 Co-presence, which goes beyond the concept of co-residence or location, is used here in the way proposed by E. Goffman (1963, 22) as something that "renders persons uniquely accessible, available, and subject to one another".
24 Rostovtzeff *et al.* 1936, 116.
25 Ibid. 117.
26 Allison 1999 and 2001.
27 Sherwin-White and Kuhrt (1993, 141) have remarked upon the tendency to "search the Middle

of local practice. The lack of detail in chronologies of local material has created an unchanging 'Other' at the site against which 'purer' Greek and Roman objects could be cast. This can be seen, for example, in the terracottas, lamps and ceramics that were excavated from the houses and the site as a whole. The terracottas have recently been thoroughly studied by S. B. Downey, who has shown that, while they are a unique group, parallels can be found at Palmyra for some of the forms and at Assur for the proportion of handmade to mould-made items. The terracottas were for the most part locally produced, mundane in form and common at the site. Downey repeatedly comments on the lack of Greek influence and lack of Greek types.[28]

The continuity of practice — for instance, in building methods and materials as well as in the production of terracottas — is not evident in other aspects of everyday life, such as dress practices. Many of the brooches and jewellery of Roman-period Dura, and other items of personal dress including footwear found at the site, have direct comparanda elsewhere in the Roman empire.[29] This would seem to indicate a selective use of portable material culture and illustrates the dangers of assessing cultural affiliations from singular categories of evidence. The presence of materials such as lapis lazuli, amber and silk attest to access to broader trade networks.

The modern influences on the interpretation of the archaeological record at Dura are evident: an obsession with Greek forms has led to the creation of archaeological typologies in which locally produced objects are grouped in such a way as to appear static, while relatively rare examples of imported Hellenic material are emphasised. Both classification and nomenclature reflect this. Thus a place was created, a Greco-Roman city as defined through 20th-c. archaeological experience, in which we lose both access to the reality of the ancient town and an appreciation of its situation in the colonial world of Syria during the French mandate.

(Re)constructing ancient Dura

I offer next a few examples of how engaging directly with the material allows us to circumvent the edifice constructed by the French-American expedition whilst still using the evidence they collected. I do not seek to create an argument wherein archaeology proves or disproves the textual sources, but rather to show that a close reading of the material evidence, and an understanding of the past from things and places, can offer a different perspective, for instance, on the power dynamic between people and empire. Roman archaeology has (but does not often exploit) the potential to construct knowledge from multiple positions and to assess how these relate to each other.

It is implicit in many archaeological studies that urban topography generally, and town planning specifically, are meaningful ways of understanding ancient cities, and the extraction of meaning from (heavily restored) town plans has become a staple method in the study of classical sites. This is due in part to the correspondence of the study of Early Roman cities with the birth of modern city planning,[30] the place of monumental architecture and

---

  East microscopically for any evidence of something Greek — almost to the exclusion of the existing cultures".
28 Downey 1993, 144; 1996, 253-55; 2003, 20-21.
29 Baird forthcoming.
30 See, e.g., the work of Haverfield on town planning as described by Laurence 1995.

its ruins in the popular imagination,[31] the legacy of Roman cities in western Europe, where many ancient authors lived, and the implicit omnipotence of the bird's-eye view offered by archaeological plans.[32]

If, however, we approach Dura not from the view of a planner but from the material remains on the ground, a different perspective emerges. Take, for instance, the relationship between the ostensibly 'Greek' élite of the site and the bulk of the population. The documents give a picture of a nominally hereditary élite who hold on to power throughout the site's history.[33] This Greek background has been leveraged by some scholars to try to show town planning in Greek cities as reflecting egalitarian ideals, of which Dura is offered up as an example.[34] At Dura, however, most instances of supposedly Hellenistic elements in architecture and material culture post-date the Hellenistic period.[35] Certainly, the manipulation of a perceived Greek heritage in the Roman period is interesting in terms of the relationship between local élite and Roman administration. But what about the materiality of the relationships between Hellenistic and Roman Dura?

The excavations of the block designated 'C3' by the excavators, which occupies the NE slope below the so-called Redoubt, revealed several houses and a bath complex, all of which are now dated to the site's Roman period. Hellenistic architecture at Dura, visible to this day in the fortifications and remains of palaces, is characterised by the use of large blocks of cut stone, a locally quarried gypsum.[36] The topography of the site itself was shaped by the quarrying of stone, both outside the walls in the wadis immediately north and south of the site, and inside, where there is evidence of extensive quarrying in the natural trough between the plateau and the citadel on the E side of the site. By the late 2nd c., houses such as those in block C3 were built within these quarries — some even used the living rock as house walls.[37] Not only was the urban landscape shaped by the removal of the building materials for the architecture of the élite, but the people of the site then lived in the negative spaces left by the materials taken away to build the fortifications and élite residences. Further changes come with the construction of the baths in C3. Alongside the mudbrick and plaster houses a structure composed largely of fired brick was built, complete with some of Dura's only traces of floor mosaic.[38] While there are new structures,

---

31   *Inter alios*, Lowenthal 1985 and Woodward 2001.
32   Other contributing factors to this include the place of Rome itself as an archetype, as well as the use of the archaeology and ruins of cities as an analogy in writings from Goethe to Gibbon to Freud. On archaeology as metaphor and analogy, see Shanks 1992.
33   Welles 1951; Welles, Fink and Gilliam 1959. For a recent critique of the notion of 'Greco-Macedonian' heritage at Dura (and some of the problems with previous understandings of this), see Pollard 2007.
34   Hoepfner and Schwandner 1994. Dura generally figures in studies of town planning as a 'Hellenistic' city: e.g., Ward-Perkins 1974, 20-21.
35   The orthogonal layout of the city has been re-dated by Leriche and his team to long after the colony's foundation (id. 1996a, 2003a, 2003b; Leriche and Al-Mahmoud 1994). Downey (2000) has shown that few structures are certainly Hellenistic. On the phenomenon of 'Hellenized' cities as a feature of the Roman period rather than the Hellenistic, see Bowersock 1989, 67-68.
36   The use of this type of stone in the buildings is also visible in certain temples, and re-used in the walls of later structures, including in block D2 and in the agora. On the palaces and the temple of Zeus Megistos, see the works of Downey (most recently 2004).
37   Dyson 1968, 5. On these houses (although with incorrect house lettering), see Allara 1988, 329-30.
38   Rostovtzeff *et al.* 1936, 95-105.

such as baths, at Dura in the Roman period, the changes occur alongside the continuation of existing building practices.

Both the architecture and the topography created by the quarries are part of the dialogue of power at the site. We should not simply seek to correlate communities extrapolated from texts with structures on the ground (as was done in naming élite structures at Dura; e.g., the so-called palace of the *dux ripae*, the strategeion, etc.), but also seek to show that urban landscapes offer a different way of expressing and understanding relationships within and between communities. We might, for example, consider who was likely to have done the quarrying and to have created the spaces into which some houses were built, and what the (temporal or power) relationships might have been among those quarrying, those inhabiting the resulting spaces, and those inhabiting spaces made from the quarried materials.[39] The site's topography, its building practices and materials, may be read in one sense as a manifestation of a sequence of shifting power dynamics. Dura's urban landscape was heavily impacted by quarrying activities, which were carried out by non-élite individuals: in the urban topography, we can read the labour of those people who are generally considered archaeologically invisible. What is perhaps more ambiguous is the extent to which urban topography continued to play an active rôle — how it reflected not only past relationships but was also constitutive of new ones.

With the coming of Rome, the space of houses is a key area of interaction in the relationship between Rome and the local people. The main impact of Roman hegemony on Dura as far as daily life was concerned, however, was not in the 160s when Roman control was extended to the middle Euphrates by the campaigns of Verus; rather, it was with the later installation of the garrison inside the walls of Dura. By the time it fell to the Sasanians, Dura was not only under Roman control but also had a substantial Roman garrison stationed within the walls.[40] The demography of ancient sites is notoriously difficult to assess, but even judging simply from the standpoint of the amount of space taken over, a substantial part of the population was displaced by the installation of Roman troops inside Dura's city walls.[41] While we do not know with precision the size of either Dura's population or the garrison, the displacement of people formerly residing on the city's N side would probably have resulted in increased population density in the rest of the town. The density of occupation in the military quarter is shown by the houses that were converted to barracks and by the increased cooking and storage arrangements in them.[42] The army was not simply taking over spaces — several houses within the area of the camp were converted for use as barracks. There is evidence that *immunes* took control of some houses outside the camp and that soldiers were present in, if not occupying, many other houses all over the site. But they are also moving around the city, not least along the walls and through the gates.[43] The

---

[39] On the relationship between labour and architecture, see Given 2004, 105-15.
[40] For the physical form of the garrison, see James 2007 on the pilot season of the renewed study and excavation program.
[41] For the population size at Dura, see Will 1988.
[42] There is evidence of such arrangements not only in excavated remains but also in the parts of the camp recently studied using geophysics (James, Baird and Strutt, forthcoming).
[43] Blocks E4 and E8 inside the camp were converted for use from houses into military residences. House L7A, the so-called House of the Scribes, contains evidence for the presence of *immunes*. The presence of, and occupation by, the military in houses elsewhere throughout the site is too extensive a topic to be dealt with here.

vantage point taken by the army not only allowed them a view toward the enemy but also a pervasive view into the town. So whatever 'being Roman' was to someone at Dura, this would have changed significantly not with the establishment of Roman control but rather with the arrival of the army in the city.[44]

To take the case of building practice, the houses of Dura are the physical manifestation of social practice not only in terms of layout but also in terms of the process of building itself. Houses were continually adapted and adjusted, doors were blocked, walls were built and continually plastered and re-plastered, both internally and externally. Thus the structure of the house can be seen to maintain and re-affirm social structures within a household, and also re-affirm identities on a collective urban level. Houses displayed particular household-level kinship structures, but they also had many elements in common, such as a shared architectural language that governed the acceptable form of adaptation, attesting to shared social practice on a town-wide scale.[45] It is interesting that in a town where we know so many different religions were practised, including some which were supposedly exclusive, these broader social norms govern house-building practices, and not (so far as we have evidence) more localised forms governed by religious practices or differing community norms. This is visible not only in building and adaptation but also in the practice of maintaining the houses. In this way, the repeated act of maintaining the houses through activities such as plastering not only responds to social identity but also forms it: building practice and social practice continuously feed into each other, materially constructing both space and place. The material of building does not simply construct spaces or places, but is a way of doing things. Architecture can thus be seen as an embodied practice from which we may deduce certain dynamics at play.[46] While the military did apparently introduce some building materials and forms, notably fired brick, the vast majority of excavated military structures at Dura were constructed with the materials that had been used at Dura for centuries: mudbrick and plaster.[47]

Frontiers, the military and change

It has been argued that the culture in zones such as the middle Euphrates broke down social and political boundaries that had been artificially drawn between the two sides.[48] On the other hand, if we accept that physical boundaries do not have to be dividing lines between cultures, then the social and political boundaries *are* the boundaries between the two. Frontier zones can be places both of confrontation[49] and of the breaking down of barriers; it is this tension that creates the new sense of place that is usually described as

---

44 The payment of taxes is an issue to be examined in this relationship, but in an area that was not new to empire the Roman taxation system would have been but one in a longer history of taxation. The building programme associated with the garrison also coincides (within a couple of years) with the *Constitutio Antoniniana*.
45 One document from Dura that is illuminating with regard to housing and kinship is *P. Dura* 19, which details the distribution of property amongst the heirs of one Polemocrates. For a revised translation in French and discussion of the text, see Saliou 1992.
46 Sørensen 2007, especially 91.
47 On the use of fired brick in the Roman East, see Dodge 1990.
48 Whittaker 2004, 13.
49 Potter 1996, 50: the frontiers are where "... different political/cultural entities confront each other".

'barbarised' by the textual sources, ancient and modern, because the culture there is not easily categorised as Greek, Roman or Other.

J. Elsner has written that Dura was part of a "permanent frontier", in that it is geographically in a frontier zone between the Roman and the Iranian empires.[50] Dura, understandably, is generally argued to be peripheral to both the Roman and Parthian spheres. However, in its uniquely Durene characteristics during the Roman period, Dura exemplifies the very essence of what it meant to live in a ordinary local town under the Roman empire. It characterizes the local response and the variability evident in what it meant to be Roman.[51] To put it another way: what makes Dura an excellent example of what it was to be Roman is precisely that it seems, in some ways, to be barely Roman at all.

To return briefly to the question of the place of the river as a boundary, as connector and as part of Dura's worldview: it has been shown that Dura was a central node for smaller agricultural communities up and down the Euphrates (and hence its sphere of influence is not sphere-shaped but river-shaped).[52] The rhythm of the river had cycles throughout the year, providing water for agriculture, constantly shaping and re-shaping the landscape, and creating an additional spatial dimension through movement. Just as the town itself was subjected to various territories of influence and control, the river too was in a constant state of flux. Dura's relationship with its region was intimately tied up with the river. While the Euphrates might have been a conceptual boundary in some sense for Rome, for the people of Dura its place would have been constantly changing and omnipresent. The Euphrates formed a barrier between Rome and Persia only inasmuch as the Roman core perceived it to be one.[53] While Rome perceived the Euphrates as emblematic of the conquered region[54] and a line in the sand between what was Roman and non-Roman, the view from Dura of the river, which was not only its water source but also its source of local power, would have been quite different. It is doubtful the river was ever perceived by the inhabitants as a boundary (the Sasanians attacked, after all, from the steppe on the W side of the town). The Euphrates was the means by which most contacts came to and went from Dura. The river is a source, a point from which places emerge, thus not a boundary. The Euphrates can be understood both as a conceptual boundary (as it is in ancient texts and representations) and as a connective feature in the landscape (as it no doubt functioned on the ground).

---

50   Elsner 2001, 271.
51   For local experiences of being Roman, we can now turn to Derks 1998, Mattingly 2004 and Revell 2009.
52   Millar 1993, 449-50. On Dura as regional capital, see Leriche 1996b. On differing "mental maps" and the imposition of archaeological maps as a universal understanding of geography, see Babić 2007.
53   No physical feature of the landscape is truly a boundary in itself. Instead, boundaries are indicated "in relation to the activities of the people (or animals) for whom it is recognised or experienced as such" (Ingold 2000, 192-93). For the Euphrates in Roman thought, see, e.g., Verg., *Aen.* 8.727. On the Euphrates in Vergil, see Clauss 1988; Jenkyns 1993. For the changing current of the river as metaphor for the newly civilized people of the region, see Jones 2005, 73-74 and 74 n.11. On the personification of rivers in Roman art, see Ostrowski 1991.
54   For instance, see the (probable) depiction of the Euphrates on the Arch of Severus at Rome or on coins of Trajan: Brilliant 1967, 129-35; *BMCRE* III, 221 no. 1033. On rivers as boundaries in Roman thought, see Braund 1996 and Whittaker 1994, 99-100. On the river as part of the defensive system of Syria, see Dąbrowa 1997.

Real change for most of Dura's population came early in the 3rd c. with the installation of the Roman garrison: in large part, we are dealing not with the response to Roman hegemony *per se*, but the response to the army. This is not to polarise military and civilian identities: in some senses the polarity between military and civilian is not a useful one, particularly as much of Rome's 3rd-c. military would have been made up of men from the East, if not from Syria itself. While corporate military identity will have had a strong, even primary rôle, in self-definition among the soldiers at Dura, other personal aspects will have had an impact too. Military identities overlapped and intertwined with 'civilian' ones.[55] Despite this, and particularly in an urban context such as Dura, the Roman military would have had a huge impact on daily life, not only in terms of the changing administration, taxation, legal institutions or economic opportunities, but also in terms of moving through the town and even within the homes of residents.

One of the larger problems highlighted by this study is that the periodization of sites within historical phasing, unchecked, and a lack of reflection on the historical production of archaeological knowledge have constrained the creation of artefactual typologies and also hampered our understanding of materialities of experience and the material construction of place. By examining small-scale, local phenomena we can understand the wider processes of which they are a part and how the urban landscape itself was manifesting the power dynamics at play. In exploring aspects of the lived experience of civilians rather than that of the army, this paper has given only part of the story. One person's homeland, however, is another's frontier,[56] and for that reason we need to begin to look in detail at the archaeology of both groups, the relationships within and between them, and their discrepant experiences.[57] Many important questions remain to be answered at Dura, including the nature of the communities within the town and the ways in which they may have interacted.[58] For instance, the assemblages and architecture are relatively homogeneous throughout the site in the Roman period, which is remarkable given the diversity in languages and religions.

While the study of frontiers and boundaries of the Roman world has been a topic of scholarly interest for some time, understandings of these zones has often proceeded, implicitly, from the stance of Roman writers. The peoples of the perceived periphery have yet to receive their own voices, and these will not, generally speaking, emerge from written sources.

At Dura, the Greek language is dominant in the textual record, and archaeologists gave elements of architecture and objects that were seen to be Greek a higher cultural currency than all of the architecture and material culture that is local in character. Interpretations have focused on the (nominally) Greek élite and the military, largely because these were the groups represented in the texts recovered. What has been neglected is the opportunity,

---

55 The classic example at Dura is *P. Dura* 32, a text detailing a divorce of a soldier from a local woman. For a study of identities at Dura using the onomastic evidence, see Sommer 2004. He shows that there was a low rate of adoption of the *tria nomina* after 212 at Dura (26% of individuals at Dura compared to 45% in rural areas evidenced in the *Papyri Euphratenses*) and that the majority of individuals who did take it up were soldiers or veterans. On military communities, see James 1999
56 Lightfoot and Martinez 1995, 473.
57 Mattingly 2004.
58 For a fascinating examination of religious communities at Dura, see Kaizer 2009a and 2009b.

given the large number of excavated houses, to look at the daily life of ordinary people. The opportunity has been missed to examine in detail the material culture of diverse religious and linguistic communities living in close spatial proximity in a frontier zone and to see the extent to which different forms of identity — civic, linguistic, and religious — were co-terminous.[59] We have only begun to scratch the surface in studying the nature of the composition of these groups and the interactions between them. First, however, there is a need to determine how much of the current reading of the material is the product of a system of archaeological classification that privileged particular forms. We need to re-evaluate archaeological knowledge that was built from a position that privileged one culture over another, evaluating the co-presence of these cultures. We must recognise a world in which mudbrick could be used alongside fired brick and in which the military could turn a town's fortifications in upon itself.

We should attempt not simply to show the local adoption of Roman material culture and customs, but also to characterize the interaction between, and negotiation with, the many identities at play: in other words, to examine discrepant experiences and specific, regional responses to Roman rule. What is needed is a more vigorous dialogue between ancient historians and archaeologists. Roman archaeologists can do better at understanding the history of the discipline in its context and its impact on the construction of knowledge. In the East, this should involve the shaking off of old ideas about the cultural supremacy of the Greek past or the polarization of eastern powers. Instead, we must develop a more nuanced approach to the complex negotiation of what it meant to live under Rome.

Bibliography

Alabe, F. 1992. "La céramique de Doura-Europos," *Dura-Europos Études* 1990 = *Syria* 69, 49-63.
Alabe, F. 2005. "Céramiques hellénistiques d'Europos à Doura: hasards ou cohérences?" *Doura-Europos Études* 5, 163-98.
Allara, A. 1988. "Les maisons de Doura-Europos: les données du terrain," *Doura-Europos Études* 1988 = *Syria* 65, 323-42.
Allison, P. M. 1997. "Roman households: an archaeological perspective," in H. M. Parkins (ed.), *Roman urbanism: beyond the consumer city* (London) 112-46.
Allison, P. M. 1999. "Labels for ladles: interpreting the material culture of Roman households," in ead. (ed.), *The archaeology of household activities* (London) 57-77.
Allison, P. M. 2001. "Using the material and written sources: turn of the millennium approaches to Roman domestic space," *AJA* 105, 181-208.
Andrén, A. 1998. *Between artifacts and texts: historical archaeology in global perspective* (New York).
Babić, S. 2007. "Greeks, barbarians and archaeologists: mapping the contact," *Ancient West & East* 6, 73-89.
Baird, J. A. 2006. *Housing and households at Dura-Europos: a study in identity on Rome's eastern frontier* (Ph.D. diss., Univ. of Leicester).
Baird, J. A. 2007. "The bizarre bazaar: early excavations in the Roman East and problems of nomenclature," in *TRAC 2006* (Oxford) 34-42.
Baird, J. A. 2011. "Photographing Dura-Europos 1928-1937. An archaeology of the archive," *AJA* 115.3, 427-46.
Baird, J. A. forthcoming. "Everyday life in Roman Dura-Europos: the evidence of dress practices," in T. Kaizer (ed.), *Religion, society and culture at Dura-Europos* (Cambridge).
Baur, P. V. C. 1947. *The excavations at Dura-Europos conducted by Yale University and the French Academy of Inscriptions and Letters. Final Report IV, Part III. The lamps* (New Haven, CT).

---

59   I hope to examine these issues more fully in a project on the communities of Dura-Europos, based on my Ph.D. thesis (Baird 2006).

Bowersock, G. W. 1989. "Social and economic history of Syria under the Roman empire," in J.-M. Dentzer and W. Orthmann (edd.), *Archéologie et histoire de la Syrie, 2: la Syrie de l'époque achéménide à l'avènement de l'Islam* (Saarbrücken) 63-80.
Braund, D. 1996. "River frontiers in the environmental psychology of the Roman world," in Kennedy 1996, 43-47.
Breasted, J. H. 1924. *The Oriental forerunners of Byzantine painting: first-century wall paintings from the fortress of Dura on the middle Euphrates* (Chicago, IL).
Brilliant, R. 1967. *The Arch of Septimius Severus in the Roman Forum* (MAAR 29).
Clauss, J. J. 1988. "Vergil and the Euphrates revisited," *AJP* 109, 309-20.
Cox, D. H. 1949. *The excavations at Dura-Europos conducted by Yale University and the French Academy of Inscriptions and Letters. Final report IV, Part I, fasc. 2. The Greek and Roman pottery* (New Haven, CT).
Dąbrowa, E. 1997. "The rivers in the defensive system of Roman Syria (from Augustus to Septimius Severus)," in W. Groenman-van Waateringe, B. L. van Beek, W. J. H. Willems *et al.* (edd.), *Roman frontier studies 1995* (Oxford) 109-11.
Derks, T. 1998. *Gods, temples and ritual practices: the transformation of religious ideas and values in Roman Gaul* (Amsterdam).
Dirven, L. 1999. *The Palmyrenes of Dura-Europos: a study of religious interaction in Roman Syria* (Leiden).
Dodge, H. 1990. "The architectural impact of Rome in the East," in M. Henig (ed.), *Architecture and architectural sculpture in the Roman empire* (Oxford) 108-20.
Downey, S. B. 1993. "Hellenistic, local, and Near Eastern elements in the terracotta production of Dura-Europos," in A. Invernizzi and J.-F. Salles (edd.), *Arabia antiqua* (Rome) 129-45.
Downey, S. B. 1996. "Terracotta plaques as evidence for connections between Palmyra and Dura-Europos," *AAAS* 42, 253-60.
Downey, S. B. 2000. "The transformation of Seleucid Dura-Europos," in E. Fentress (ed.), *Romanization and the city* (JRA Suppl. 38) 155-72.
Downey, S. B. 2003. *Terracotta figurines and plaques from Dura-Europos* (Ann Arbor, MI).
Downey, S. B. 2004. "Excavations in the temple of Zeus Megistos, 1994-1998," in P. Leriche, M. Gelin and A. Dandrau (edd.), *Doura-Europos Études 5, 1994-1997* (Paris) 41-55.
Dyson, S. L. 1968. *The excavations at Dura-Europos conducted by Yale University and the French Academy of Inscriptions and Letters. Final Report IV, Part I, fasc. 3. The commonware pottery, the brittle ware* (New Haven, CT).
Dyson, S. L. 1995. "Is there a text in this site?" in D. B. Small (ed.), *Methods in the Mediterranean: historical and archaeological views on texts and archaeology* (Leiden) 25-44.
Edwell, P. M. 2008. *Between Rome and Persia: the middle Euphrates, Mesopotamia and Palmyra under Roman control* (London).
Elsner, J. 2001. "Cultural resistance and the visual image: the case of Dura-Europos," *CPh* 96, 269-304.
Gelin, M. 1997. "Les fouilles anciennes de Doura-Europos et leur contexte: documents d'archives conservés dans les institutions françaises et témoignages," in P. Leriche and M. Gelin (edd.), *Doura-Europos Études* 4 (Beirut) 229-44.
Given, M. 2004. *The archaeology of the colonized* (London).
Goffman, E. 1963. *Behavior in public places* (New York).
Hamilakis, Y. 1999. "La trahison des archéologues? Archaeological practice as intellectual activity in postmodernity," *JMedArch* 12.1, 60-79.
Herbert, S. C. (ed.) 1997. *Tel Anafa* II,i: *the Hellenistic and Roman pottery* (JRA Suppl. 10.2).
Hoepfner, W. and E.-L. Schwandner 1994. *Haus und Stadt im klassischen Griechenland* (Munich).
Hopkins, C. 1934. "The tragedy of a buried city told by its ruins," *Illustrated London News*, Sept. 22, 421-23.
Ingold, T. 2000. *The perception of the environment: essays in livelihood, dwelling and skill* (Abingdon).
James, S. 1999. "The community of soldiers: a major identity and centre of power in the Roman empire," in *TRAC 98* (Oxford) 14-25.
James, S. 2007. "New light on the Roman military base at Dura-Europos: interim report on a pilot season of fieldwork in 2005," in A. S. Lewin and P. Pellegrini (edd.), *Proceedings of the later Roman army in the East conference, Potenza, 2005* (Oxford) 29-47.
James, S., J. A. Baird and K. Strutt (forthcoming). "Magnetometry survey of Dura's Roman military base and vicinity," in P. Leriche, S. de Pontbriand and G. Coqueugniot (edd.), *Europos-Doura Études* 6.
Jenkyns, R. 1993. "Virgil and the Euphrates," *AJPh* 114, 115-21.

Jones, P. J. 2005. *Reading rivers in Roman literature and culture* (Oxford).
Kaizer, T. 2009a. "Religion and language in Dura-Europos," in H. M. Cotton *et al.* (edd.), *From Hellenism to Islam: cultural and linguistic change in the Roman Near East* (Cambridge) 235-53.
Kaizer, T. 2009b. "Patterns of worship in Dura-Europos: a case study of religious life in the classical Levant outside the main cult centres," in C. Bonnet, V. Pirenne-Delforge and D. Praet (edd.), *Les religions orientales dans le monde grec et romain: cent ans après Cumont (1906-2006)* (Bruxelles) 153-72.
Kemash, Z. 2008. "What lies beneath? Perceptions of the ontological paradox of water," *WorldArch* 40, 224-37.
Kennedy, D. L. (ed.) 1996. *The Roman army in the East* (JRA Suppl. 18).
Laurence, R. 1995. "The organization of space in Pompeii," in T. Cornell and K. Lomas (edd.), *Urban society in Roman Italy* (New York) 63-78.
Leriche, P. 1996a. "Le *Chreophylakeion* de Doura-Europos et la mise en place du plan hippodamien de la ville," in M.-F. Boussac and A. Invernizzi (edd.), *Archives et sceaux du monde hellénistique* (Paris) 157-69.
Leriche, P. 1996b. "Dura-Europos (Archaeology)," *Encyclopaedia Iranica*, 589-93.
Leriche, P. 2003a. "Europos-Doura hellénistique," *La Syrie hellénistique* (TOPOI Suppl. 4) 171-91.
Leriche, P. 2003b. "Le phénomène urbain dans l'Orient hellénistique," in M. Reddé *et al.* (edd.), *La naissance de la ville dans l'antiquité* (Paris) 141-54.
Leriche, P. and A. Al-Mahmoud 1994. "Doura-Europos: bilan des recherches récentes," *CRAI*, 395-420.
Lightfoot, K. G. and A. Martinez 1995. "Frontiers and boundaries in archaeological perspective," *Annual Review of Anthropology* 24, 471-92.
Lowenthal, D. 1985. *The past is a foreign country* (Cambridge).
Mattingly, D. J. 2004. "Being Roman: expressing identity in a provincial setting," *JRA* 17, 5-25.
Millar, F. 1993. *The Roman Near East 31 BC–AD 337* (Cambridge, MA).
Moreland, J. 2003. *Archaeology and text* (London).
Ostrowski, J. A. 1991. *Personifications of rivers in Greek and Roman art* (Warsaw).
Pollard, N. 2007. "Colonial and cultural identities in Parthian and Roman Dura-Europos," in R. Alston and S. N. C. Lieu (edd.), *Aspects of the Roman East* I (Studia Antiqua Australiensia 3; Turnhout) 81-102.
Potter, D. 1996. "Emperors, their borders and their neighbours: the scope of the imperial *mandata*," in Kennedy 1996, 49-66.
Revell, L. 2009. *Roman imperialism and local identities* (Cambridge).
Rostovtzeff, M. I., *et al.* (edd.) 1936. *The excavations at Dura-Europos conducted by Yale University and the French Academy of Inscriptions and Letters. Preliminary report of the sixth season of work, October 1932–March 1933* (New Haven, CT).
Saliou, C. 1992. "Les quatre fils de Polémocratès (P. Dura 19)," *Doura-Europos Études 1990* = *Syria* 69, 65-100.
Sauer, E. W. (ed.) 2004. *Archaeology and ancient history* (London).
Shanks, M. 1992. *Experiencing the past: on the character of archaeology* (London).
Sherwin-White, S. and A. Kuhrt 1993. *From Samarkhand to Sardis: a new approach to the Seleucid empire* (London).
Sommer, M. 2004. "A map of meaning: approaching cultural identities at the Middle Euphrates (1st to 3rd centuries AD)," *Egitto e Vicino Oriente* 27, 153-83.
Sørensen, M. L. S. 2007. "Gender, things, and material culture," in S. M. Nelson (ed.), *Women in antiquity: theoretical approaches to gender and archaeology* (Lanham, MD) 75-105.
Toll, N. 1943. *The excavations at Dura-Europos conducted by Yale University and the French Academy of Inscriptions and Letters. Final report IV, Part I, fasc. 1. The green glazed pottery* (New Haven, CT).
Velud, C. 1988. "Contexte historique régional des fouilles de Doura entre les deux guerres mondiales," *Doura-Europos Études 1988* = *Syria* 65, 363-82.
Ward-Perkins, J. B. 1974. *Cities of ancient Greece and Italy: planning in classical antiquity* (New York).
Welles, C. B. 1951. "The population of Roman Dura," in P. R. Coleman-Norton (ed.), *Studies in Roman economic and social history in honor of Allan Chester Johnson* (Princeton, NJ) 251-73.
Welles, C. B. 1959. "The Hellenism of Dura-Europos," *Aegyptus* 39, 23-23.
Welles, C. B., R. O. Fink and J. F. Gilliam 1959. *The excavations at Dura-Europos conducted by Yale University and the French Academy of Inscriptions and Letters. Final Report V, Part I. The parchments and papyri* (New Haven, CT).

Wharton, A. J. 1995. *Refiguring the post classical city: Dura Europos, Jerash, Jerusalem and Ravenna* (Cambridge).

Whittaker, C. R. 1994. *Frontiers of the Roman empire: a social and economic study* (London).

Whittaker, C. R. 2004. *Rome and its frontiers: the dynamics of empire* (London).

Will, E. 1988. "La population de Doura-Europos: une évaluation," *Doura-Europos Études 1988 = Syria* 65, 315-21.

Woodward, C. 2001. *In ruins* (London).

Yon, J.-B. 1997. "Les conditions de travail de la mission américano-française à Doura-Europos à travers les archives de l'Université de Yale," in P. Leriche and M. Gelin (edd.), *Doura-Europos Études* 4 (Beirut) 245-52.

Fig. 1. View down the Embolos, toward the Library of Celsus from the State Agora (author).

Bodies in motion: civic ritual and place-making in Roman Ephesus
Cecelia Feldman Weiss

> "Humans are not placed. They bring place into being".
> J. Z. Smith (1987, 28)

Introduction: setting the stage

At Buckingham Palace the changing of the guard is a spectacle so thoroughly integrated into the character of the complex that it contributes to the identity of the location. Likewise, at St. Peter's Basilica the presence and actions of the Swiss Guards are so vital to the environment that they draw more of a crowd than does Michelangelo's Pieta. Ritualized performances have become integral to the character of both locations. These performances become part of a cultural landscape, embedded in the physical landscape. How, then, does this relate to ancient Ephesus?

Much of the earlier discussion on urban space in Ephesus, one of the major cities in Roman Asia Minor, has focused on its architectural and artistic programs.[1] These programs have been addressed using archaeological, art historical, architectural and historical approaches.[2] Such interpretations of the material world tend to flatten its multiple, dynamic meanings and disaggregate the phenomenological aspects of lived space from its material remains (fig. 1).[3] In this tradition, treatment of the ancient city accords primacy to the way in which we experience it as a static and overwhelmingly visual entity. Too often such treatments come at the expense of investigating daily, ritual and civic activities that have the potential to shape the city's physical environment, as it was animated by the action of its inhabitants, and to contribute to the characterization of a location as 'place'.[4]

S. R. F. Price and G. Rogers have pointed to the need to consider the concepts of ritual and performance when conceptualizing life in antiquity.[5] In a similar vein, I argue that performative action is not merely a superficial part of the cultural landscape but rather an essential component of urban space.[6] Performance should be considered a vital element within the urban built environment and integral to the creation of city as place. I draw on previous scholarship concerning the urban environment and civic performance at Ephesus but with the intent of examining how the space within the city was animated by the practices of those who inhabited it. I use as a case study the procession outlined in the civic

---

1 Koester 1995; Sherwood 2000; Kalinowski 2002; Klose 2005.
2 Friesen 1993; D. P. Crouch (2004) investigates the geological resources in and around Ephesus and W Asia Minor; see also Ng 2007 for the connection between élite patronage, mythology and sculptural programs in Ephesus.
3 Ö. Harmanşah, pers. comm.; Wandsnider and Athanassopoulos 2004.
4 These aspects of life in antiquity are often unavailable to us due to the nature of the archaeological record and our means of interrogating it. Because our investigation always deals with the material remains of human actions, it is often difficult to identify the subtleties of lived experience. I do not, however, advocate a strictly phenomenological perspective; instead, I suggest that we consider the ways in which the dynamism of human action was integral to the shape and meaning of lived places.
5 Price 1984; Rogers 1991.
6 Muir 1981; see Trexler 1983 for examples of other studies that address civic performance.

dedication by C. Vibius Salutaris and carried out possibly as often as every fortnight, to examine civic performance as a place-making practice.[7]

Theoretical considerations: ritual and place

The terms 'place' and 'ritual' have a long history of use and have been deployed in different disciplines to different ends. E. Casey highlights the distinction between 'space', an all-encompassing reality that allows things to be located within it, and 'place', which, being more than simply the reciprocal influence between people and the world, is "their constitutive co-ingrediance", such that each is essential to the being of the other.[8] Over and against spatial theory, which regards space as the original entity from which place is derived, this perspective views place and space as two fundamentally different orders of reality.[9] Here, 'place' is considered to be a basic unit of lived experience and a nexus of human praxis.[10] In other words, place is produced by human engagements and associations with the world. Employing a similar conception of place in his work on the Western Apache, K. Basso focused on the idea of 'dwelling', which consists of the multiple lived-relationships that people maintain with places. He argued that space acquires meaning only through the intimate connections established between people and the places they inhabit.[11] The Western Apache associate stories with specific features in their landscape which are not created *de novo* but rather are the result of sustained interaction between people and their world, each influencing and informing the other. Continued and intimate interaction with the material world is thus an essential component in the act of place-making.

As Casey suggests, "places actively solicit bodily motions".[12] I will emphasize the sense of embodiment and movement that underlies this notion of place and place-making. T. Ingold illustrates the connection between place and movement by drawing on the perspectives of the Walbiri people of Central Australia. From this anthropological perspective, Ingold suggests that place consists of the lines along which people live and move, just as the Walbiri consider a person's life to consist of the sum of his or her trails. Where there is a density of movement, the lines bunch together to form a knot, which Ingold considers to be a metaphor for place. According to him, this contrasts markedly with modern conceptions of place, which is instead reconfigured as a "nexus in which all life, growth and activity are *contained*".[13] The reciprocity between movement and place is also demonstrated by the humanist geographer Y.-F. Tuan, who uses the metaphors of movement and pause to illustrate his definition of place-making: "... if we think of space as that which allows movement, then place is pause; each pause in movement makes it possible for location to be transformed into place".[14] Approaching 'place' from an experiential perspective, Tuan emphasizes how embodied action, both in moving and in not moving, is a necessary component in the place-making process.

---

7   The major editors of this text include Hicks 1890; Heberdey 1912, vol. II; and Wankel 1979 = *IvE* I, 27.
8   Casey 2001, 406.
9   Ibid. 404.
10 Id. 2008, 44-45.
11 Basso 1996, 54. He bases his concept of dwelling largely on the work of M. Heidegger (1977).
12 Casey 1996, 24.
13 Ingold 2007, 96 (original emphasis).
14 Tuan 1977, 6.

Ritual action is one venue in which to examine this engagement between people and place. I use 'ritual' to refer to circumscribed and iterative action that need not occur only in a religious context.[15] J. Z. Smith argues that ritual action serves as a nexus for the intersection of people and place, in that both place and ritual are modes of paying attention. According to him:

> Ritual is, first and foremost, a mode of paying attention. It is a process for marking interest. It is the recognition of this fundamental characteristic of ritual that most sharply distinguishes our understanding from that of the Reformers, with their all too easy equation of ritual with blind and thoughtless habit. It is this characteristic, as well, that explains the role of place as a fundamental component of ritual: place directs attention.[16]

Although his focus is on the theorization of ritual, not place, Smith makes a case for an intimate, interrelated connection between the two. He suggests that ritual focuses attention on place because it cannot exist in a vacuum; rather, the location in which ritual action occurs is an essential element of the ritual performance. Place and ritual reciprocally direct attention.

"*Lived bodies belong to places* and help to constitute them ... By the same token, however, *places belong to lived bodies* and depend on them".[17] In other words, just as surely as human actions and engagements make place, place shapes human identity. The study of urban environments has largely neglected the centrality of human engagement as an integral component of the urban landscape. There are undeniable challenges implicit in our project, which attempts to invoke impermanent actions and human experience through examination of a text; however, the detailed instructions of the Salutaris dedication coupled with the extraordinary preservation of the urban fabric of Ephesus provide a productive starting point.

The Salutaris dedication: the script

C. Vibius Salutaris presented the donation under discussion to Ephesus in A.D. 104. Salutaris was a Roman equestrian whose *cursus honorum* is imprecisely known, who owned estates near Ephesus and had already bestowed benefactions on the city, where he was both a citizen and member of the *boule*.[18] The dedication was inscribed on the marble wall of the S *parados* of the Great Theater and in the Artemision (the temple to Artemis), two of Ephesus' most conspicuous locations. The lengthy inscription (568 lines survive) was in 6 columns, placed on the wall at a height varying from 2.08 to 4.30 m. The small size of the letters (ranging from *c*.1-4 cm tall) suggests that the inscription was not intended to be read, but rather served as a material symbol of Salutaris' generosity toward the city.[19]

The inscription was published and extensively interpreted by G. Rogers in his book *The sacred identity of Ephesus* (1991). While I draw heavily on Rogers' interpretation of the

---

15   Bell 1992; for other perspectives on ritual, see Insoll 2004 and Alexander 2006.
16   Smith 1987, 103; see also Trexler 1983. C. Renfrew (2007, 115) also suggests that ritual is attention-focusing, one of four main aspects of religious ritual.
17   Casey 1996, 24 (original emphasis).
18   Rogers 1991, 16-19; M. E. H. Walbank (1994, 90) suggests that the reference in the dedication to Salutaris' tribe, Oufentina, one of the Roman tribes originating from Terracina (*IvE* I 27, line 452), may indicate that his origins were Italian rather than Ephesian.
19   Rogers 1991, 19-24.

mechanics of the dedication itself, I depart from his interpretation of the meaning of the civic ritual performance as it was based largely on the perspective of the dedicator, his motivations and intentions. In contrast, I consider this dedication and its enactment to have had multiple meanings in different contexts. This approach is supported by C. Renfrew's assertion that the meaning of ritual need not be something that is defined prior to its enactment: it does not necessarily remain constant through time, but "instead, the ceremony itself, the ritual *is* the point".[20] In the following, I explore ritual performance as a place-making practice through its interaction with the urban fabric and its frequent repetition within Ephesus.

The text of the dedication calls for the distribution of money to various civic and religious bodies. These lotteries were to have been carried out at the Artemision during the annual celebration of the goddess' birthday. In addition to the distribution of money, Salutaris specified that a procession was to be enacted, and that is my focus here. The Salutaris dedication called for a procession of people and statues in a prescribed route along the major thoroughfares in and around Ephesus. They interacted with city gates, civic and religious architecture, euergetistic monuments, residential areas and the surrounding landscape.

The procession's route was explicitly outlined in the dedication (fig. 2).[21] The participants would have passed major points of interest both inside and outside the city walls. Beginning at the Temple of Artemis, one of the two locations where the inscription was located, the participants crossed the temenos of the sacred precinct and followed the Sacred Way to the Magnesian Gate. The Sacred Way skirted the E side of the Panayir Dağ (the hill of ancient Pion)[22] and led from the Artemision to the sacred Ortygian Groves, Artemis's mythological birthplace.[23] This was also the beginning of the route used for the sacred annual procession in celebration of Artemis' birthday.[24] Along this route the procession also crossed the Selinous and Marnas rivers. The Marnas was a major source of water for the city. Testament to its centrality in civic life is its appearance on several coins issued by the Ephesian mint.[25] At the Magnesian Gate, the main S entrance, the procession moved into the center of the city. It then traveled along the major thoroughfare stretching between the Magnesian Gate on the southeast and the Koressian Gate on the northeast.

---

20   Renfrew 2007, 117 (original emphasis).
21   *IvE* I 27, lines 49-52, 210-13 and 423-25; translation by Rogers (1991).
22   In Turkish, Panayir Dağ means 'Festival' or 'Panegyric Mountain'. Here we see the uses of landscape and practices from antiquity memorialized in modern toponyms.
23   Several locations have been suggested as the birthplace for Artemis and her twin brother Apollo. The Cycladic island of Delos was widely held to be the birthplace of the twins, while the *Hom. Hymn Delian Apollo* (15) claims that Apollo was born on Delos and Artemis was born in Ortygia, commonly believed to be located near Syracuse in Sicily. However, the Ephesians maintained that the twin gods were born in the groves outside their city walls, an opinion echoed by Strabo (14.20): "On the same coast, slightly above the sea, is also Ortygia ... where Leto is said to have bathed after the birth of her travail. For here is the mythical scene of the birth, and of the nurse Ortygia, and the holy place where the birth took place, and of the olive tree nearby, where the goddess is said first to have taken rest after she was relieved from her travail".
24   For more on the festivals celebrated in honor of Artemis, see Strabo 14.20; Xenophon of Ephesos, *The Ephesian Tale of Anthia and Habrocomes*; and Ach. Tat., *The Adventures of Leucippe and Clitophon*.
25   Rogers 1991; Karwiese 2006; see also Scherrer 2001.

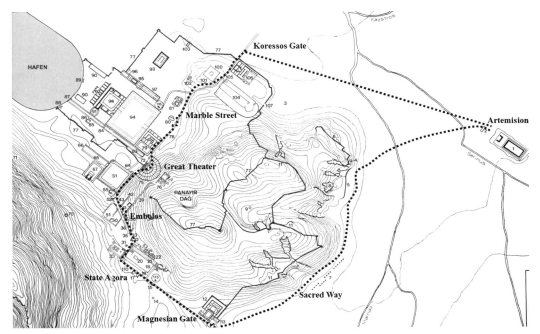

Fig. 2. Plan of Ephesus with route as outlined in the Salutaris dedication (after Scherrer 2006, fig. 1, with modifications).

The gathering passed through the State Agora and the Embolos, a crowded commercial district, then continued down the Marble Street, the longest artery, its length embellished with statues and colonnades. About halfway down the Marble Street stands the Great Theater, the second location of the dedication's text, where the procession made its only stop inside the city. Curiously, the dedication is not explicit about what happened during that pause. The procession then continued down the street leading to the Stadium, out the Koressos Gate and back to the Artemision, completing a full circuit.

The dedication specified that the procession should occur "during the first new moon's sacrifice of the archieratic year, and on the occasions of the 12 sacred gatherings and regular assemblies every month, and during the Sebasteia and the Soteria and the penteteric festivals", during all gymnastic games and on all other occasions determined by the *demos* and the *boule*.[26] Rogers estimates that this procession occurred as frequently as once every two weeks.[27] Regardless of the precise number of annual enactments, the impression from the dedication is that this performance occurred regularly over the course of the year. The procession, in other words, was an iterative performance, one that happened frequently and followed a consistent framework.

Rogers suggests that the primary purpose of the dedication was to inculcate the *paides* and the ephebes into the Ephesian social hierarchy and to teach them about the "history of Ephesos through physical participation in these civic rituals".[28] While he acknowledges that the ritual procession fulfilled other social functions, he does so in passing without

---

26 *IvE* I 27, lines 48-56.
27 Rogers 1991, 83.
28 Ibid. 136-37.

exploring any other possibilities. He argues that the 'message' of the procession was more completely internalized by its frequent enactment:

> When the ephebes carried the statues into the theatre, and acted out the history of the city, they also advertised the *philotimia* of Salutaris, held up that *philotimia* as worthy of imitation by rival benefactors, and entertained the spectators in the streets of the city. These various social functions (and no doubt more) integrated and reinforced each other through the medium of the repeated performance.[29]

While Rogers may be right to suggest that Salutaris provided the endowment in order to reproduce certain social structures, the procession was nonetheless experienced by a variety of people as a part of the Ephesian cultural landscape. While the framework of the act is the same — the processional route was fixed and the ritual implements and statues were unchangeable, otherwise the dedication promises grave consequences[30] — the spontaneous and diverse responses to the performance must have varied with each subsequent iteration. Moreover, the experience of the procession would have differed for each person based on his or her level of participation, civic position, social station, age, and any number of other relevant factors. In contrast to Rogers' interpretation that the dedication was an educational tool, I prefer to focus on the relationship among the performers, the built environment and extra-urban landscape.[31] I propose that the procession itself became part of the urban landscape through the frequent enactment of the performance and the participants' continuous engagement with the urban environment. Not only was the action of the civic performance circumscribed in time and location, but the procession also physically circumscribed the city. By tracing a path from the extra-urban Artemision through the city and back again, these performers were kinetically engaged with the landscape by means of their movement through it. Ritual focuses attention on place,[32] and one can imagine that this civic ritual created in participants and observers alike an awareness of the places through which it moved.

The players

Who would have participated in the procession? Renfrew suggests that not all people present at a ritual performance need be actors in it, nor must they all act in the same way.[33] The dedication offers detailed information about the responsibilities of certain participants as well as about the groups receiving money from the lottery. Rogers estimates that at least 1,500 citizens, plus civic and religious attendants, obtained some donation from Salutaris at the annual lottery.[34] The dedication is also explicit that the ephebes, *neopoioi*, the beadle,[35]

---

29 Ibid. 112.
30 *IvE* I 27, lines 210-20: "Nor let it be possible for anyone to make changes in the administration either of the type-statues of the goddess, or the images with a view toward changing the names or melting down, or in any other way to do evil, since the one who does any of these things, let him be liable for sacrilege and impiety, and none the less let the same weight be shown in the aforementioned type-statues and images, 111 pounds, having the prosecution about these things by necessity [half-line missing] ... " (transl. Rogers 1991, 162-65).
31 Casey 2001, 406.
32 Smith 1987, 103.
33 Renfrew 2007, 115-16.
34 Rogers 1991, 41-65.
35 The dedication reads *skaptouchios*, which Rogers translates as 'beadle', but 'staff bearer' might be a more appropriate translation.

and guards should carry the statues during the procession.[36] Given that there were c.250 ephebes in A.D. 104, Rogers suggests that there were 260 participants: the ephebes plus 10 additional attendants.[37]

And what of those going about their daily business, who acted as a potential audience? As ritual has the ability to direct attention, the people watching the performance with close consideration, in effect, may also have become participants.[38] The inscription refers to the procession's audience in passing when it mentions "the care of the aforementioned sacred images, *and the conveyance before everyone* (koin[on]), from the temple into the theater, and from the theater into the temple of Artemis …".[39] What is meant by 'everyone' is vague. Rogers concludes that "except for slaves and foreigners, virtually the whole adult male population of Ephesus either took part in or watched these public rituals".[40] Rogers gives no explanation for excluding slaves and foreigners from his estimate. As Ephesus was a bustling metropolis that attracted a variety of people, it is likely that people of various social stations moving about town may have been witness to the procession. The interpretation of the civic ritual would vary depending on the perspective of the viewer, but it does not necessarily exclude those who were not adult male citizens from participating as active observers. If we assume that the procession actually happened in the way it is outlined in the text — with relative frequency, through the major city streets, and during major civic and religious occasions — it is fair to conclude that the majority of the inhabitants of Ephesus either participated in or witnessed it.

The statues dedicated by Salutaris participated too. Artemis, the city's patron deity, figured prominently in the performance. The procession began and ended at her sanctuary, and the dedication describes in detail the 9 gold and silver statues in her image: seven of the statues were silver, one image was silver-gilt, and the single gold statue depicted Artemis flanked by two silver stags. This was not an iconographical type unique to Ephesus (the so-called Ephesian Artemis), but rather a more universal representation of the goddess as huntress.[41] Also in the procession were 20 statues representing notable individuals, groups, and topographical features that played a central rôle in the Ephesian civic imagination.[42] The statues dedicated by Salutaris, all in silver, were as follows: Trajan and his wife Plotina; the Roman senate, Ephesian *boule*, equestrian order, and ephebes; deified Augustus accompanied by Sebaste, the Ephesian tribe named in his honor; "the loyal

---

36 Rogers 1991, 61; *IvE* I 27, line 48: " … by the guards, and two of the *neopoioi* attending and the beadle, to be brought and brought back, the ephebes receiving and escorting from the Magnesian Gate into the theater, and from the theater in the same manner …";
line 210: "After the assemblies have been dismissed, the type-statues and the images should be carried back to the sanctuary of Artemis and should be handed over by the guards, two of the *neopoioi* and a beadle attending, to Mousaios, sacred slave of Artemis, custodian of the things deposited, the ephebes receiving and escorting from the Magnesian gate …";
line 423: "That it may be permitted to the gold-bearers for the goddess to bring into the assemblies and the contests the type-statues and the images dedicated by Caius Vibius Salutaris from the pronaos of Artemis, the *neopoioi* sharing in the care, and the ephebes sharing in receiving them from the Magnesian Gate, and in escorting the procession up to the Koressian Gate".
37 Rogers 1991, 86.
38 Smith 1987, 103; Renfrew 2007, 115.
39 *IvE* I 27, line 91 (emphasis mine).
40 Rogers 1991, 136.
41 *IvE* I 27, lines 158-59.
42 See ibid., lines 135-97 for the enumeration of the dedicated statues.

demos of the Ephesians", and the tribe of the Ephesians;[43] Androklos, the city's mythological founder;[44] and of Lysimachos, (re)founder of the city in the 3rd c. B.C.[45] There were also statues of the other 4 Ephesian tribes — the Karenaioi, Teioi, Bembinaioi, and Euonumoi — as well as Pion, the god associated with the mountain around which Ephesus was built.[46] All the images were carried in the procession and installed on their own statue bases above the block of the *boule* in the Great Theater. Although none of the statues survives, bases for statues of the 4 tribes were uncovered during excavations in the Great Theater.[47] Consistency between the description of the statues in the dedication and the inscriptions on the excavated bases suggests that the procession as it was practiced conformed with Salutaris' instructions.[48]

Rogers has proposed that the statues were a visual manifestation of the social hierarchy of Ephesus.[49] I suggest that they were more than just visual representations and actually stood in for the people and institutions they depicted.[50] Through them, the emperor, goddess, Roman senate, and the civic councils and tribes of the city were participating in this ritual. The statues were essential participants in the procession.

The urban theater: performance in place

More specific data on the nature of the procession would influence our reading of the intricacies of the performance, but the basic conclusion remains the same. It was a regular part of the urban rhythms in Ephesus, a part of the cadence of life. With the ritual performance being regularly enacted in that location, it produced a uniquely Ephesian place.

By their nature, urban environments convey an element of spectacle and theatricality.[51] Although the mundane actions of individuals within cities rarely survive in the archaeological record, human engagements are important in our consideration of cities as places. Basso suggests that meanings are attached to the world through the process of dwelling, which is the result of continued and intimate interaction.[52] Meanings connected to the built environment and to the surrounding landscape form a palimpsest of stories, experiences and associations. Performance interacts with these associations and enlivens the physical realities of place, transforming itself into an essential component within the fabric of the

---

[43] Ibid., lines 134-67.
[44] The name Androklos in line 183 is restored on the suggestion of R. Merkelbach: see Rogers 1991, 117, n.16.
[45] *IvE* I 27, lines 168-97.
[46] Pion is restored in line 195 by Heberdy; see Rogers 1991, 117, n.16.
[47] *IvE* I 28-31; see also Rogers 1991, 102 and 123, n.170.
[48] Rogers (1991, 102) avers that this consistency proves that the procession took place "exactly as Salutaris planned it". I prefer not to assume a definitive correlation between the material evidence and the way in which the procession was actually carried out. We can only infer a connection between material remains and the enactment of the dedication.
[49] Ibid. 1991, 137; see also Ng 2007.
[50] B. Latour (2005) discusses the concept of representation from a political perspective. He argues that, as in a representational system of government, one individual stands in for the constituency that he or she represents. When thinking about images that represent an individual or collective body, it is helpful to see them from this perspective as agents standing in for the individuals and collective bodies they depict. See also Price 1984 and Strathern 1999.
[51] Bergmann and Kondoleon 1999.
[52] Basso 1996.

built environment.[53] Through physical engagement with place, new meanings and memories are created, while previously held associations are maintained through sustained interaction.[54] The setting for the performance provides the context within which the ritual becomes meaningful. The visual climate of Ephesus was rich and diverse. Its prosperity was echoed in the material richness of large-scale building programs sponsored by imperial or élite patrons.[55]

The text of the dedication was erected in two of the city's most significant locations: on the marble wall of the S *parados* of the Great Theater, and in the Artemision.[56] Its height (well above eye level), the small size of the letters, and the length and breadth of the text suggests that it was not intended to be read.[57] However, the ceremonies outlined by the dedication occurred in the theater and the cult temple to Artemis, so the inscription itself was physically present during the performances.[58] At other times, the inscriptions remained as a conspicuous feature in the cityscape, ensuring that traces of this civic performance became a permanent part of the built environment.

Unlike other euergetists who influenced urban life through contributions to the built environment, Salutaris' benefaction came in the form of civic lotteries and ritual performance, yet his procession still played into the architectural and topographical setting of Ephesus. Its processional route took advantage of the directional and spatial cues embedded in Ephesus' urban fabric.[59] Important moments in the ritual performance were underscored by the locations where they occurred. For example, the Magnesian Gate, the point where the procession crossed into the city and the statues were transferred to the ephebes, played on the physical and ritual distinction between city and country.[60] The processional route also followed the city's topographical setting. It started by winding through the low valley between the Artemision and the city center. Once within the city limits, the performers moved between the towering buildings of the State Agora. Then, processing down the Embolos, they descended a slope toward the harbor, which would have been visible at the base of the hill.[61] Rogers suggests that the route of the Salutaris procession retraced the history of Ephesus in reverse: beginning with its present, symbolized by the State Agora built by imperial patrons, and ending with its mythological foundation, expressed by the Koressian Gate located in the area of Ephesus' foundation. Artemis' importance to the performance is shown by the procession beginning and ending at her temple.[62] While Rogers rightly points out that there is a loosely chronological logic to the route of the procession, it is debatable whether this historical narrative was the

---

53 Favro 1994.
54 Alcock 2002.
55 Gleason 1995; Kalinowski 2002.
56 Rogers (1991, 20) suggests that, although the exact location of the inscription has not been determined, it is likely that it was positioned in a conspicuous place within the temple.
57 For the dimensions, see above p. 53 n.19.
58 Ibid. 20-22. Both of these locations were integral to the civic ritual performance. The Artemision was the location where the procession both began and ended; the procession paused for ceremonies in the Great Theater.
59 MacDonald 1936.
60 *IvE* I 27, lines 49-50.
61 Yegül 1994.
62 Rogers 1991, 113-15.

primary motivation for the path chosen. In her review of Rogers' book, M. E. H. Walbank suggests that there may simply have been practical considerations to the route: namely, that it was the simplest downhill path that passed along the major thoroughfares and led to the theater.[63]

But other factors make the path meaningful. The landmarks past which the procession moved also had a long history of performance, both ritual and routine. The accretion of activities and meanings within the urban environment and the consciousness of them on the part of its residents further contribute to the intensity of engagement with place. Use of the Sacred Way for part of the processional route illustrates the build-up of meanings within the landscape and the ways in which the urban residents might activate those meanings. The Sacred Way was the processional route from the Artemision to the sacred Ortygian Groves. The path extended from the Artemision along the Embolos and the valley between the Panayir Dağ and Bülbül Dağ and then exited the city to the groves located on the Bülbül Dağ. The Salutaris procession followed the Sacred Way for a substantial segment of its route through the city, and Salutaris may well have intended to capitalize on the sacredness of its path.

Sacred rites were held annually to celebrate the birth of Artemis; they included sacrifices, lavish banquets, and a re-enactment of Artemis's birth in the Ortygian Groves. The festival of Artemis Ephesia is described in the *Ephesian tale of Anthia and Habrocomes* by Xenophon of Ephesus:

> The local festival of Artemis was in progress, with its procession from the city to the temple nearly a mile away. All the local girls had to march in the procession, richly dressed, as well as all the young men ... There was a great crowd of Ephesians and visitors alike to see the festival, for it was the custom at this festival to find husbands for the young girls and wives for the young men. So the procession filed past — first, the sacred objects, the torches, the baskets and the incense; then horses, dogs and hunting equipment ... And when the procession was over, the whole crowd went into the temple for the sacrifice, and the files broke up; and the men and women, girls and boys came together (1.2-3).

These rites included a procession from the Temple of Artemis to the Ortygian Groves. This path served to connect the birthplace of the goddess with her temple and perhaps ritually re-created the story of the birth of the goddess. By taking part in the annual rite, the participants also re-enacted the myth. Taking the same path for the Salutaris procession, the participants engaged with the route's previous associations and, through its action, produced additional layers of meaning.

Also highlighting the association of stories with place, and of place with human activity, is the Koressian Gate's presence in the procession. The gate's name refers to the story of Ephesus' mythological founding by Androklos, who, in fulfillment of a prophecy, settled his town on the slopes of the Koressos, the NW slope of the Panayir Dağ.[64] The gate served as the architectural manifestation of this Greek foundation myth and was the last monument with which the procession interacted before exiting the city on its way back to the Artemision. The presence of the statue of Androklos in the location where he fulfilled the prophecy and founded the city added meaning to the performance.[65]

---

[63] Walbank 1994, 90.
[64] Ibid. 106; Ath. 8.361.
[65] Rogers 1991, 106-7.

Bodies in motion: civic ritual and place-making in Roman Ephesus

The segment of the processional route that followed the Embolos illustrates the contrast between the chaotic heterogeneity of daily life and the circumscribed action of ritual performance. The Embolos was home to shops, houses, fountains, temples, a bath and a latrine. In her discussion of the built environment and activities performed in the Athenian Agora, S. Alcock captures the spectacle of a city:

> Why would people go to the Agora, and what would they do there? Some would be on their way to sacrifice at temples; others would call at buildings still active in civic administration; others would be sightseeing; still others would merely be passing through, on their way to the Market of Caesar and Augustus, to the Acropolis, or to ends known best to themselves ... They would each move through their own version of the space for their own purposes: to visit different monuments, to perform different rituals, to seek different services, and to enjoy different things.[66]

Alcock highlights here the multi-directional, multi-purpose movements of people. As Casey states, "the basis of the density of engagement between self and place in this world is the set of *habitualities* by which its rich fabric is woven".[67] The multiplicity of daily actions along the Embolos is distinct from the ordered performance of the Salutaris procession. According to Smith, "ritual is, above all, an assertion of difference ... Ritual is a relationship between 'nows' — the now of everyday life and the now of ritual place; the simultaneity, but not the coexistence of 'here' and 'there'".[68] He also says that the assertion of difference is most thoroughly expressed in built ritual environments, particularly with the construction of temples.[69] However, the structured action of the procession within the city would have emphasized the difference between the ritual time and place of the performance *versus* all other time. From this, the action of the procession had the ability to create sacred space within the urban fabric, if only while it was moving through it.

Performance activates and enlivens the urban landscape, drawing on stories and meanings already present in the environment and creating new associations with every subsequent enactment. The people of Ephesus acted out the dedication within their lived environment through the theatricality and ritual repetition of the procession. Using physical engagement with the urban and extra-urban landscape, the people of Ephesus focussed attention on place, through participation and observation in this civic ritual performance. This frequent procession became an integral component of the urban rhythms and character of Ephesus. Through its staging and participants (human, architectural, topographic, and its statuary), the civic ritual performance played upon associations present within both the urban landscape and the collective memory. It also had the potential to create new meanings through its iterative action.

Conclusion: as the curtain falls

A close, contextual examination of civic ritual performance in Ephesus can shed light on processes that make place. I have argued that performance was a vital part of urban experience in antiquity and was a means through which place was conceived and produced. Performance engenders bodily interaction with the world which, as Casey suggests, is the

---

66   Alcock 2002, 64-65.
67   Casey 2001, 409 (original emphasis).
68   Smith 1987, 109-10.
69   Ibid. 104.

most fundamental component in the creation of place.[70] Movement, as described by Ingold, forms the ontological basis of what happens in place. He stresses that place is neither static nor a container within which life and activity happen, but rather a density of movement in one location.[71] The movement within and around Ephesus in the context of the Salutaris procession furnishes an example of physical interaction with the world through ritualized and iterative action. The kinetic engagement with the world engendered by ritual performance in turn serves to focus attention on place.[72] As part of "dwelling in place", which is the result of sustained and intimate interaction with the landscape and the built environment, stories and meanings are created and associated with the world.[73] Within the framework of this civic ritual performance, the stories associated with Ephesus' urban and extra-urban landscape would have been perceived through the structure of the ritual. Reciprocally, place directs attention to ritual action.[74]

Thus, the procession within the urban environment is itself another kind of (ephemeral) monument dedicated by Salutaris, but, unlike architectural monuments, the performance has evaporated with the passing of millennia. Yet like the changing of the guard at Buckingham Palace or the Swiss Guards at St. Peter's Basilica, the performative action of Salutaris' procession and other civic rituals should be considered integral to Ephesus-as-place. Performance is a vital component in the act of place-making — both in the relationships that people make to their lived environments through physical interaction and in the ways the built and natural landscape is enlivened by human action.

Bibliography
Alcock, S. 2002. *Archaeologies of the Greek past: landscape, monuments, and memories* (Cambridge).
Alexander, J. 2006. "Cultural pragmatics: social performance between ritual and strategy," in J. Alexander, B. Giesen and J. Mast (edd.), *Social performance: symbolic action, cultural pragmatics, and ritual* (Cambridge) 29-90.
Basso, K. 1996. "Wisdom sits in places: notes on a western Apache landscape," in Feld and Basso 1996, 53-90.
Bell, C. 1992. *Ritual theory, ritual practice* (Oxford).
Bergmann, B. and C. Kondoleon (edd.) 1999. *The art of ancient spectacle* (New Haven, CT).
Casey, E. 1996. "How to get from space to place in a fairly short stretch of time: phenomenological prolegomena," in Feld and Basso 1996, 13-52.
Casey, E. 2001. "Body, self, and landscape: a geophilosophical inquiry into the place-world," in P. C. Adams, S. Hoelscher and K. Till (edd.), *Textures of place: exploring humanist geographies* (Minneapolis, MN) 403-25.
Casey, E. 2008. "*Place* in landscape archaeology: a western philosophical prelude," in B. David and J. Thomas (edd.), *Handbook of landscape archaeology* (Walnut Creek, CA) 44-50.
Celik, Z., D. Favro and R. Ingersoll (edd.) 1994. *Streets: critical perspectives on public space* (Berkeley, CA).
Crouch, D. P. 2004. *Geology and settlement: Greco-Roman patterns* (Oxford).
Favro, D. 1994. "The street triumphant: the urban impact of Roman triumphal parades," in Celik, Favro and Ingersoll 1994, 151-64.
Feld, S. and K. Basso (edd.) 1996. *Senses of place* (Santa Fe, NM).
Friesen, S. 1993. *Twice Neokoros: Ephesus, Asia, and the cult of the Flavian imperial family* (Leiden).
Gleason, M. 1995. *Making men: sophists and self-presentation in ancient Rome* (Princeton, NJ).
Heberdey, R. 1912. *Forschungen in Ephesos*, vol. II (Vienna).

---

70   Casey 1996 and 2001.
71   Ingold 2007, 96-103.
72   Smith 1987; Casey 2001; Renfrew 2007.
73   Basso 1996.
74   Smith 1987, 103.

Heidegger, M. 1977. "Building dwelling thinking," in id., *Poetry, language, thought* (transl. A. Hofstadter; New York) 141-60.

Hicks, E. L. 1890. *Ancient Greek inscriptions in the British Museum*, III.2 (Oxford).

Ingold, T. 2007. *Lines: a brief history* (London).

Insoll, T. 2004. *Archaeology, ritual, religion* (London).

Kalinowski, A. 2002. "The Vedii Antonini: aspects of patronage and benefaction in second-century Ephesos," *Phoenix* 56, 109-49.

Karwiese, S. 2006. "ΠΟΛΙΣ ΠΟΤΑΜΩΝ — Stadt der Flüsse: die Gewässer auf den ephesischen Münzen," in Wiplinger 2006, 17-22.

Klose, D. 2005. "Festivals and games in the cities of the East during the Roman empire," in C. Howgego (ed.), *Coinage and identity in the provinces of the Roman empire* (Oxford) 125-33.

Koester, H. (ed.) 1995. *Ephesos, metropolis of Asia: an interdisciplinary approach to its archaeology, religion and culture* (Cambridge, MA).

Latour, B. 2005. "From Realpolitik to Dingpolitik — or how to make things public," in B. Latour and P. Weibel (edd.), *Making things public: atmospheres of democracy* (Cambridge, MA) 14-41.

MacDonald, W. 1986. *The architecture of the Roman empire* (New Haven, CT).

Muir, E. 1981. *Civic rituals in Renaissance Venice* (Princeton, NJ).

Ng, D. 2007. "Ephesos: the significance of the legendary founder to an internal audience," in *Manipulation of memory: public buildings and decorative programs in Roman cities of Asia Minor* (Ph.D. diss., Univ. of Michigan) 183-233.

Price, S. R. F. 1984. *Rituals and power: the Roman imperial cult in Asia Minor* (Cambridge).

Renfrew, C. 2007. "The archaeology of ritual," in E. Kyriakidis (ed.), *The archaeology of ritual* (Los Angeles, CA) 109-22.

Rogers, G. M. 1991. *The sacred identity of Ephesos* (London).

Scherrer, P. 2001. "The historical topography of Ephesos," in D. Parrish (ed.), *Urbanism in western Asia Minor* (JRA Suppl. 45) 57-95.

Scherrer, P. 2006. "Die Fernwasserversorgung von Ephesos in der römischen Kaiserzeit: Synopse der epigraphischen Quellen," in Wiplinger 2006, 45-58.

Sherwood, A. 2000. *Roman architectural influence in provincial Asia: Augustus to Severus Alexander* (Ph.D. diss., Princeton Univ.).

Smith, J. Z. 1987. *To take place: toward a theory in ritual* (Chicago, IL).

Strathern, M. 1999. *Property, substance, and effect: anthropological essays in persons and things* (London).

Trexler, R. 1983. "Ritual behavior in Renaissance Florence: the setting," *Medievalia et Humanistica* 34, 125-44.

Tuan, Y.-F. 1977. *Space and place: the perspectives of experience* (Minneapolis, MN).

Walbank, M. E. H. 1994. Review of Rogers, *Sacred identity of Ephesos*, in *Phoenix* 48, 89-91.

Wandsnider, L. and E. Athanassopoulos 2004. *Mediterranean archaeological landscapes: current issues* (Philadelphia, PA).

Wankel, H. (ed.) 1979. *Die Inschriften von Ephesos*, vol. I (Bonn).

Wiplinger, G. (ed.) 2006. *Cura Aquarum in Ephesus* (Leuven).

Yegül, F. 1994. "Ephesus: the street experience in ancient Ephesus," in Celik, Favro and Ingersoll 1994, 95-110.

Social spaces at the end of the Empire: the *limitanei* of Hadrian's Wall
Rob Collins

In Roman frontier studies over the past 20 years, there has been a shift toward emphasizing the dynamic and transitional nature of frontiers.[1] Interest in the Roman army has also moved away from investigation of structural organization to focus on the social aspects of military life.[2] While such changes are welcome in both frontier and military studies, the two branches have yet to converge. This is not to suggest that the study of frontiers and the Roman army should be conflated, as they tended to be in earlier scholarship.[3] Local demographics, economics, political agendas and military logistics determined the formation and maintenance of frontiers,[4] showing that a frontier was something larger and much more complex than its occupying army. The study of the army, given its size and institutional longevity, can benefit from theoretical approaches that move it beyond the "total institution" debate.[5] To accomplish this, structural aspects of military organization must be married to social theory so that the Roman army can be contextualized historically and geographically in a frontier. The intersection of political/military dominance and place is recognized in the remains of ancient fortifications as much as in modern social theory,[6] but there is a tendency to focus on the advantages with respect to power-relations conferred by terrain or built-space rather than on place-making or place-makers *per se*.

A brief case study is offered here, focused on Hadrian's Wall in N England (fig. 1), where archaeological data have revealed important transformations dated to the later 4th c. A.D. These changes offer insight into the *limitanei*, the frontier soldiers, and can be understood through the combined perspective of G. Salaman's 'occupational community theory' and the concept of place-making.[7] While the imposition and construction of a military-held

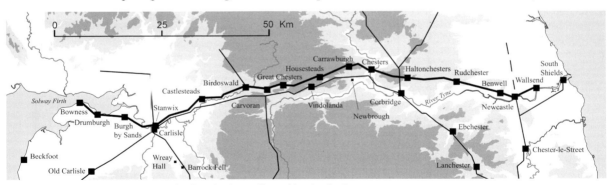

Fig. 1. Hadrian's Wall and the forts in the wall corridor (author).

---

1 E.g., Whittaker 1994; Elton 1996.
2 E.g., Goldsworthy and Haynes 1999.
3 James 2002.
4 Isaac 1990; Fulford 1992; Whittaker 1994; Elton 1996.
5 Shaw 1983; Alston 1995; Pollard 1996.
6 Summarized in Gieryn 2000, 474-76; cf. Woodward 2004.
7 Salaman 1974. The terms "occupation" and "occupational" will be used here only in the sense of a job or profession, not in the sense of a military occupation or occupational forces.

frontier is clearly indicative of place-making, the later 4th c. saw a more localized frontier army, subject to decreasing centralized institutional authority, in which the local soldiers actively transformed their host environment. Such localized occupational place-making in association with a key imperial institution suggests a need for us to re-assess our current understanding of the Late Roman army and imperial frontiers in order to see beyond the regional devolution of administration and logistics.

The frontier of N England

Hadrian's Wall was constructed in the 120s, although there had been an earlier military presence and the establishment of a frontier on the Tyne-Solway isthmus had already come about during the last three decades of the 1st c. A.D.[8] There were 15 forts along the length of the Wall (with another 5 forts immediately south of it) along with numerous milecastles and turrets, as well as other installations south and north of the curtain. By the mid-4th c., the installations north of the Wall had been abandoned, but *c.*30 forts remained south of the Wall corridor.[9] By then, most units posted in the N British frontier had been there for at least a century, to judge by inscriptions and the *Notitia Dignitatum*.[10] Compared to other parts of the empire and elsewhere in Britain, there was also exceptional architectural conservatism on the N frontier, which mostly retained its Hadrianic forms until the 4th c.[11] It was only in the mid-4th c. and later that significant deviation from the Hadrianic arrangement occurred, and at greater frequency.[12] Unbroken inhabitation from the Late Roman into the post-Roman period is attested at South Shields, possibly Newcastle, probably Corbridge, Housesteads, Vindolanda, Birdoswald and Carlisle in the Wall corridor, as well as at a number of frontier forts and towns south of the Wall, such as Piercebridge, Binchester, Catterick, Malton and the legionary fortress at York.[13] Evidence for post-Roman activity is often ephemeral and limited in its spatial extent, and it can appear strikingly 'un-Roman' when compared to evidence from the Roman period. The changes of the later 4th c. indicate the regular occurrence of specific activities at numerous forts and allow for a series of trends to be identified (Table 1), which prompts a reconsideration of the *limitanei* while

---

[8] Breeze and Dobson 2000.
[9] Most turrets along the Wall had not been used since the end of the 2nd c. Late ceramic scatters suggest the milecastles still functioned, though their rôle is largely unknown, with the exception of the metalworking site at Sewingshields milecastle in the 4th c. (Haigh and Savage 1984).
[10] Breeze and Dobson 2000, 256-62.
[11] Johnson 1983. Hadrianic forts had a standardized plan consisting of playing-card shaped defenses, arranged symmetrically on the interior around a central range containing all the important buildings: the *principia* or headquarters building in the center, flanked by *horrea* or large storehouses, and the *praetorium* or commanding officer's house. The majority of remaining buildings were barracks in the front and rear ranges, but there were also separate workshops that could be found along street frontages or set within the ramparts. Like the arrangement of the fort itself, its interior buildings also followed standard plans. For example, barracks were designed to hold a century of *c.*80 men, with 8-10 apartments each housing a *contubernium* of *c.*10 men and a larger apartment at one end for the centurion commanding the century (Hodgson and Bidwell 2004). While some variations can be found in both building plans and fort arrangement, these are usually minor in detail and conform to the primary elements of the Hadrianic period.
[12] Collins 2007.
[13] Wilmott 2000.

TABLE 1
4th-c. AND LATER TRAITS AT FORTS ON HADRIAN'S WALL

Confirmed are indicated by a square; probable/possible are indicated by a circle. Compiled from: Bidwell 1985; Bidwell and Speak 1994; Birley 2002; Birley and Blake 2007; Bishop and Dore 1988; Breeze 1972 and 2006; Breeze and Dobson 2000; Gibson 1903; Hodgson 2003; McCarthy 2002; Petch 1927 and 1928; Rushworth 2009; Snape and Bidwell 2002; Welsby 1982; Wilmott 1997; Zant 2009.

	Barrack repair/refurbishment	*Praetoria* repair/refurbishment	*Principia* repair/refurbishment	Increase use of timber	Decreasing road quality	Infringement on road space	Gate blocking	Changed use of gate space	Accommodation expanded into formerly specialized space	Metalworking no longer restricted to purpose built *fabricae*	Barrack demolition/conversion	Subdivision of rooms	Extension/addition of bath suites	*Horrea* demolition/conversion	Changed use of *principia* space	Patterned coin loss	Refurbishment of defenses in earth banks & timber/stone revetment
South Shields	■	■	■	■	■	■	■	■	■	■	■	■	■	■	■		■
Wallsend	●				■	■	■									■	■
Newcastle		■	■		■					■					■	■	■
Benwell		■				■	●						■		■		
Rudchester	■	●				●		■									
Halton Chesters	■	■		●			■	■									
Corbridge			■							■					■		
Chesters		■					●	■									
Carrawburgh	■		■				■						●	■		●	
Housesteads	■	■	■	■		■	■		■	■	■		■	■	■		■
Vindolanda	■	■				■	■			■				■	■		
Great Chesters	■	●					■										
Carvoran							■										
Birdoswald	■	●		■	■	■	■	■	■	■	■			■			■
Castlesteads																	
Stanwix	●		■		●				●			●			●		
Carlisle	■		■	■	■	■						●			●	■	●
Burgh-by-Sands																	
Drumburgh																	
Bowness-on-Solway						■		■									

further contextualizing post-Roman activity. These trends can be considered in terms of changes to fortifications, the plans and functions of internal buildings (see below), and in the economy.

Changes to the fortifications are seen in three separate but inter-related defensive features: gates, ditches and curtain walls. Alterations to fort gates occur throughout the Roman period, although with increased frequency and consistency in the 4th c. In most cases alterations include the narrowing or blocking of passageways and the overall reduction of functioning gates. Infilling of ditches and the cutting of new ones correspond to changes in the gate-systems, indicating a desire to minimize access into forts, whether for defensive purposes or for better management of traffic into and out of a fort. Further defensive refurbishments are seen along curtain walls. Most, perhaps all, of the 4th-c. repairs and refurbishments of curtain walls were carried out using roughly-hewn stone which was laid with varying degrees of skill. Subsequent repairs consisted of earthen ramparts with timber or stone revetments rather than freestanding stone walls backed by a rampart, but dating these refurbishments is difficult and they cannot date before the final years of the 4th c. These changes did not fundamentally alter the tactical advantage or function of this kind of architecture; indeed, despite their modified appearance, such a makeover would have made little difference to the efficacy of the defenses if the fort were to have been directly attacked.

From the mid-4th c. and later, a number of changes can be seen in the internal layout of forts and the use of space, including the blocking or narrowing of the gates, inferior road paving, and the encroachment of buildings onto roads. Functional changes to buildings suggest that defined zones of accommodation, storage and industry were less discrete than before. Barracks changed from the Hadrianic stone-built barrack blocks to chalet-style barracks of freestanding structures.[14] *Principia* (headquarters buildings) seem to have assumed new functions, with the offices in the rear range often taking on a domestic use. The perimeters of forecourt verandahs and porticoes were walled up, with further walls dividing the space internally. Some spaces were used for metalworking or butchery. *Praetoria* (commanders' residences) continued to be occupied, but the second half of the 4th c. saw a decline in their opulence, again with evidence for subdivision of rooms, the introduction of metalworking or other craft-production, or even the reduction in the size of the building, as at Vindolanda.[15] The demolition or conversion of *horrea* (granaries/stores) occurred at several forts along the Wall. The replacement of a *horreum* at Birdoswald with a timber hall is perhaps the best known and most drastic example.[16] At Housesteads, one *horreum* was converted for domestic use, while another was converted into a small bath suite;[17] at Newcastle, a *horreum* was converted for industrial use, probably metalworking.[18] In terms of supply and storage issues, these conversions were in part a result of a change of scale in the arrangements of military supply. There were also structural changes to many late 4th-c. buildings within forts, such as the increased use of timber for framing or post-built structures.

Significant economic changes begin in the mid-4th c. and continue until at least the early to mid-5th c. The most obvious trends relate to economic activities of the military communities and their supply. The demolition or conversion of *horrea* resulted from military and economic re-organizations by the 4th-c. emperors.[19] *Horrea* were designed to store supplies in bulk and presumably to receive them in bulk. The demolition or conversion of granaries indicates that supplies were no longer being imported and stored in bulk. This further suggests that foodstuffs were acquired relatively locally and that the scale of production

---

14 Chalet-style barracks first appeared in the mid- to late 3rd c., but are encountered with more frequency in the 4th c. The evidence is reviewed most recently in Hodgson and Bidwell 2004.
15 Birley 2002.
16 Wilmott 1997.
17 Rushworth 2009.
18 Snape and Bidwell 2002.
19 Units were smaller than their 2nd-c. precursors, and the 4th-c. tax system was suited to local supply (Nicasie 1998, 67-74 and 147-48).

was high enough to support the population of a military community year-round. The shifting of metalworking and other craft activities to areas scattered throughout the fort was probably related to a less formally organized production and repair of metal objects. Artifactual evidence, particularly ceramics but also environmental remains, indicates a shift in the dietary economy and supply sources, drawing more on N England in preference to imports from S England.[20] Another indicator of the changed economic rôle of forts is the evidence that forts were hosting marketplace activity. At Newcastle and Carlisle, the extensive coin spreads found along the streets and adjacent building fronts of the *via principalis* and *via praetoria* have been interpreted as loss resulting from regular and frequent monetary exchanges, as would occur in a marketplace.[21] These trends suggest increasing regionalization through the 4th c., in the sense that there are few significant economic links outside the region. Those that did exist tend to be with manufacturers/suppliers in other parts of Britain. Coinage, the only plentiful indicator of long distance, state-subsidized supply, decreased in the later 4th c. Does that mean that the frontier was increasingly economically self-sufficient in the 4th c., or does it mean the N British frontier was not a high priority for the imperial authorities? By the late 4th to early 5th c. (the end of Roman rule in Britain), forts were probably drawing on supplies almost entirely from within the region.

The transformation of social spaces in the frontier

Previous scholars have noted some of the modifications occurring in later 4th-c. forts along Hadrian's Wall,[22] but new evidence has revealed the consistency of these changes throughout the frontier. Further, such changes have often been interpreted through the lens of historical events (e.g., the "barbarian conspiracy" or British usurpations) and with implicit value judgments that see these years as a time of stagnation or decline. It has been assumed that the Roman frontier garrison withdrew from Britain in the first decade of the 5th c., under the orders of continental imperial authorities or British usurpers, or that only small numbers of the poorest soldiers remained.[23] Such interpretations inherently cast the soldiers as individuals inserted into the frontier rather than social entities integral to the frontier.

J. Casey and T. Wilmott, however, have argued that a military withdrawal should not be assumed, given the archaeological evidence that indicates continued inhabitation in forts into the early post-Roman period, and they suggest a number of scenarios to explain such continuity.[24] Wilmott's model argues that the Late to post-Roman transition can be explained by the transformation of the frontier garrison into local warbands, the primary élite social formation of the post-Roman to Early Mediaeval period. A critic of this model would argue that the latest Roman inhabitation cannot be considered military in nature, seeing it as squatters, or perhaps a local militia.[25] Such criticism, however, rests largely on a notion that a Late Roman military presence would leave a clear archaeological footprint.

---

20 Huntley 2000; Stallibrass 2000; Bidwell and Croom 2010.
21 Snape and Bidwell 2002; Zant 2009.
22 E.g., Welsby 1982.
23 E.g., Jones and Mattingly 1993, 140 and 308.
24 Casey 1993; Wilmott 1997 and 2000.
25 Cf. Gardner 1999 for squatter inhabitation and the doubts regarding the identification of squatters. A militia, as a pseudo-military force comprised of individuals primarily engaged in other professions, should not be conflated with a warband, composed of trained warriors who are socially bound to serve a patron.

The changes in the Wall corridor and throughout the frontier zone indicate a transitional situation somewhere between structured military groups and locally-raised militias. I would argue that the *limitanei* became a regionally-distinct military community in the north due to a combination of local and regional circumstances with imperial decisions and priorities. The separation of the Roman empire into three prefectures by the sons of Constantine, and the later permanent splitting of the empire into West and East by Valentinian and Valens, led to the fracturing of territories into smaller regions with largely self-sufficient administrative systems that in turn produced further separation between provincial authorities, prefectural offices, and the imperial court.[26] In addition to this administrative distancing, there was a reduction of the presence of central imperial authorities. Throughout the 4th c., there are only 7 instances of military operations in Britain recorded by the sources, of which 6 required military assistance from central imperial authorities on the continent.[27] Compared to the number of campaigns along the Rhine or Danube, the problems in Britain seem to have been fewer, lower in priority and not as frequently requiring the emperor's presence. This is not to say that there were no problems — only that most difficulties could be dealt with by the *limitanei* themselves, without requiring much long-distance movement of soldiers. With the long-term posting of units and a reliance on local recruitment, the British frontier was in practice more independent than other imperial frontiers. Theoretically, this can be best explained as the transformation of an occupational community from having cosmopolitan or universal military identity into one that is geographically limited to a specified region.

Occupational community theory

The transformations in the frontier noted above provide good examples of localized place-making, in which the frontier soldiers modified existing built-space to better suit their situation. However, the fact that this activity has occurred in the context of the military, a key institution of the Roman state, requires further consideration. The concept of occupational communities provides a theoretical lens through which to understand the Roman military.[28] According to Salaman, an occupational community is a group of "people who are members of the same occupation or who work together, ... have some sort of common life together and are, to some extent, separate from the rest of society".[29] Occupational communities represent the relationship between a person's work and life outside of work, in which the nature and conditions of their profession permeate his or her social relationships, interests and values. There are three key components of an occupational community:

---

26   Errington 2006.
27   Breeze and Dobson 2000, 234-44.
28   In the following discussion, 'profession' will be used interchangeably with 'occupation', even though the definitions of these words are somewhat different in sociological literature.
29   Salaman 1974, 19, n.4. This definition of an occupational community is superficially similar to that of a total institution, which has been proposed as an appropriate theoretical model for understanding the Roman army (supra n.5). However, a total institution model removes soldiers from broader society through the claim that the military was a self-contained microsociety, which was demonstrably not true (Alston 1995) and undermines the relationship of military communities with 'civilian' and barbarian societies. The importance of occupational community theory is that the occupation is the primary, but not the only, influence in identity formation. A soldier can still be subject to an occupational community and fulfill other, non-military social rôles.

1. Members of occupational communities see themselves in terms of their occupational rôles, which form the foundation of their self-image; they see themselves as persons with specific qualities, interests and abilities.
2. Members of occupational communities share a reference group composed of members of the occupational community.
3. Members of occupational communities associate and form friendships with other members of their occupation in preference to outsiders, and they carry work activities and interests into their non-work lives.

In terms of self-image, members of an occupational community do not see themselves solely in this rôle, as each individual's identity is composed of multiple rôles determined through various social relationships.[30] However, the member places a higher emphasis on his or her occupational identity, which dominates much of his life outside of work. Membership creates a value system that emphasizes the qualities and abilities needed for that profession, which becomes relevant not only to work but also to aspects of life outside that work.[31] This feature strengthens relationships with work colleagues, as they generally share the same value system, attitudes and viewpoints. The member can best relate to and interact with co-workers — their primary reference group. The reference group is particularly important since its members can exercise powerful social sanctions that strongly influence the behavior of the member, permeating life outside work and sharing the same work-based collection of knowledge, meanings, symbols, and language.[32]

Once an occupational community is identified, membership in such a community can be determined by three factors: physical and/or emotional involvement in work tasks, the possession of a defined status, and the inclusiveness of the work or organizational situation.[33] There are also three primary types of 'inclusivity': 'pervasiveness', 'organizational embrace', and 'restrictions' (otherwise known as 'restrictive factors').[34] Of the three types of inclusivity, organizational pervasiveness is the most important because pervasiveness affects occupational self-identity, the prime component of an occupational community. Pervasiveness facilitates the internalization of a value system that allows a person to identify with work colleagues. These determining factors, along with inclusivity, decide the type of occupational community formed.

The determinants are important because the factors that govern the profession will decide whether the occupational community can be identified as 'cosmopolitan' or 'local'.[35] Cosmopolitan occupational communities are based on the profession as a whole and

---

30   Hitlin 2003; Hogg, Terry and White 1995.
31   Salaman 1974, 24.
32   Ibid. 24-26
33   Gerstl 1961; Salaman 1974, 27-37. 'Involvement' in work is always to some extent a result of external factors (e.g., familial obligations or physical limitations), but certain situations generate a greater sense of involvement. These include: potential danger, a sense of responsibility, and a high level of expertise or training. The 'status' of the job relative to other occupations, particularly if it is high-status when compared to other local jobs, will generate increased involvement, just as marginal status relative to other occupations increases involvement. When membership in an occupational community is attained or granted, features of the job affect non-work activities and interests, which in turn restrict opportunities to establish and maintain relationships both with co-workers and persons outside the occupational community.
34   Salaman 1974, 34-36.
35   Ibid. 38-41.

composed, potentially, of all the members of that profession. Members of cosmopolitan communities perceive their occupation in the context of broader society, and they are likely to identify with any colleagues from that profession without any geographic limitations or restrictions. Local occupational communities, on the other hand, are composed of members who share a specific work situation, creating a geographic correlation that can be described as 'occupational place-making'. Members of this type will not identify as strongly with others in the same profession outside their specific work location, and they may also have more social ties to their locality outside of the occupational community. Social links outside the occupational community will have contributed to local place-making.

Roman soldiers had a strong notion of identity that encouraged separation from other social groups. A high degree of 'involvement' was achieved through physical (and presumably mental) conditioning, shared responsibility amongst soldiers, and regular routines/duties. Soldiers enjoyed an exclusive 'status' marked by legal privileges such as tax exemptions and visual symbols (e.g., uniforms and arms). Numerous factors reinforced the 'inclusivity' of soldiers, from indoctrination during training, through provision of food and equipment, to the regulation of official activities, religious or ritual behavior, and disciplinary measures.[36] The very willingness and ability to engage in combat and commit other forms of violence demonstrates the ability of a military authority to set norms and affect the values of recruits and soldiers. In this way, military practice, reinforced by laws distinguishing soldiers from other citizens and subjects of the emperor, allowed for the creation of a strong occupational identity for soldiers. This identity construct enabled soldiers across the empire to recognize and relate to each other, superseding the divergent relationships cultivated by units long-garrisoned in one locality.[37] However, factors that reinforced inclusivity among soldiers could, and probably did, vary.

Interpreting occupational place-making

Identifying the Late Roman military as an occupational community allows a distinction to be made between the empire's military communities and a state institution, between the soldiers and the formal organization in which they served. An occupational community is archaeologically visible, particularly when the focus is not on individual identity but on that of the community. Architectural changes, variations in the use of space and of artifacts within spatial contexts can be clearly related to material manifestations of inclusivity — pervasiveness, embrace and restrictions.[38] While explicable through occupational community theory, these spatial changes attest to place-making activity distinct from that of the formation of the frontier, in which the *limitanei* of N Britain were recasting their frontier homes in a fashion that demonstrated their difference from other, physically-distant Roman soldiers. Place-making by the *limitanei*, however, was superseded by the needs of the Roman state on the frontier. Roman frontiers, particularly those with monumental delineations, offer case studies in place-making that can be examined from multiple perspectives, such as landscapes of transition, but also as landscapes of control, contention or disruption. Such place-making is observed from the formation and initial construction of frontier installations as well as their subsequent habitation. By the 4th c., the location of the

---

[36] James 1999, 15.
[37] Haynes 1999; James 1999.
[38] See above n.33, also noting conditions that impact on involvement.

settlements and central places for the military communities, the forts, were already fixed in the landscape based upon considerations of tactical deployment and supply, constraining place-making activity to the settlement and its structures.

The fort itself was an important symbol of the military community. The outer defenses acted as a form of restriction for its occupants and those who lived outside it.[39] Inside the fort, the provision of certain facilities (accommodation, food storage, bathing, etc.) is evidence for embrace, while the standardization in the form of these structures is a manifestation of pervasiveness. In this way one can compare the internal layout of a fort, the form of the buildings and the defenses themselves with other forts in the region, or even elsewhere in the empire. Any changes that deviate from the 'standard' military architecture of the time suggest a rejection of regularized, institutional military practices imposed from above. When there are deviations, this suggests localized place-making activity, although the reasons for it may vary. In N Britain, these later 4th-c. changes indicate a shift from a cosmopolitan military community, seen in garrisons across the empire, to one that is more locally situated, namely, the *limitanei* of N Britain.

The construction, repair and habitation of chalet-style barracks created a small-scale social unit (fig. 2). A row of chalets probably housed a single infantry century or cavalry *turma* (although these terms were redundant in the 4th c.[40]), preserving

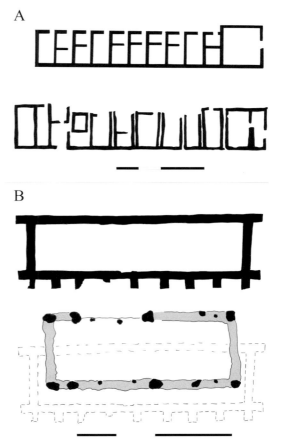

Fig. 2. A. The typical Hadrianic barracks (top) compared to chalet-style barracks at Housesteads (bottom). B. The plan of a *horreum* from Birdoswald (top) compared to the plan of the timber hall that succeeded it in the 5th c. (bottom), in which the capacity for bulk storage is replaced with a new social space. Scale is 20 m (author).

---

39 The presence of a *vicus* (dependent settlement of a fort) or of an adjacent town does not undermine the concept of the fort as a material manifestation of the occupational community. Soldiers are members of a military occupational community, but they are also members of the broader military community, which includes their spouses/partners, relatives, slave/servants and other dependants, as well as other residents of the extra-mural settlements. In N England, military *vici* seem to have been abandoned by the late 3rd c.

40 Centuries were subdivisions of infantry legions and cohorts and *turmae* were subdivisions of cavalry *alae* in the army of the Principate. A century had a paper-strength of c.80 men organized into 10 *contubernia*, and a cavalry *turma* a paper-strength of c.30 men. Unit sizes in the 4th-c. army are uncertain: there is some evidence for the reduction of *contubernia* from 10 men to 6 men but no evidence for the size of cavalry sub-units; cf. Nicasie 1998, 52 and 60-65.

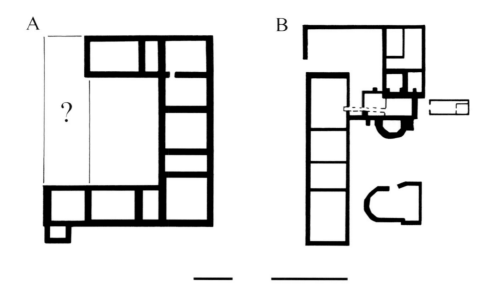

Fig. 3. The 3rd-c. *praetorium* at Vindolanda (A) compared to that of A.D. 370 and later (B) (reproduced by permission of the Vindolanda Trust). Scale is 20 m.

traditional sub-unit organization but in a different form.[41] On the other hand, chalets lacked the standardized regularity found in the Hadrianic barrack-blocks, and adjacent chalets varied in size and internal layout. The implication is that a *contubernium* was responsible for a chalet, which suggests that each *contubernium* had more independence than in previous eras with regard to its own quarters.[42] Thus, there are indications of both continued sub-unit formations — centuries and *contubernia* — with less standardization exerted on their housing by the local commanding officer (*praepositus*) and his regional commander.

These changes in barracks indicate the importance of the *praepositus* as a figure who can impose or dispose of perceived tradition and conformity, but the rôle of *praepositi* also changed in the late frontier. The *praetorium* (the residence of the *praepositus*) at South Shields was less opulent in its subsequent phases of habitation in the later 4th c. than in its first phase belonging to the first half of the 4th c.[43] The *praetorium* at Vindolanda changed in plan from a Mediterranean-style courtyard house to a smaller L-shaped house (fig. 3).[44] While the declining opulence suggests that the material differentiation between the *praepositus* and his soldiers was decreasing, the substantial space occupied by the modified *praetoria* still indicates that he was the social pinnacle of the settlement. The shift in plan of the *praetorium*, abandoning that of the Mediterranean-style courtyard house, is also significant. Both factors indicate the *praepositus* did not (or could not) differentiate himself to the same degree as before. Decreased opulence can be related to increased regionalization of the frontier, specifically the geographically-reduced social and economic links with

---

41   Hodgson and Bidwell 2004.
42   Coello 1996. The notion that chalet-style barracks were occupied by married soldiers and their families (Daniels 1980) has been generally refuted by recent studies (e.g., Hodgson and Bidwell 2004). Note also a shift in 4th-c. terminology away from *contubernium* to *manipulum* or *familia* (Nicasie 1998, 52-53).
43   Bidwell and Speak 1994; N. Hodgson, pers. comm.
44   Birley 2002.

people inside the frontier and in the imperial core. In other words, commanding officers were more locally situated, with fewer links to the imperial élite and to the socio-economic benefits that such links entailed. The change in architectural form may also relate to a different model of social power. Put simply, the pinnacle of social authority in the fort no longer emulated the housing of the Mediterranean élite and did not maintain links with those Mediterranean communities.[45] Since reduced material wealth affected status, the *praepositus* needed to maintain and enhance his position in other ways. As his access to high-status individuals and goods was geographically reduced, the *praepositus* had to rely increasingly, I suggest, on regional and local social relationships. Indeed, the presence of 'mead' halls at Birdoswald — if we accept the excavator's interpretation of these structures as standard Early Mediaeval halls[46] — indicates that the *praepositus* socialized with his soldiers more, using enhanced personal loyalties and relationships to reinforce his institutional authority. The open, communal space of a hall must be contrasted with the restricted and private spaces of a Mediterranean-style *praetorium*. The *praetorium* at Birdoswald has yet to be excavated but, given the presence of these halls, one might expect either a reduction in the size of the *praetorium* or a less opulent (though still élite) residence, or both. Further, the 'small pig horizon' dating to the early 5th c. at York suggests an élite feasting culture in the basilica crosshall of the legionary *principia*,[47] which may indicate reinforcement of patronage and social ties amongst the officers.

The construction of churches at forts was a valuable asset to the *praepositus* as a patron because he could thereby promote a unifying, imperially-sanctioned ideology.[48] By providing a church, he became the patron of religious space in the fort, through which he could further enforce his position of authority — and perhaps beyond the military settlement into the countryside. The *praepositus* also seems the person most likely to have organized the refurbishment of fort defenses. The defenses further acted to enhance socially the *praepositus*' seat of power while reminding his soldiers of their social position and military identity. These activities can all be interpreted as forms of reinforcement of social status, most explicable in the context of a restriction of the *praepositus*' influence to a limited geographic area and reduced social network due to increased political and economic distance from the imperial court(s).

The most significant indication of social change in late 4th-c. forts comes in changes in *principia*. Traditionally, *principia* acted as the official and ceremonial focus of a fort, but by the late 4th c. changing uses of the buildings indicate the transformation of those functions. The offices situated at the back of the building were no longer only offices: some seem to have provided accommodation, probably to the same clerks who had used them before. There is evidence in *principia* of butchery and metalworking. Forecourt verandahs and

---

[45] This is further reinforced by the insignificant quantity of imported ceramics in the frontier: Bidwell and Croom 2010.
[46] Wilmott 1997. Early Mediaeval halls are a distinct form of architecture found in slightly varying forms across N Europe. They served as the focus of élite activities, including domestic, diplomatic, and military activities (Alcock 2003, 248-51), combining the functions of the private residence of wealthy *honestiores* with a basilica.
[47] Gerrard 2007.
[48] For South Shields, see Bidwell and Speak 1994; for Housesteads, Rushworth 2009; for Vindolanda, Birley 2002.

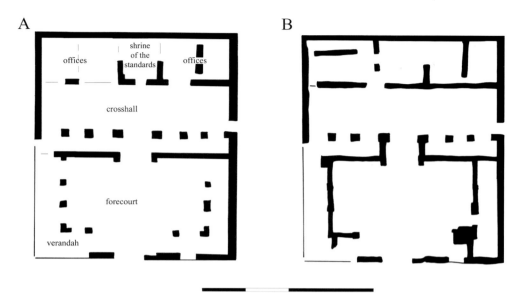

Fig. 4. The Hadrianic *principia* at Housesteads (A) compared to the 'Theodosian' plan (B). Scale is 20 m (author).

porticoes have walls inserted, creating a number of small chambers (fig. 4). Such changes are seen in the legionary *principia* at York[49] and at *principia* throughout the frontier. At South Shields, a church seems to have been built in the forecourt of the *principia*.[50] At Newcastle, and possibly at Carlisle, there are suggestions that uses of the *principia* were related to marketplace activity in the fort.[51] Where could the essential functions of *principia* be carried out, and was a single building dedicated to those functions necessary? There is no evidence that clerical functions had ceased or that the shrine of the standards was no longer maintained or permitted. Forecourts also seem to remain intact. The changes are to other areas, notably the verandahs and cross-halls. Are different activities now given official sanction or priority by the fact of their taking place in the *principia*? Is there no other available space, or is the *principia* no longer the semi-sacred building it once was? The central placement of the *principia* was still important, demonstrated by the intermittent feasting at York and marketplace activities at Carlisle and Newcastle; these activities could have taken place in other areas of the fort, but their occurrence in the center is significant. Overall, it seems likely that *principia* had lost their semi-sacred and exclusive status.

 The shifts outlined here for the forts on Hadrian's Wall indicate a reduced institutional control of the activities in military installations. The new and various activities in previously specialized spaces demonstrate altered priorities at the local level, with *principia* being not only the headquarters of a regiment but also the focus of social and economic activities unrelated to clerical work or official ceremonies. These physical changes to the structure of the fort and its buildings will have reflected the perspective of the soldiers. A well-travelled Roman would recognize that the overall plans of N British forts were relics from earlier times. As social rôles were renegotiated in the later 4th c., the spaces within

---

49 Phillips and Heywood 1995.
50 Bidwell and Speak 1994.
51 Snape and Bidwell 2002; Zant 2009.

these forts reflected the changes. The hierarchical divisions of the fort garrison were no longer stark: the *praepositus* still had the largest accommodation, but the common soldier now shared a freestanding structure with just a few colleagues. Supplies received by the *limitanei* were no longer exotic imports but relatively local, from within the region, and foodstuffs were similar to, if not virtually the same as, those consumed outside military communities.[52] These changes in the material conditions imply transformations in social relationships and distinctions. The commanding officer, perhaps with fewer long-distance prestige goods to his name, needed to reinforce his authority. To do so, he could build a church, perhaps over or within the *principia*, as at South Shields, or he could reduce his own household for the sake of his soldiers' spiritual well-being, as at Vindolanda. An alternative method was to forge closer bonds through shared space and activities such as feasting, as is suggested by the timber halls at Birdoswald. This is not the Late Roman army we find on the Rhine, the Danube or along the Persian border.

Some may even question whether the members of these military communities were truly soldiers. Supply patterns support my belief that the residents of forts in the late 4th c. were military units, albeit with a regionally-distinctive identity. The ceramic assemblages at forts across N England are almost identical, with minor variations accounted for by geographic proximity to other major producers of ceramics.[53] The major supplier of coarseware in the later 4th c. was based in East Yorkshire, and its industry dominated assemblages even on the opposite side of the country, despite the requirement of overland travel and the presence of alternative sources more easily brought by sea along the W coast of Britain. Coin assemblages are nearly identical across the region, and contrast with numismatic profiles at urban and rural sites.[54] These two classes of material culture and their similarity across many military sites suggest an organized supply-system. Such a system is only found in reference to state-sponsored activity, in this case a frontier army, indicating that the Late Roman forts in the frontier were still being supplied by imperial authorities. The transformations of the later 4th c. are indicative of a transition in the institutional authority of the empire to a regionally-distinct entity. Roman 'authority' can be seen in the consistency of changes at forts throughout the frontier, as well as in the similar ceramic and numismatic profiles. Truly localized occupational place-making by the *limitanei* or their descendants is seen in the 5th c., when there is no evidence for an overarching authority, although the foundations for such small-scale communities are to be sought in the socio-economic changes of the 4th c. The presence of élites at most former Roman forts seems to have come to an end by the 6th or 7th c. (although non-élite inhabitation may have continued), as new political entities emerged with different frontiers.[55] This shift in the political geography of the Roman frontier zone further reinforces an interpretation of occupational place-making by the *limitanei* and their descendants.

Conclusion

Archaeological evidence from 4th-c. forts in N England show a number of structural changes in the second half of the 4th c. that can be understood as localized place-making activities. Such place-making in the context of a key imperial institution, a frontier army,

---

52 Bidwell and Croom 2010; Rushworth 2009, 311-14.
53 Bidwell and Croom 2010.
54 Brickstock 2000.
55 Rollason 2003.

links these activities to significant social transformations amongst the *limitanei*. These changes are indicative of an increasingly regionalized and localized military, in which the soldiers were no longer imposed on the area by an external imperial power, but were instead a local community that made the frontier 'their own'. The placement of the *limitanei* in the frontier was significant in this process, binding the military communities with a discrete spatial identity, a process identified as occupational place-making. This process was not inevitable: it was a result of historical circumstances, chiefly the stability of the N British frontier by contrast with other Roman frontiers.

By the end of the 4th c., the *limitanei* of N England were materially distinct from other soldiers in the empire. This distinction helps to explain subsequent post-Roman settlement. An examination of other frontiers may reveal a similar trend toward increased regionalization, particularly where those frontiers were relatively stable, as in the case of N Africa. Studies of the *limitanei* not only reveal their situation with respect to the frontier, but also bear testimony to the relationship of that frontier to the imperial core.

Acknowledgements

Thanks are due to Lindsay Allason-Jones (Newcastle University) for comments on a draft of this paper, and to the dedicated efforts of the editors for innumerable improvements. All mistakes remain my own.

Bibliography

Alcock, L. 2003. *Kings and warriors, craftsmen and priests in Northern Britain AD 550-850* (Edinburgh).
Alston, R. 1995. *Soldier and society in Roman Egypt: a social history* (London).
Bidwell, P. 1985. *The Roman fort of Vindolanda at Chesterholm, Northumberland* (London).
Bidwell, P. and A. Croom 2010. "The supply and use of pottery on Hadrian's Wall in the 4th century AD," in R. Collins and L. Allason-Jones (edd.), *Finds from the frontier: material culture in the 4th-5th centuries* (York) 20-36.
Bidwell, P. and S. Speak 1994. *Excavations at South Shields Roman fort,* vol. 1 (Newcastle upon Tyne).
Birley, A. 2002. *All Vindolanda excavation reports 1997-2000* (CD-ROM produced in December 2002).
Birley, A. and J. Blake 2007. *Vindolanda excavations 2005-2006* (Hexham).
Bishop, M. and J. Dore 1988. *Corbridge: excavations of the Roman fort and town, 1947-80* (London).
Breeze, D. 1972. "Excavations at the Roman fort of Carrawburgh, 1967-1969," *ArchAel* 4th ser. 50, 81-144.
Breeze, D. 2006. *J. Collingwood Bruce's handbook to the Roman Wall* (14th edn.; Newcastle upon Tyne).
Breeze, D. and B. Dobson 2000. *Hadrian's Wall* (4th edn.; London).
Brickstock, R. 2000. "Coin supply in the north in the late Roman period," in Wilmott and Wilson 2000, 33-37.
Casey, P. J. 1993. "The end of fort garrisons on Hadrian's Wall: a hypothetical model," in F. Vallet and M. Kazanski (edd.), *L'armée romaine et les barbares du IIIe au VIIe siècle* (Rouen) 259-67.
Coello, T. 1996. *Unit sizes in the Late Roman army* (BAR S645; Oxford).
Collins, R. 2007. *Decline, collapse, or transformation? Hadrian's Wall in the 4th-5th centuries A.D.* (Ph.D. diss., Univ. of York).
Daniels, C. 1980. "Excavations at Wallsend and the fourth-century barracks on Hadrian's Wall," in W. S. Hanson and L. J. F. Keppie (edd.), *Roman frontier studies 1979* (BAR S71; Oxford) 173-93.
Elton, H. 1996. *Frontiers of the Roman empire* (London).
Errington, R. 2006. *Roman imperial policy from Julian to Theodosius* (Chapel Hill, NC).
Fulford, M. 1992. "Territorial expansion and the Roman empire," *WorldArch* 23, 294-305.
Gardner, A. 1999. "Military identities in Late Roman Britain," *OJA* 18, 403-18.
Gerrard, J. 2007. "Rethinking the small pig horizon at York Minster," *OJA* 26, 303-7.
Gerstl, J. E. 1961. "Determinants of occupational community in high status occupations," *Sociology Quarterly* 2, 37-48.
Gibson, J. P. 1903. "On excavations at Great Chesters (*Aesica*) in 1894, 1895, and 1897," *ArchAel* 2nd ser. 24, 19-62.

Gieryn, T. F. 2000. "A space for place in sociology," *Annual Review of Sociology* 26, 463-96.
Goldsworthy, A. and I. Haynes (edd.) 1999. *The Roman army as a community* (JRA Suppl. 34).
Haigh, D. and M. Savage 1984. "Sewingshields," *ArchAel* 5th ser. 12, 33-147.
Haynes, I. 1999. "Military service and cultural identity in the *auxilia*," in Goldsworthy and Haynes 1999, 165-74.
Hitlin, S. 2003. "Values as the core of personal identity: drawing links between two theories of self," *Social Psychology Quarterly* 66, 118-37.
Hodgson, N. 2003. *The Roman fort at Wallsend (Segedunum): excavations in 1997-8* (Newcastle upon Tyne).
Hodgson, N. and P. Bidwell 2004. "Auxiliary barracks in a new light: recent discoveries on Hadrian's Wall," *Britannia* 35, 121-57.
Hogg, M., D. Terry and K. White 1995. "A tale of two theories: a critical comparison of identity theory with social identity theory," *Social Psychology Quarterly* 58, 255-69.
Huntley, J. P. 2000. "Late Roman transition in the North: the palynological evidence," in Wilmott and Wilson 2000, 67-71.
Isaac, B. 1990. *The limits of empire: the Roman army in the East* (Oxford).
James, S. 1999. "The community of soldiers: a major identity and centre of power in the Roman empire," in *TRAC 98* (Oxford) 14-25.
James, S. 2002. "Writing the legions: the development and future of Roman military studies in Britain," *ArchJ* 159, 1-58.
Johnson, S. 1983. *Late Roman fortifications* (London).
Jones, B. and D. Mattingly 1993. *An atlas of Roman Britain* (London).
McCarthy, M. 2002. *Roman Carlisle and the lands of the Solway* (Stroud).
Nicasie, M. J. 1998. *Twilight of empire: the Roman army from the reign of Diocletian until the Battle of Adrianople* (Amsterdam).
Petch, J. 1927. "Excavations at Benwell (Condercum): first interim report (1926)," *ArchAel* 4th ser. 4, 135-92.
Petch, J. 1928. "Excavations at Benwell (Condercum): second interim report (1927 and 1928)," *ArchAel* 4th ser. 5, 46-74.
Phillips, D. and B. Heywood 1995. *Excavations at York Minster* (London).
Pollard, N. 1996. "The Roman army as 'total institution' in the Near East? Dura-Europos as a case study," in D. Kennedy (ed.), *The Roman army in the East* (JRA Suppl. 18) 217-27.
Rollason, D. 2003. *Northumbria, 500-1100: creation and destruction of a kingdom* (Cambridge).
Rushworth, A. 2009. *Housesteads Roman fort — the grandest station: excavation and survey at Housesteads, 1954-95, by Charles Daniels, John Gillam, James Crow and others* (Swindon).
Salaman, G. 1974. *Community and occupation* (Cambridge).
Shaw, B. 1983. "Soldiers and society: the army in Numidia," *Opus* 2, 133-59.
Snape, M. and P. Bidwell 2002. "Excavations at Castle Garth, Newcastle upon Tyne, 1976-92 and 1995-6: the excavation of the Roman fort," *The Roman fort at Newcastle upon Tyne = ArchAel* 5th ser. 31, 1-249.
Stallibrass, S. 2000. "How little we know, and how much there is to learn: what can animal and human bones tell us about the late Roman transition in northern England?" in Wilmott and Wilson 2000, 73-79.
Welsby, D. 1982. *The Roman military defence of the British provinces in its later phases* (BAR 101; Oxford).
Whittaker, C. 1994. *Frontiers of the Roman empire: a social and economic study* (London).
Wilmott, T. 1997. *Birdoswald, excavations of a Roman fort on Hadrian's Wall and its successor settlements, 1987-92* (London).
Wilmott, T. 2000. "The late Roman transition at Birdoswald and on Hadrian's Wall," in id. and Wilson 2000, 13-23.
Wilmott, T. and P. Wilson (edd.) 2000. *The Late Roman transition in the North: papers from the Roman Archaeology Conference, Durham 1999* (BAR 299; Oxford).
Woodward, R. 2004. *Military geographies* (Malden, MA).
Zant, J. 2009. *The Carlisle millennium project: excavations in Carlisle 1998-2001* (Lancaster).

Carved in stone: long-term modification of the landscape as place-making practice at Fasıllar (Turkey)

Bradley M. Sekedat

Issues of place and space are increasingly relevant to Roman archaeology. Whereas places traditionally have been addressed in terms of their cultural affiliations, recent thinking assigns greater emphasis to local circumstance in the constitution of place. In Roman archaeology, this shift in thinking is perhaps most clear on the peripheries of the empire. Because Roman influence is thought to be less tenable there, more attention has been paid to local interactions with areas that were already socially meaningful,[1] and greater variation is detected in the 'cultural' process of making place.

This paper follows this shift in thinking through an exploration of place-making practices in central Anatolia. I look specifically at how quarries reveal traces of place-making practices from the distant past that influence the maintenance of place in later periods. The site and quarry of Fasıllar (central Turkey) is used as a case study of specific engagements between people and quarried stone in order to highlight the ability of the surviving traces to inform later interactions with the site. Hittite-, Roman-, and Byzantine-period evidence shows how modification of the abundant stone outcrops became part of the place (see the definition of place below) of Fasıllar through continual re-inscribing of the (stone) material of the site itself. I aim to re-assess how quarries are understood. Scholarship on Roman quarries has tended to address their economic rôles, regarding quarries as less significant than the features constructed from their material. I suggest that the knowledge and craftsmanship involved in locating, extracting and working stone, as well as in transporting it, were instrumental in the composition of quarries as places,[2] and that these practices leave indelible traces that influence and frame subsequent engagements with a site and thereby the sense of place.

First, how is 'place' understood? For the purposes of this paper, place is regarded as being a result of interactions amongst people, their practices and the material aspects of a location. Conceptually, place is not something that is predetermined in the human mind: it arises from physical interactions with locations. I follow E. Casey, who states that

> any effort to assess the relationship between self and place should point not just to reciprocal influence (that much an ecologically sensitive account would maintain) but, more radically, to constitutive co-ingredience: each is essential to the being of the other.[3]

In other words, places and people are intimately entwined with each other. Critically, this definition obviates a notion of place as derived from space. Spatial theory often regards the two as differentiated: space is empty, only to be filled by the places that people create.[4] My understanding emphasizes the simultaneous constitution of the two, so that meaning (the

---

1   See, e.g., Mattingly 1997 on discrepant experience.
2   Cf. Barrett 1994; Edmonds 1999; Sinopoli 2003.
3   Casey 2001, 406.
4   This dichotomy is well-established in spatial theory; it is articulated and critiqued by Casey (2001), where he advocates a return to pre-Cartesian and Euclidean models, which will enable space and place to be developed separately from each other, rather than one being subordinate to, or deriving from, the other.

mental construct of place) does not precede location (the spaces occupied by those mental constructs): they arise together.

Second, 'place' is understood here as the numerous physical interactions with locations, as well as the interactions of broader social forces with locations. These interactions are simultaneous, frequent, and of different temporal rhythms. As T. Ingold notes, a given landscape or place comprises a variety of tasks that occur at different time scales, so that there are multiple temporal rhythms present in a landscape.[5] To demonstrate this, he gives the example of the country setting depicted in Pieter Bruegel's *The Harvesters* in which some people are sleeping while others thresh wheat, all over a short period of time. Trees, a road and a church compose the background, which together provide simultaneous but more durable elements to the landscape's temporality, comprising slow-moving and fast-moving rhythms of action. A multitude of tasks and landscape features come together in this setting to constitute a location. Place is therefore understood as including many traces of past activities that are materially simultaneous in the present, just as the church and the thresher's tools are both present in the Bruegel painting scrutinized by Ingold.[6] From an archaeological perspective, these traces are not already sequenced and seriated, but are encountered in a relational, almost narrative, way through "bodily relationships with the material world".[7] It is only later that we separate them and categorize them. A look at Fasıllar will highlight how practices and temporalities co-exist and relate to one another.

Fasıllar: a case study

Located near the Beyşehir Lake basin between the modern cities of Beyşehir and Konya, Fasıllar today evokes several questions about how to regard the site as a place. The site lies in the steppes on the N edge of the Taurus mountains, overlooking the Konya plain to the east and the Beyşehir Lake basin to the west. It therefore sits at the intersection of these three topographic zones, each with its own economic, communication and trading spheres.[8] The archaeological site sits in an upland zone with numerous limestone and basalt outcrops, a wide, low valley, a cliff face, and a quarried plateau. Below and to the southeast, *c.*500 m down the valley, the modern village (fig. 1) occupies a transitional zone between the plain and the foothills.[9] Although no systematic archaeological work has been done, the site preserves surface remains spanning thousands of years. The valley is the main orienting feature: it runs roughly E–W between the carved cliff face on the N side and the gentler hill on the S side on which a massive Hittite monument sits. Two dirt roads run through the middle of the valley, one circling the S hill down to a paved road leading to a second village, Çavuş, while the other runs directly down the valley to modern Fasıllar.

The Hittite monument (fig. 2) on the N slope is the primary tourist attraction and one of the only aspects of the site that receives scholarly attention.[10] The 7.40-m-tall block of local

---

5   Ingold 1993; id. 2000, 154.
6   Importantly, this simultaneous character of place differs from L. R. Binford's (1981) emphasis on duration and layered practices. See Lucas 2005 and Bailey 2007 for the metaphor of a palimpsest, wherein traces intermingle in the same locations.
7   Witmore 2004a, 58.
8   The boundaries of the three zones also more or less follow the borders between different Bronze Age kingdoms that inhabited the region.
9   Note that all measurements are approximate, except for that pertaining to the Fasıllar monument, which has already been published. No new measurements were taken during my visits.
10 E.g., Hall 1959; Mellaart 1962; Ehringhaus 2005. In its present state, it rests horizontally, on its

Long-term modification of the landscape as place-making practice at Fasıllar

Fig. 1. View of the modern village of Fasıllar, looking east; the monument is not in this view (author).

Fig. 2. The Fasıllar monument (author).

basalt depicts the Hittite Rock God standing on the Sun God, who is flanked by frontal lions.[11] Scholars have debated the origin of this stone. Some argue that it was brought to

---

back, with the top of the carving upslope of the bottom. A full-scale replica of the monument was erected in the garden outside of the Museum of Anatolian Civilizations in Ankara.

11 See Ramsay 1908, Alexander 1968 and Ehringhaus 2005 for more in-depth discussions of the monument.

Fasıllar from nearby sources as late as the Classical or Roman period.[12] Others have speculated that it was quarried locally and intended for use at the nearby monumental spring of Eflatupınar,[13] near which a similar stone monument has been found.[14] The deities are paralleled in Assyrian relief-carvings, which may speak to Fasıllar's position on a communications network linking Pamphylia, Cilicia and eventually N Assyria.

Fig. 3. The Lucianus monument, seen from the Fasıllar monument, looking north (author).

The other side of the valley, c.100 m from the Hittite monument, is dominated by an E–W running cliff face into which numerous reliefs are carved. There is almost no trace of Bronze Age activity in the reliefs, as the carvings are dated primarily to the Classical and Roman periods. The most famous is the Lucianus monument (fig. 3). This high-relief carving shows two columns supporting an archway (naming the dedicatee) that frames a now-empty niche. The base of the niche shows a heavily worn section, suggesting that a statue once stood in the center. To the right of the archway is a life-size horse in high relief, its head facing the niche. Below and to the right is a long Greek inscription in a pedimented frame.[15] Of the two other prominent carvings further west along the cliff face,

---

12   Mellaart 1962; Alexander 1968.
13   Mellaart 1962.
14   Hall (1959), however, provides a more convincing argument about the dissimilarities between the two monuments, suggesting that it is less likely that they were intended for use on the same spring monument.
15   S. Mitchell (1993, 172) notes that Greek inscriptions in rural Anatolia at the time are more common than non-Greek ones.

one has a repeating floral motif on the two exposed sides, while adjacent and to the east is a low-relief carving of a male figure with a bundle of grass over his shoulder. Whereas the Lucianus monument is an element of public display deliberately set in the rock face, these two reliefs do not appear monumental in character. Instead, it appears that they were readied for removal from the cliff face once carving was finished. The various carvings on this cliff face were created for different audiences — one present at the site, the other not.

J. Mellaart argued that the shape of the valley along with the displays on the cliff face, both sculptural and inscriptional, belong to a "Roman stadium above a Classical site".[16] He conceived of the valley as a coherent space. While there may have been a stadium in this portion of the site, the quarrying carried out on the rock face seems to continue the quarrying practices on the plateau above it to the north; thus, while the cliff face looks onto the valley, the practices employed do not point to an explicit relationship with the valley.

The plateau — which cannot be seen from the valley — reveals intensive engagement with its stone surface during the process of carving sarcophagi. Many sarcophagi remain attached to the surface with crude preparation marks along their bases.[17] Rectangular depressions where sarcophagi were removed appear in greater numbers, some near the cliff edge. An area of $c.300$ m E–W x 150 m N–S is pocked with similar traces of quarrying. Additional features include a series of stone walls in the E portion of the plateau and several sections of removed stone, $c.3$ m deep, at the E point of the plateau and descending the cliff. It is possible that the N limit of quarrying on this plateau continues beyond a stone field boundary that encloses an agricultural zone. Further evidence for quarrying is seen around the E edge of the valley. A large outcrop that juts out at the crest of the valley east of the plateau bears many signs of scarring and undercutting. To the west, toward Beyşehir Lake, a wide wall sloping down to the flat plain was probably built to stop large rocks from washing done the slope.[18]

Limited archaeological work has been conducted at this site. In the 1980s a team mapped sarcophagi on the S side of the valley at Fasıllar. Later, M. Waelkens[19] recorded evidence for Bronze Age quarrying, noting Bronze Age workers chose to engage with surface stone, rather than develop deep-cutting industrial-scale quarries, such as those that existed in Egypt.[20] Based on many distinctively-shaped rock features, it is thought that a N–S depression may be the location of a Bronze Age settlement.[21] The extreme S portion of the site — a steep, jagged basalt cliff several hundred meters high — overlooks the road between Fasıllar and Çavuş.

Understanding these site characteristics is critical for comprehending the place-making process. How would the archaeologist go about characterizing this place? What aspects are the most critical for identifying place-making practices? Do we find a sequence of places,

---

16   Mellaart 1962, 111; Hall 1959.
17   For parallels of partially-prepared stone elsewhere in the Roman world, see Ward-Perkins 1973. For comparanda of sarcophagus types in Anatolia, see Mitchell 1993.
18   If through erosion the landscape itself was moving, it had a rôle in determining which surface stones were prepared and which were not. Cf. Massey 2005 for a discussion of the significance of constant changes in geography for understanding place and space.
19   Waelkens 1992.
20   Arnold 1991; Peacock and Maxfield 1997; Waelkens 1990 and 1992.
21   O. Harmanşah, pers. comm.

layered one on top of the other, or should we focus on spatial and material relationships? If we use chronological sequencing to phase the site, how do we account for the impact of early practices on later encounters with respect to the physical appearance of the site as a result of quarrying activity? I will highlight two patterns of place-making that are particularly salient. First, places are products of long-term or multi-temporal engagements.[22] Second, quarries as a category are under-theorized as places in their own right. The place of Fasıllar results from the specific practices of many periods, quarrying being the most important of them. Quarries can be the setting for social interactions, knowledge sharing and landscape production: far from being negative places or mere resource locations, they bring together different materials, practices and people into a single specific location, the foundation of which is moved beyond the site.[23] The site is, in this regard, both a particular location and a distributed entity.

The long-term and the multi-temporal at Fasıllar

When dealing with sites that have long-term histories, archaeologists traditionally divide those histories into sequential phases. Analytically, this implies that a city such as Athens is periodically re-invented because each chronological phase is taken to represent a different city. Re-emplacement would therefore occur as a previous architectural program in the city is replaced by the one which follows it, with an assumption that each phase can be discretely separated from what came before.[24] While there is certainly an element of re-emplacement at play in discussions of 'place', this is only one avenue to understanding places. Focusing on the material qualities of sites and the practices associated with them provides a sense of place that breaks down strict temporal boundaries.

In our case, the obvious starting point is the Hittite monument on the N-facing slope of the narrow valley cutting through the site. It is the product of Bronze Age craftsmanship that drew on influences from as far away as Assyria,[25] but its rôle in place-making is not restricted to the Bronze Age. The Fasıllar monument is large in stature, and later inhabitants would have interacted with it. Phenomenological perspectives of the kind developed by C. Tilley suggest that there are strong connections between a person and the landscape.[26] In an effort to avoid using a human as a subject model, B. Latour describes the significance of materials through the construction of a relational ontology.[27] The significance of materials, he suggests, is not limited to human perception and interpretation of them. Instead, humans and things reinforce each other through their co-existence and interaction. Therefore, the relationships between individuals and the materiality of the site are significant, since these set up subsequent relationships between persons and things as interdependent. While the meaning of these encounters must have changed over time, place-making at Fasıllar was wrought through the stone itself, the carvings of revered deities (if they were recognized as such), and the ubiquitous physical traces of human interaction with the rock.

---

22 Lucas 2005; Witmore 2004b.
23 Edmonds 1999; Dobres 2000, 110; Sinopoli 2003.
24 'Re-emplacement' is used in the sense that each chronological phase is characterized as a new place because of the constructed (literally 'emplaced') elements that arise in them.
25 Alexander 1968.
26 Tilley 1994 and 2004.
27 Latour 1993a, 1993b and 2005.

Bronze Age modification and interaction with the landscape transformed that landscape into the form encountered by people and material in later periods, so that past actions influence place-making in subsequent time periods. In other words, the place fashioned during the Hittite period continued, in a material sense, to fashion subsequent permutations of place at Fasıllar.

This temporal component of the site is manifested through the various periods of monumentalization, illustrated by the carving of the Lucianus monument 100 m from the Fasıllar monument. They interact with each other locationally and materially in that they are positioned close to each other and they evoke each other's monumental character. Rather than approaching these temporally-distinct episodes as separate phases of the site, here I follow R. Bradley, who states that "all monuments were built in places, and many of those places were selected precisely because they already enjoyed a special social significance".[28] Using sites such as Stonehenge, he demonstrates that their significance persisted by means of continuous ritual activity, which encouraged repeated ritual occurrences, although they were not necessarily identical in form.[29] Similarly, J. Barrett writes that the henge site of Avebury is

> the physical remnant of a number of abandoned projects and not the culmination of a series of planned phases. These projects were undertaken at different locations within the landscape, and at these *locales* actions and exchanges between people created the material conditions which then helped, in turn, to sustain those particular human relations.[30]

Thus we should examine the various instances of monumentalization at Fasıllar with a view to how they relate to each other. While Fasıllar may not be characterized by the same degree of successive use and re-use as other sites, the Bronze Age monument can be considered a marker of the site's 'social significance', which was still in effect when the Lucianus monument was constructed.

Fasıllar displays both commemorative and non-commemorative, conscious and unconscious acts of engaging with the past. The processes of stone-cutting in different periods of time recall each other. The quarrying of stone in the Bronze Age and Roman periods created an altered landscape that is akin to Ingold's multi-temporal landscape: the traces of quarrying present in the landscape are effectively different temporalities.[31] The discussion of place-making at Fasıllar needs to account for the cross-temporal relationships between materials. Modification of Fasıllar's material fabric leaves marks that are continuously interacted with over time. The specific meaning of such landscape modification undoubtedly took different forms depending on the prevailing social context, but social context is in part informed by the landscape with which humans interact. This approach is neither deterministic nor mentalist; it suggests that the specific context in which people encounter and engage with a site is part of Casey's "constitutive co-ingredience".[32] Material reality is an active part of any 'constructed' place, so that what people are interacting with matters, even if meaning is not directly attributable to this material.[33]

---

28   Bradley 1993, 44.
29   Id. 1991 and 1998.
30   Barrett 1994, 13.
31   Ingold 1993.
32   Casey 2001, 405.
33   A discussion of the full complexity of this issue must be reserved, hopefully, for when much more work has taken place at the site.

The discourses that surround places are significant, too, although sometimes place is endowed with conflicting sets of meanings and associations. For the post-Classical periods, uncertainty abounds at Fasıllar, including everything from the site's full extent, the nature of the activities that occurred there, and even its name. Fasıllar was once thought to be the Late Roman town of Misthia. Based on a Greek inscription discovered out of context and *c*.30 km distant at Beyşehir, W. M. Ramsay posited that Misthia was located at Fasıllar.[34] A Byzantine castle at Kale Daği, directly north of Fasıllar, supported the idea that a town of substantial size might lie nearby. A. Hall, however, argued against Fasıllar being Misthia because nothing more than ritual and possibly athletic activity (in the supposed stadium) is attested, noting also that there is no known road-system nearby. He suggests that Classical to Late Roman Fasıllar was more likely to be a regional meeting-point for several towns and villages, possibly with ritual overtones. Nevertheless, even if only in academic scholarship, Fasıllar at one time *was* Misthia. Since our engagements with the site today are not isolated from earlier ones — whether they occurred 3,000 years ago or 50 — the place incorporates them all, allowing for multiple interpretations and senses of place. It also warns of the consequences of essentializing the meaning of a place into a single moment, function or intention, since these things are fluid — even in scholarship.

Quarries and the maintenance of place

Quarries deserve greater attention as places within landscapes. Traditionally, quarries are discussed from an economic perspective that favors questions pertaining to the nature of the labor, who controlled quarries, where the stone was going and how it got there. Quarries are frequently seen as part of an economic structure, the control of which lies somewhere else. They provide building blocks for other places. Yet when we find instances where quarries exist alongside monumental structures, certain other questions arise. For example, how did the sense of place change as the very material of the place was transformed? Quarries are not static places that can be reduced to their functional rôle within a broader landscape: rather, they change due to the activities carried out in them, and, as they change, their character as places changes too. The same can be said of any city. Often it takes the form of construction (both addition to and subtraction from the built environment). Where quarries differ from cities is in the durability of the traces left by subtraction. This calls for a contextual look at place-making, since it speaks to the relevance of both a place's material qualities and the practices that engage those material qualities. The outcomes of those engagements leave lasting traces on the landscape. Later populations interact with an ever-changing site. In the case of Fasıllar, Hittite monumentalization and quarrying left traces of the practices that actively constructed this place, traces later confronted by Roman-period quarrying and monumentalization. Bronze Age stone-cutting left durable markers, literally 'carved in stone', of practices imposed on the physical landscape, which influenced subsequent place-making in the Roman era. Casey's "constitutive co-ingredience" must necessarily cross temporal boundaries.

Fasıllar is a place of lived practices. The presence of a Roman sarcophagus quarry on the N plateau suggests that this area also played a part in the relationship between the living and the dead. During the use-life of the quarries, other contemporary practices included actions such as the sharing of crafts knowledge; the procurement and consumption of food

---

[34] Hall 1959, 120.

and water; the movement of materials and movement by herders and traders; and the distribution of stone between this location and those where it would be used. Engagement with such issues provides a sense of the place that is literally distributed through its material being. A productive way to look at quarries is what D. Massey (following others) calls a "throwntogetherness":[35] all of the practices that shape the site are brought together in a way that transcends temporal divisions. Roman Fasıllar depends on Bronze Age Fasıllar and all of the attendant practices, relationships, material and social networks at the site. Quarries are not just quarries: quarry sites involve networks of people and materials and their movement.[36] To define a place according to one function is not sufficient, and archaeologists should incorporate as much of a site's complexity as possible in their interpretations of place.

Conclusions

I have argued for an account of places that includes the multi-temporal components of each site, based on Hittite, Classical, Roman and later interactions with the site of Fasıllar, which are never independent of prior interactions. The Hittite practices and the site's layout during the Late Roman period are not mutually exclusive: they come together as a collection of practices that shapes and reshapes this location as a place, whether through direct changes to the physical environment or through subtle recollections of the past in the present. Fasıllar has variously been considered a Hittite center with a large monument, a (misnamed) Roman town, a Roman site lacking the significance of a civic center, and a modern village. All of these things, however, hold significance for understanding Fasıllar as a place both in the past and present.

Bibliography

Alexander, R. L. 1968. "The Mountain-God at Eflatun Pınar (Pl. II-IV)," *Anatolica* 2, 77-85.
Arnold, D. 1991. *Building in Egypt: pharaonic stone masonry* (New York).
Bailey, G. 2007. "Time perspectives, palimpsests and the archaeology of time," *JAnthArch* 26, 198-223.
Barrett, J. 1994. *Fragments from antiquity: an archaeology of social life in Britain, 2900-1200 BC* (Oxford).
Binford, L. R. 1981. "Behavioral archaeology and the 'Pompeii Premise'," *Journal of Anthropological Research* 37, 195-208.
Bradley, R. 1991. "Ritual, time and history," *WorldArch* 23.2, 209-19.
Bradley, R. 1993. *Altering the earth: the 1992 Rhind Lectures* (Edinburgh).
Bradley, R. 1998. *The significance of monuments: on the shaping of human experience in Neolithic and Bronze Age Europe* (London).
Casey, E. 2001. "Body, self and landscape: a geophilosophical inquiry into the place-world," in P. C. Adams, S. Hoelscher and K. E. Till (edd.), *Textures of place: exploring humanist geographies* (Minneapolis, MN) 403-25.
Dobres, M.-A. 2000. *Technology and social agency* (Oxford).
Edmonds, M. 1999. *Ancestral geographies of the Neolithic: landscapes, monuments and memory* (London).
Ehringhaus, H. 2005. *Götter, Herrscher, Inschriften: die Felsreliefs der hethitischen Grossreichszeit in der Türkei* (Mainz).
Hall, A. S. 1959. "The site of Misthia," *AnatSt* 9, 119-24.
Ingold, T. 1993. "The temporality of landscape," *WorldArch* 25.2, 152-74.
Ingold, T. 2000. *The perception of the environment: essays in livelihood, dwelling and skill* (London).
Ingold, T. 2007. *Lines: a brief history* (London).
Latour, B. 1993a. "Ethnography of a 'high-tech' case: about Aramis," in P. Lemonnier (ed.), *Technological choices: transformation in material cultures since the Neolithic* (London) 372-98.

---

35   Massey 2005, 140.
36   Ingold 2007, 96-103.

Latour, B. 1993b. *We have never been modern* (Cambridge, MA).
Latour, B. 2005. *Reassembling the social: an introduction to actor-network-theory* (Oxford).
Lucas, G. 2005. *The archaeology of time* (London).
Massey, D. 2005. *For space* (London).
Mattingly, D. J. (ed.) 1997. *Dialogues in Roman imperialism* (JRA Suppl. 23).
Mellaart, J. 1962. "The Late Bronze Age monuments of Eflatun Pınar and Fasıllar near Beysehir," *AnatSt* 12, 111-17.
Mitchell, S. 1993. *Anatolia: land, men, and gods in Asia Minor,* vol. 1 (Oxford).
Peacock, D. P. S. and V. A. Maxfield 1997. *Mons Claudianus, survey and excavation 1987-1993,* 1: *topography and quarries* (Cairo).
Ramsay, W. M. 1908. *The cities of St. Paul: their influence on his life and thought. The cities of Asia Minor* (New York).
Sinopoli, C. M. 2003. *The political economy of craft production: crafting empire in South India, c.1350-1650* (Cambridge).
Tilley, C. 1994. *A phenomenology of landscape: places, paths and monuments* (Oxford).
Tilley, C. 2004. *The materiality of stone: explorations in landscape phenomenology* (Oxford).
Waelkens, M. 1990. "Extraction et prémanufacture dans le monde hittite," in id. (ed.), *Pierre éternelle du Nil au Rhine* (Bruxelles) 37-44.
Waelkens, M. 1992. "Bronze Age quarries and quarrying techniques in the Eastern Mediterranean and the Near East," in id., N. Herz and L. Moens (edd.), *Ancient stones: quarrying, trade and provenance: interdisciplinary studies on stones and stone technology in Europe and Near East from the Prehistoric to the Early Christian period* (Leuven) 5-20.
Ward-Perkins, J. B. 1973. "Quarrying in antiquity: technology, tradition and social change," *ProcBritAc* 57, 137-58.
Witmore, C. 2004a. "Four archaeological engagements with place: mediating bodily experience through peripatetic video," *Visual Anthropology Review* 20.2, 57-71.
Witmore, C. 2004b. "On multiple fields. Between the material world and media: two cases from the Peloponnesus, Greece," *Archaeological Dialogues* 11.2, 133-64.

Problematising privacy at the imperial villas
Dirk Booms

The study of privacy in the Roman world has been heavily influenced by modern, Western preconceptions of 'public' and 'private', especially regarding domestic space. As a result, studies that aim to contribute to a theoretical framework of the rôles of specific spaces in a Roman context often generate contradictory and vague conclusions.[1] Privacy is a cultural construct that differs across cultures, classes and times, but, generally, interactions between different actors determine how 'privacy' as a concept is defined. The nature of privacy is further determined by the relations between the different actors who participate in these interactions. In order to provide an appropriate setting that facilitates this social interaction, places are created, and space is organized.[2] While other papers in this section examine how people in the provinces, sometimes unintentionally, shaped and reshaped space and place(s) under Roman rule, this paper looks at how and why both private place and the sense of private place (i.e., privacy) were deliberately created within a straightforward Roman domestic context, namely three imperial villas in Italy. For this analysis of privacy, I will focus on the relationship between the status of the people and the places they occupy in the villas, through the ways in which access to the emperor's personal space was regulated, and through the ways in which different spaces were created for and assigned to guests of different status.

The relationship between public and private spaces has been studied for smaller domestic contexts (particularly at Pompeii and Herculaneum) using literary and archaeological sources.[3] However, it is often difficult to identify spaces, because several areas in the traditional *domus* (e.g., the *atrium*, *tablinum* and *cubiculum*) had several different uses, depending on the time of day and the needs of the moment. This is probably due to the relatively small size of the *domus*, which renders boundaries between functionally-distinct areas permeable and often invisible on a plan. One of the strengths of studies of domestic contexts, however, has been their use of different types of decoration to argue not just for a division between public and private spaces, but also for the existence of several layers of privacy, depending on the relationship of the visitor to the master of the house. In a society where daily life was dominated by social status, richly-decorated spaces displayed the wealth and status of the owner and were intended for the entertainment of high-status visitors.[4] In this way, a system of 'controlled access' filtered guests through the house, where a higher status allowed deeper penetration into the core.

Imperial villas (i.e., villas in the possession of the emperor) do not pose the same problems as small residential contexts. As the largest expression of domestic space, there was no need for rooms with multiple functions. Since the villas were meant to illustrate the luxury that accompanied the emperor, any limitation in the use of space would have been viewed as a shortcoming. Furthermore, because of their compartmentalised nature,

---

1   George 1997, 300; Nevett 1997, 283-85.
2   Nevett 1997, 282.
3   Wallace-Hadrill 1994; Zaccaria Ruggio 1995; Berry 1997; George 1997; Grahame 1997; Leach 1997; Riggsby 1997; Allison 2004.
4   For example, while intimate friends were invited into the *cubiculum*, less intimate *clientes* were allowed merely in the *vestibulum* and *atrium*. All spaces were decorated accordingly (Wallace-Hadrill 1988, 80-81; id. 1994, 44).

there were connection routes and boundaries between spaces, which often remain visible. Details about the occupants of imperial villas can be reconstructed to a considerable degree, because references to them appear frequently in literary and epigraphic sources.

Assuming the existence of several levels of privacy in an imperial villa, I provide a brief survey of the literary evidence for different types of guests. It shows that, along with high-status guests who were in residence, lower-status visitors were admitted when public events were organised at the villa. Boundaries and access ways isolated guests in residence from the emperor's personal space, but guests did have direct access to the entertainment areas. Day visitors, on the other hand, were guided directly to the entertainment areas through specially planned and controlled routes, which kept them away from other parts of the villa. In the case of Hadrian's Villa, the existence of such a route was recognised in the underground network by E. Salza Prina Ricotti (2001), but a similar design is found at other villas. Entertainment areas were thus purposely located in the peripheries of a complex.

Peopling the imperial villa

While previous spatial studies have used a bipartite structure of interactions in domestic space (i.e., between inhabitants, or between inhabitants and strangers[5]), it is more accurate to assume a multipartite scheme, composed of guests of different status, guards and personnel. At imperial villas there is enough evidence to identify these different groups.

Whenever the emperor was present, the imperial villa became his palace and place for conducting official business. Caligula and Domitian welcomed embassies at villas in Baiae and Albanum.[6] From the villa at Baiae, Claudius issued an important edict allowing foreigners to become senators.[7] Domitian signed a municipal law at his villa in Circeii.[8] Domitian and Trajan held trials at Albanum and Centumcellae,[9] and Trajan and Hadrian replied to embassies from Delphi at Antium and Tivoli, respectively.[10] Literary sources mention public events at these villas: Claudius asked the consuls for permission to hold fairs on his estates,[11] and Nero instituted public games for the birth of his daughter at the Antium villa.[12] Better known are the *Quinquatriae Minervae*, a public festival in honour of Minerva, held annually by Domitian at his villa at Albanum. Numerous sources mention the games, which included not only literary and theatrical performances but also hunting and gladiatorial events.[13] These examples show that there were two categories of guests at the villas: visitors in residence on official business (among them, embassies of cities or provinces, petitioners,[14] and members of the Senate) and visitors to public events.

The organisation of such events at the villas implies that, apart from the emperor, his immediate family and other members of the court, a permanent working staff must have

---

5 Grahame 2000, 21-22.
6 Caligula: Philo, *Leg.* 29; Jos., *AntJ* 18.7.2. Domitian: *CIL* IX 5420.
7 *CIL* V 5050.
8 González 1986.
9 Domitian: Plin., *Ep.* 4.11.6; Suet., *Dom.* 8.4; Juv. 4. Trajan: Plin., *Ep.* 71.
10 Plassart 1970, 36 (Trajan) and 82-83 (Hadrian).
11 Suet., *Claud.* 12.2.
12 Tac., *Ann.* 15.23.
13 Stat., *Silv.* 3.5.28-31 and 4.2.64-68; Dio Cass. 67.1.2 and 67.14.3; Suet., *Dom.* 4.4; Juv. 4.99-101.
14 Juv. 4.60-63.

been present in the form of a substantial corps of slaves.[15] With so many visitors, the safety of the emperor was a crucial issue. Emperors were often surrounded by personal bodyguards (e.g., the *Germani corporis custodes*),[16] and guards and soldiers are attested at the villas of Sperlonga, Capri, Albanum and Sorrento.[17]

Case studies: three imperial villas

Many of the villas were originally constructed in the Late Republic, but some emperors chose to build new and lavish complexes. Because they were built for the emperor, careful attention was given to his personal preferences, with regard not only to design and decoration but also to access and safety. Villas can give insight into the way that spaces with different functions were intentionally demarcated. I will discuss three of the best preserved examples of imperial villas: Domitian's at Albanum, Trajan's at Arcinazzo and Hadrian's at Tivoli. Of these three, the latter is the best preserved and studied and will therefore serve as the starting point.

Hadrian's Villa at Tivoli

Built during the 120s and 130s, several structures at Hadrian's Villa have been identified as slave-quarters and guest rooms based on their architecture and decoration. Because of the lower quality of the decoration and the inclusion of a large number of small rooms, slave-quarters have traditionally been recognised in the *Cento Camerelle* (fig. 1, CC),[18] the architecturally-similar *Pretorio* (fig. 1, no. 2)[19] and, more recently, the *Caserma dei Vigili* (fig. 1, no. 5), although these last were thought to have been a military complex.[20] Similar in layout are the so-called *Hospitalia* (fig. 1, no. 4), whose longstanding interpretation as barracks for the praetorian guards is still generally accepted, although it has been suggested recently that they were guest quarters.[21] Guest quarters have also been identified in the rooms richly decorated with marble floors and wall veneer on the top floor of the *Pretorio*, where occupants had a panoramic view over the W part of the villa,[22] and in the block of houses decorated with lavish wall-paintings and mosaics with a view over the *Canopo* (fig. 1, no. 3).[23]

Recently, Salza Prina Ricotti has shown that the internal communication of the villa was organised around a system of underground passages. At one point, the access route split into two directions. While the main road continued towards the *Vestibulo* (fig. 1, no. 6), the other one went around the villa (fig. 1, A), passing by the *Teatro greco* and the *Palaestra*

---

15 Although their quarters will be mentioned, this study is not directly concerned with slaves at the villas.
16 E.g., Suet., *Tib.* 24; *Calig.* 45, 52 and 55; *Claud.* 26.2, 29.3 and 39.1; Tac., *Ann.* 1.24 and 11.12; Dio Cass. 60.31.2-5.
17 Sperlonga: Tac., *Ann.* 4.59.2; Capri: Tac., *Ann.* 4.67.2-4; Albanum: *CIL* XIV 2286 and 2287; Sorrento: *CIL* X 711.
18 Salza Prina Ricotti 2001, 163. The names in italics used to label the different parts of the villa are the traditional ones, given to them by the villa's first excavators.
19 Aurigemma 1961, 147-50.
20 Salza Prina Ricotti 2001, 157 and 393-96.
21 Ibid. 153 and 215.
22 Aurigemma 1961, 147-50.
23 MacDonald and Pinto 1995, 63.

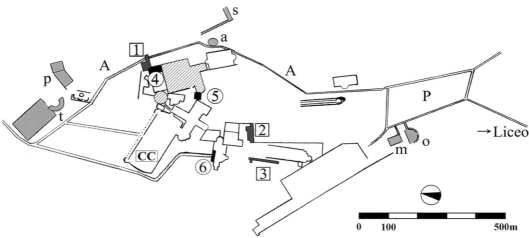

Fig. 1. Schematic plan of Hadrian's Villa.
Entertainment buildings (light grey): a - *Arena*; m - *Mimizia*; o - *Odeon*; p - *Palaestra*; s - *Stadio*; t - *Teatro greco*.
Guest quarters (dark grey with numbers in squares): 1 - *Triclinio Imperiale*; 2 - *Pretorio*; 3 - *Canopo*.
Guards (black with numbers in circles): 4 - *Hospitalia*; 5 - *Caserma dei Vigili*; 6 - *Vestibulo*.
Emperor's personal space (hatched lines): A - Route A; CC - *Cento Camerelle*; P - *Parking* (after Salza Prina Ricotti 2001, fig. 158).

(fig. 1, t and p). It then led to the underground network, which was designed to accommodate carriages and which included a trapezoidal network of passages where guests could leave carriages and animals, the so-called *Grande Trapezic* (fig. 1, P). Apart from its function as a supply-route, Salza Prina Ricotti attaches another use to the passage, based on the trajectory of the road and the structures it connects. It passes the *Teatro greco* before going underground at the *Triclinio Imperiale* (fig. 1, no. 1), then passes the *Arena* and the *Stadio* (fig. 1, a and s), before giving access to the *Grande Trapezio*, from which the *Liceo*, *Odeon* and *Mimizia* (fig. 1, o and m) could be reached. In this way, while bypassing the residential areas of the villa, it connected all the entertainment buildings (fig. 1, light grey), which were located on the peripheries of the complex. Salza Prina Ricotti concludes that the entertainment buildings, which could hold relatively large numbers of people, were at times the setting for public events that guests could attend. These guests were probably aristocrats from nearby villas or inhabitants of the town of Tibur, who, after leaving their horses and carriages in the *Grande Trapezio,* could be led to their destination without entering the residential part of the villa.[24]

Based on the spatial relationship between the communication network and the emperor's personal space (fig. 1, hatched lines), it is clear that the guest quarters were positioned specifically to be under constant surveillance of the guards. At the entrance to the underground network, one would have expected to find guards controlling access to the villa,[25] so the traditional interpretation of the *Hospitalia* is probably correct. The neighbouring *Triclinio Imperiale* could have acted as the villa's secondary vestibule as it shares several of the traditional characteristics of a vestibule.[26] Its lavish marble decoration and the architectural

---

24 Salza Prina Ricotti 2001, 415-17.
25 Guards at the entrance of an imperial villa are mentioned by Juvenal (4.61-63).
26 In fact, Lugli (1932, Tav. II) labels it *vestibolo*, as do MacDonald and Pinto 1995, 70; *contra* Salza

similarity to the other guest areas suggest that guests were also housed here and had access to a personal belvedere. Although located next to the emperor's quarters, neither the *Hospitalia* nor the *Triclinio Imperiale* had doors that gave access to the emperor's space. Similarly, the guest quarters at the *Pretorio* and the *Canopo* did connect to the reception and dining areas at the *Vestibule* and the *Canopo*, while the *Pretorio* had its personal belvedere, but both were located at some distance from the emperor's personal space. Since the guests at the *Triclinio Imperiale* lacked direct access to the emperor, the guards at the *Hospitalia* lacked access too. Thus, different guards must have been in charge of the emperor's personal safety. Only the *Caserma dei Vigili* (fig. 1, no. 5), ideally located between the *Vestibulo*, the guest quarters and the emperor's palace, had direct access. These considerations support its original interpretation as a military complex.[27]

In short, guests were not accommodated close to the emperor's personal space. While his personal guests and permanent members of the court were housed in the emperor's quarters, we have to imagine that the separate housing was intended for guests of lesser status, such as emissaries and ambassadors of cities or provinces. That would apply, for example, to the embassy from Delphi that stayed at the villa in A.D. 125.[28] Moreover, the underground network made it possible for day visitors to go to the entertainment areas without entering either the emperor's space or the guest quarters.

Domitian's villa at Albanum

Several decades earlier, Domitian had constructed an impressive villa-complex near Albanum (Castel Gandolfo) (fig. 2). Although the area has been continuously occupied since antiquity, the villa is relatively well-known architecturally and from literary evidence. The actual entrance to the complex, however, is still poorly understood. Excavations in the 1970s identified two structures close to the *via Appia*[29] that have recently been interpreted as the main entrance (fig. 2, no. 3 [black square]).[30] Although no complete plans have been published, one of the structures may have been a *nymphaeum* acting as vestibule.[31] From this structure, a road (fig. 2, A) led to the main body of the villa. It branched off to a series of rooms, interpreted as stables (fig. 2, P),[32] while the main road continued towards the entrance of a cryptoporticus (fig. 2, no. 2) lavishly decorated in two different styles. The N part, which was closest to the entrance from the road, had a richly-decorated coffered vault, large windows in the W wall, and painted architectural patterns all around. The

---

    Prina Ricotti 2001, 216-17.

27   Chiappetta 2008, which was published at the same time that I wrote this article, focuses specifically on the connection routes within the villa. Some of our interpretations coincide — Triclinio Imperiale, Canopo — while others do not — Pretorio (upper level would be restricted to Hadrian's use), Grande Trapezio (would also be used by Hadrian, which is highly unlikely), Caserma dei Vigili (for servants, not guards; Chiappetta [p. 199] places the guards at the Palaestra, far away from any central building). On the whole, Chiappetta is much more confident in uncritically assigning guest status to certain areas, but, within this, fails to distinguish between access for Hadrian, court, or eminent guests, and does not consider locating guards within the compounds of the villa.

28   See supra n.10.

29   Crescenzi 1979 and 1981.

30   von Hesberg 2006, 222.

31   Id. 2005, 380.

32   Lugli 1918, 63-64; all were 4.20 m wide and 2.95 m deep, with their back wall serving as a terrace wall. A small triangular outlet provided each room with water.

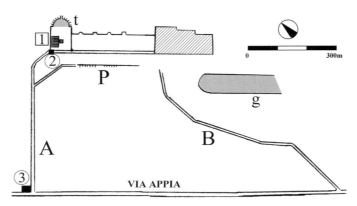

Fig. 2. Schematic plan of Domitian's villa.
Entertainment buildings (light grey): g - garden-stadium; t - theatre.
Guest quarters (dark grey): 1.
Guards (black with numbers in circles): 2 - cryptoporticus; 3 - entrance.
Emperor's personal space (hatched lines): A - Route A; B - Route B; P - Parking (after Lugli 1917, pls. III-V and von Hesberg 2006, fig. 1).

S part, on the other hand, had a plain ceiling without coffering, smaller windows, painted architectural elements and, curiously, painted centurions on the walls (fig. 3).[33] The stables could also be reached from another road that branched off the *via Appia* a little farther south than the first one (fig. 2, B). Before arriving at the stables, this road passed by the garden stadium (fig. 2, g).[34] Those arriving by the first road at the cryptoporticus found a series of rooms connected to a bath complex (fig. 2, no. 1).[35] These were the substructures for a large *porticus post scaenam* that was, according to tradition, connected to the villa's theatre (fig. 2, t). The true residential area of the villa was located in the southeast, overlooking a large open garden area set between the theatre and the residence, and accessible both from the garden and through the large cryptoporticus.

The villa's layout is a simple precursor of the more complex design at Hadrian's Villa. The two access routes led towards the villa's entertainment buildings (fig. 2, light grey), located on the periphery of the villa. They also gave access to the stables, where guests could leave their carriages. Although guest quarters have not yet been identified, the rooms beneath the *porticus post scaenam* are good candidates (fig. 2, dark grey). As they have never been excavated, their decoration remains unknown,[36] but they had their own bath complex and direct access to the entertainment areas of the villa. As at Hadrian's Villa, they were removed from the emperor's space (fig. 2, hatched lines), which could only be reached through the (guarded) cryptoporticus. Too little is known about the entrance to this complex to make any comparisons with other villas. However, to have no guards at the access road on the *via Appia*, one of the busiest roads into and out of Rome, is unthinkable. Thus, the *nymphaeum* might have been part of a larger guard structure.[37]

---

[33] von Hesberg 2006, 229.
[34] Originally it was believed to have been a hippodrome, but a new plan, the presence of water conduits and the comparison with Domitian's palace in Rome make it more plausible that the structure functioned as a garden.
[35] von Hesberg 2005, 379.
[36] Lugli 1918, 37-38.
[37] As at Hadrian's Villa, but also at later imperial villas, such as the villa of Maxentius and the villa of the Quintilii.

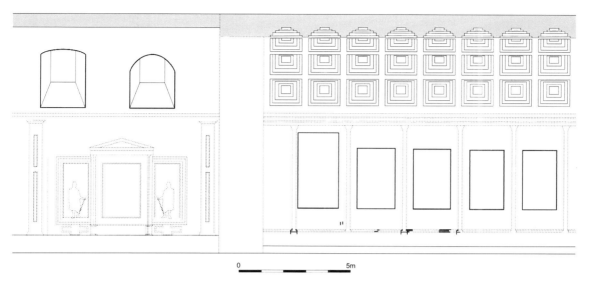

Fig. 3. The two different types of decoration (south at left, north at right) of the cryptoporticus of Domitian's villa (from von Hesberg 2006, fig. 5).

Literary sources report that, apart from guests in residence, day visitors were also welcomed at the villa on the occasion of the annual *Quinquatriae Minervae*. An entrance token to the games in the shape of a lead tessera carries the legend IVVEN(es) AVG(ustales) on one side and ALBAN(i) with a bust of Minerva on the other.[38] Such tokens indicate that not only close friends of the emperor but also members of lower social classes were invited.[39] Thus, when Suetonius (*Dom.* 19) writes that "there are many who have more than once seen him (i.e., Domitian) slay a hundred wild beasts of different kinds on his Alban estate", he does not mean the personal friends of the emperor or members of the court but rather visitors to the *Quinquatriae Minervae* or other events held at the villa. These day visitors could be led to the theatre via the first access road (fig. 2, A) without passing near the emperor's personal space.[40] Furthermore, when passing by the cryptoporticus, which gave access to that space, the visitor was first awed by the decoration of the N part, then dissuaded from entering by posted guards and by painted soldiers in the distance. These could have acted as a *trompe l'oeil* or a visual cue not to enter.

Trajan's villa at Arcinazzo

A very simple version of the same villa design appears in Trajan's villa at Arcinazzo (fig. 4). At its entrance on the *via Sublacense*, a rectangular building has been interpreted by the excavators as a service building or storage room (fig. 4, no. 2). Its walls are much thicker than any of the other walls in the villa, and buttresses were added to its exterior

---

38 Rostovtseff 1898, 276, no. 19; the *Iuvenalia* were without doubt identical to the Νεανισκεύματα, which Dio Cassius (67.14.3) locates at the villa and which were part of the *Quinquatriae Minervae* (Hardie 2003, 135).
39 von Hesberg 2006, 239-42.
40 Although the theatre was only constructed during the last years of Domitian's reign, the games had been instituted earlier, and a predecessor in the same place can be supposed. Certainly it seems that the theatre formed part of the villa's original design: von Hesberg 1978-80, 319-20.

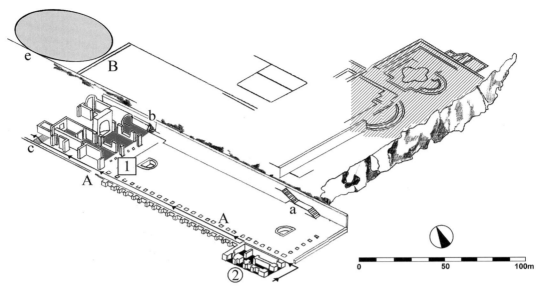

Fig. 4. Axonometric drawing of Trajan's villa.
Entertainment building (light grey): e - elliptical building.
Guest quarters (dark grey): 1.
Guards (black): 2.
Emperor's personal space (hatched lines): A - Route A; B - cryptoporticus; a, b and c - staircases
(after Fiore and Mari 2003a, fig. 5 and iid. 2003b, fig. 12).

wall. It must have been a tower of several levels, possibly serving as a belvedere.[41] Next to the building, steps led up to a large *platea* in front of a complex consisting of several rooms around a large *nymphaeum-triclinium* (fig. 4, no. 1). The structure has been interpreted as the guest quarters of the villa, in which the rooms flanking the *nymphaeum* were able to house both guests and their retinue.[42] They were luxurious in their decoration, with *opus sectile* floors in imitation of the *triclinium* of the Domus Flavia. These quarters were located on the lower terrace, while a higher terrace held more buildings that are not yet excavated but are known through an extensive geophysical survey. Based on their plan, they have been interpreted as the private *palatium* or the emperor's personal quarters (fig. 4, hatched lines); they include a centralised room with two *exedrae* and a bath building. Farther east, an elliptical structure (fig. 4, e) hints at the existence of an amphitheatre or garden stadium, while a vaulted cryptoporticus (fig. 4, B) functioned as an underground road linking different areas of the villa.[43]

This design is comparable with that of the two villas just discussed. Located at the entrance of the villa, the tower would have been both a guard tower and accommodation for the guards. As at Hadrian's Villa, the traffic in and out of the villa was controlled. The tower made it possible for the guards to see who was coming towards the villa and presumably also what was happening on the second terrace, where the emperor's quarters lay. The guest rooms on the lower terrace are isolated from the emperor's space, with no

---

41 Fiore and Mari 2003a, 40.
42 Ibid. 42.
43 Ibid. 44.

known stairs connecting the two. While a marble set of stairs that climbed to the higher terrace was located in view of the guardhouse (fig. 4, a), another set, hidden to the north of the guest quarters, was narrow, undecorated, and plainly not meant for guest use but rather for slaves and servants (fig. 4, b). The only stairs reserved for the guests are found on the other side of the complex and are paved in marble (fig. 4, c). They seem to have led to the only identified entertainment building, which, as at Hadrian's Villa, was located on the periphery.

At Trajan's villa, guests had no direct access to the emperor or his personal space and would have needed to pass guards to enter that space. Day visitors could be led straight to the elliptical entertainment building — without passing through the residential area and without disturbing the guests staying in the guest quarters — by taking the route along the SW side of the *platea* and going up the southern stairs (fig. 4, A). There they could enter the cryptoporticus that connected to the villa's entertainment venue. However, since most of the villa is unexcavated, this must remain a hypothesis.

Summary

The results of this study can be summarised by diagrams of the communication routes within the three villas (fig. 5). They show that entrances were not simply guarded to see who entered the villa but also to control internal movement within the villa. Guests were removed from the emperor's space, and in the cases of Trajan's and Hadrian's villas they had to pass by the guards at the entrance (and sometimes other guards subsequently, as at Hadrian's Villa) to gain access to his quarters. In Domitian's villa, additional guards (both real and painted) were stationed within the villa at a location that every visitor had to pass. By contrast, guests had direct access to entertainment areas. For day visitors, this was by means of a specially designed route (Route A) taking them directly to the entertainment buildings. Although guests in residence would also take this route, their quarters could be closed off from it so that day visitors would not disturb them.

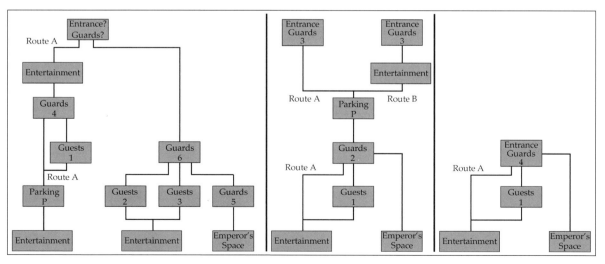

Fig. 5. Diagrammatic representations of the internal communication at Hadrian's, Domitian's and Trajan's villas (from left to right), using the numbers from figs. 1, 2 and 4 (author).

Conclusion

I have utilized the grander expressions of residential architecture to investigate notions of privacy. Imperial villas contain what a *domus* usually does not, namely the remains of boundaries between functionally distinct areas and a clear indication of internal communication routes. Nevertheless, the analytical framework proposed here can be transferred to the study of other spaces. Access to and within the *domus* is likely to have been organised in a similar manner to that described here for imperial villas. There were doors that could be closed, and access could be controlled by slaves, even though traces are more difficult to find on the smaller scale.[44]

The imperial villas were frequently the scene of public games, to which many outsiders were invited. A practical system for leading them to the entertainment areas located on the periphery used architecture and decorative patterns, as well as guards, so that they would not trespass on other areas of the villa and disturb guests in residence or the emperor and his court. Personal guests of the emperor were also carefully isolated from his personal space. Although they had easy access to the entertainment areas, guards made sure that they could not reach the emperor without his permission. This is in line with what we know from literary sources, if we may believe Pliny's *Panegyric*, in which Pliny praises Trajan and contrasts his policies to those of his evil predecessors:

> There are no obstacles, no grades of entry to cause humiliation, nor a thousand doors to be opened only to find still more obstacles barring the way ... this is the place where recently that fearful monster built his defences with untold terrors ... menaces and horror were the sentinels at his doors (47.5-48.4).

In this passage, Pliny specifically contrasts the admittance policy of Trajan to that of Domitian, to whom access was more difficult, he says, and obstructed by several doors and guards. In fact, the diagrams show that, while Hadrian's and Domitian's communication systems were more complex, movement in Trajan's villa appears to be organised more simply, as Pliny mentions. It also appears that some basic principles regarding the interaction between guests and host in the layout of Hadrian's Villa — which has been praised as being innovative compared to earlier imperial villas, as well as being distinct from them[45] — were conceived by the Flavian period. The diagrams show that the same organisational model of Trajan's villa had been used previously at Albanum, where it was expanded with another entrance, and it appeared again in Hadrian's Villa in a more elaborate form, with extra guest and guard quarters. The cryptoporticus at Albanum, however, can serve as a more specific example of the model. As H. von Hesberg has recently shown, the cryptoporticus was the villa's space for representation, where the emperor received his guests and *clientes* for the *salutatio*.[46] The fact that this did not happen in the emperor's personal space suggests that strict boundaries between the emperor and visitors were established as early as Domitian. Other studies have shown that space in the Roman world is deliberately constructed to facilitate the different types of behaviour and interaction that are required in a particular setting, which in turn are heavily influenced by the structured setting in

---

[44] Dickmann 1999, 278. Sometimes a *domus* had an *ostiarius* or porter, while most employed an *atriensis*, who was in charge of the daily running of the house. Part of the job was to make sure no person went where he was not invited (Petron., *Sat.* 72).
[45] Gros 2001, 363.
[46] von Hesberg 2006.

which they occur.[47] Thus, boundaries at the villas protected the privacy of the emperor with regard to visitors, but they also heavily affected the visitor's experience of the villa and the emperor. This analysis shows that emperors and architects made use of deliberate, multi-layered 'place-making'. They thoroughly and systematically considered how different areas of the villas related to each other and for whom they were destined, unwittingly marking the way in which domestic contexts should be studied by us.

To the modern eye, the high level of control by guards stationed around the villa and the circumscribed movement within it appear to limit that experience and affect it in a negative way. However, it is possible these boundaries were not perceived as such by the subjects. Guests were housed in lavishly decorated spaces, and day visitors were directed to view the magnificence of the place, such as the cryptoporticus at Albanum or the lavishly-decorated guest quarters at Arcinazzo. The physical proximity to the emperor of some guest quarters would probably have made an ambassador feel valued, even if he did not have direct access to the emperor. Such a sentiment at the palace is expressed by Statius (*Silv.* 4.2.10-12), who felt highly favoured by being invited to dine in the presence of the emperor, even if no direct contact between them occurred. Further, inviting members of the lower classes to his villas and letting them 'share' in the luxury would have made the emperor seem like a 'man of the people'. Hence, the boundaries within the villa served a dual purpose: the villa retained its very private character for the emperor, but at the same time was perceived, organised, designed and decorated as a public building, where public duties were performed by both the emperor and his guests.

Bibliography

Allison, P. M. 2004. *Pompeian households: an analysis of the material culture* (Los Angeles, CA).
Aurigemma, S. 1961. *Villa Adriana* (Rome).
Berry, J. 1997. "Household artefacts: towards a re-interpretation of Roman domestic space," in Laurence and Wallace-Hadrill 1997, 183-95.
Chiappetta, F. 2008. *I percorsi antichi di Villa Adriana* (Rome).
Crescenzi, L. 1979. "La villa di Domiziano a Castel Gandolfo," *QArchEtr* 3 = *Arch.Laz.* 2, 99-106.
Crescenzi, L. 1981. "La villa di Domiziano a Castel Gandolfo: nuove prospettive," *QArchEtr* 5 = *Arch. Laz.* 4, 181-84.
Dickmann, J.-A. 1999. *Domus frequentata: anspruchsvolles Wohnen im pompejanischen Stadthaus* (Munich).
Fiore, M. G. and Z. Mari 2003a. "Villa di Traiano ad Arcinazzo Romano: risultati dei nuovi scavi," in J. Rasmus Brandt, X. Dupré Raventós and G. Ghini (edd.), *Lazio & Sabina*, 1. *Atti del convegno 2002* (Rome) 39-45.
Fiore, M. G. and Z. Mari 2003b. *Villa di Traiano ad Arcinazzo Romano: il recupero di un grande monumento* (Tivoli).
George, M. 1997. "Repopulating the Roman house," in Rawson and Weaver 1997, 299-319.
González, J. 1986. "The *Lex Irnitana*: a new copy of the Flavian municipal law," *JRS* 76, 147-243.
Grahame, M. 1997. "Public and private in the Roman house: the spatial order of the *Casa del Fauno*," in Laurence and Wallace-Hadrill 1997, 137-64.
Grahame, M. 2000. *Reading space: social interaction and identity in the houses of Roman Pompeii* (BAR S886; Oxford).
Gros, P. 2001. *L'architecture romaine*, 2: *maisons, palais, villas et tombeaux du début du IIIe siècle avant J.-C. à la fin du Haut-Empire* (Paris).
Hardie, A. 2003. "Poetry and politics at the games of Domitian," in A. J. Boyle and W. J. Dominik (edd.), *Flavian Rome: culture, image, text* (Leiden) 125-47.

---

[47] Nevett 1997, 282.

Laurence, R. and A. Wallace-Hadrill (edd.) 1997. *Domestic space in the Roman world: Pompeii and beyond* (JRA Suppl. 22).
Leach, E. W. 1997. "Oecus on Ibycus: investigating the vocabulary of the Roman house," in S. E. Bon and R. Jones (edd.), *Sequence and space in Pompeii* (Oxford) 50-72.
Lugli, G. 1917. "La villa di Domiziano sui Colli Albani: topografia generale," *BullCom* 45, 29-78.
Lugli, G. 1918. "La villa di Domiziano sui Colli Albani: le costruzione centrali," *BullCom* 46, 3-68.
Lugli, G. 1932. "Studi topografici intorno alle antiche ville suburbane: V — Villa Adriana," *BullCom* 55, 111-50.
MacDonald, W. and J. Pinto 1995. *Hadrian's Villa and its legacy* (New Haven, CT).
Nevett, L. 1997. "Perceptions of domestic space in Roman Italy," in Rawson and Weaver 1997, 281-98.
Plassart, A. 1970. *Inscriptions de la terrasse du temple et de la région nord du sanctuaire. Nos. 276 à 350, Les inscriptions du temple du IVe siècle* (Fouilles de Delphes III.4.3; Paris).
Rawson, R. and P. Weaver (edd.) 1997. *The Roman family in Italy: status, sentiment, space* (Oxford).
Riggsby, A. M. 1997. "'Public' and 'private' in Roman culture: the case of the *cubiculum*," *JRA* 10, 36-56.
Rostovtseff, M. 1898. "Études sur les plombs antiques," *RevNum* 4, 251-86.
Salza Prina Ricotti, E. 2001. *Villa Adriana: il sogno di un imperatore* (Rome).
von Hesberg, H. 1978-80. "Zur Datierung des Theaters in der Domitiansvilla von Castel Gandolfo," *RendPontAcc* 51-52, 305-24.
von Hesberg, H. 2005. "Nutzung und Zurschaustellung von Wasser in der Domitiansvilla von Castel Gandolfo. Fragmente der Austattung von Brunnen und Wasserkünste," *JdI* 120, 373-422.
von Hesberg, H. 2006. "Il potere dell'otium," *ArchCl* 57, 221-44.
Wallace-Hadrill, A. 1988. "The social structure of the Roman house," *PBSR* 56, 43-97.
Wallace-Hadrill, A. 1994. *Houses and society in Pompeii and Herculaneum* (Princeton, NJ).
Zaccaria Ruggio, A. 1995. *Spazio privato e spazio pubblico nella città romana* (CollEFR 210).

Commentary: Roman places in the making
Peter van Dommelen

'Place' in the widest sense of the term has long been a concern of Roman archaeologists, as is evident from the long-standing traditions of studying architecture, settlement topography and landscape organisation. Analyses of the plans of buildings and settlements such as villas, theatres and military forts, as well as studies of centuriation and road systems, share a deeply engrained interest in the ways in which Roman material culture helped to create, maintain or re-organise spaces. The prominence of much of this material culture has no doubt played a major rôle in this interest. Precisely because of their prominence and relative uniformity, understanding how such architectural or regional structures worked in different environments has long been the object of comparative studies across the Roman world. Villa studies exemplify this approach best, as the internal architectural layouts of these sites and their rôles in structuring the wider landscape have been studied extensively across the Roman world.[1] The most spectacular example of this concern with space and, in particular, boundaries to delimit places is in *Limesforschungen*. It is surely no coincidence that this entire field, with its own conferences and publication series, has developed around the study of material culture as spectacular as Hadrian's Wall and some of the other *limites*.

Nevertheless, it is outside of Roman archaeology that spatial studies have been transformed in recent decades. One key influence has been spatial analysis in quantitative and statistical terms that was originally promoted by the 'New Archaeology' and in recent years has benefitted tremendously from technological developments such as Geographic Information Systems. The publication of *Spatial analysis in archaeology* (1976) was particularly influential, and its impact on Roman archaeology may be seen in P. M. Allison's spatial analyses of artefact distributions in Pompeian houses and Roman military forts.[2]

Another critical trend emerged a decade later from post-processual and cognitive archaeology's call to give attention to the social and symbolic dimensions of space and place. Particularly influential studies included S. Kent's *Domestic architecture and the use of space* and M. Parker Pearson and C. Richards' *Architecture and order*.[3] In the last decade, these issues have been taken up in Roman archaeology and applied to traditional topics, such as roads and domestic architecture, making use in particular of 'access analysis' to investigate how people's movements within buildings were socially controlled.[4] How space, in general, and specific places, in particular, may be differently or even selectively perceived by different social groups, and accordingly claimed and used by them, is a new approach that has come to the fore recently and shifted attention away from architecture towards landscapes and regional contexts. Following anthropologists like T. Ingold and B. Bender, this approach has been rapidly adopted across the wider discipline of archaeology, although interest within Roman studies has remained more limited.[5]

---

1   E.g., Dyson 2003, 13-35.
2   Hodder and Orton 1976; Allison 2004 and 2006.
3   Kent 1993; Parker Pearson and Richards 1994.
4   See Grahame 1998 and 2000; Laurence 1999.
5   Bender 1993; Ashmore and Knapp 1999; Ingold 2000; Bender and Winer 2001; Ashmore 2002. For Roman studies, see several of the TRAC volumes and Lafrenz Samuels and Totten in this volume.

Transforming Roman places

It is against this background, however briefly and cursorily sketched here, that the present set of papers must be understood. Collectively, they represent a productive response to the call to "investigate the construction of social space and the fluidity of these constructions at different scales of experience".[6] As this statement signals, the papers explicitly focus their attention on the social and symbolic dimensions of space; moreover, they do so unambiguously from a constructivist perspective, whereby meanings, perception and identity are not somehow 'given' or fixed but understood as actively constructed by the people and societies involved.

Three key themes characterise the five papers in this section. The heading under which the whole set of papers may be grouped is that of the construction of places in both physical and social terms. It explores how empty spaces or previously inhabited places were appropriated and transformed into 'Roman places' (or their opposite) to varying degrees and in different ways that were recognised as such by the social actors and groups involved. Associated with, and partially overlapping, this theme are the topics of interaction and memory. The former concerns the spaces in which contact and interaction took place (perhaps more appropriately glossed as 'contact zones') as people from a variety of backgrounds met and mingled. The latter foregrounds the rôle of memory in the construction of places; it investigates how memories were either drawn upon and used to construct new places or were actively manipulated to create and maintain pre-existing places.

As these brief characterisations suggest, these three themes are far from mutually exclusive, and most of the papers may be classified under more than one of them. The papers of this section also represent the rich variability of, and differences within, the Roman world as they cover contexts ranging from military N Britain to Imperial central Italy to urban Syria. Chronologically, they focus on the empire between the 1st and 4th c. A.D., but also draw on Bronze Age rock-art and contexts in Anatolia.

Constructing places

The construction of physical space is addressed by J. Baird and D. Booms. The latter examines three imperial villas at Tivoli, Albanum and Arcinazzo that were built for Hadrian, Domitian and Trajan, respectively. His analysis of these large architectural complexes starts from and builds upon conventional architectural studies, but in order to understand how public and private spaces were literally and conceptually constructed he uses access analysis or 'space syntax'.[7] These insights enable him to demonstrate how visitors would have experienced these imperial places in ways quite different from their inhabitants. Baird's study of Dura Europos of the 2nd to 3rd c. A.D. deals with a very different context. Precisely because this is a place situated on the very edge of the empire, she concentrates on examining the extent to which and in what ways Dura Europos was transformed into a Roman settlement after its occupation by the military. The presence of a Roman garrison from the 3rd c. A.D. has usually been regarded as both cause and evidence of the city's 'Romanisation', but Baird shows that the places used to house the Roman troops were created through close interaction with existing places and that this contributed

---

6   This was part of the call for papers distributed by the conference organisers.
7   This method was first proposed by B. Hiller and J. Hanson (1984) and has since been applied to Roman spaces by M. Grahame (1998 and 2000), albeit on a more modest scale.

to their integration in the settlement as a whole. A critical examination of the artefact typologies used to study the finds of the older excavations suggests that the amounts of Roman objects in the settlement have been overestimated, and she has good reason to conclude (p. 44) that the evidence from Dura Europos "characterizes the local response and the ... variability evident in what it meant to be Roman".

At the opposite end of the empire, and a later date, a related instance of constructing places is proposed by R. Collins, who explores the changes that had been occurring in the forts and settlements of Hadrian's Wall in the later 4th c. A.D. He interprets the gradual dissolution of many of the military practices that had been maintained for several centuries as evidence that the troops had steadily become more integrated in the local communities of N Britain, and he proposes that the transformation of the physical spaces of the forts was a crucial part of this process. As at Dura Europos, therefore, new places were created along Hadrian's Wall by integration rather than by differentiation; the crucial difference between the two situations is that the troops in Syria were relative newcomers, whereas those stationed on Hadrian's Wall had a long presence in N Britain.

Other ways of constructing places are highlighted by C. Feldman Weiss and B. Sekedat. Feldman Weiss's innovative paper studies the social constitution of social space in Ephesus of the 2nd c. A.D. through the so-called Salutaris dedication, a record of a gift made to fund a regularly-held procession. She uses this text to go beyond conventional topographic studies of Ephesus and to emphasise the performative dimensions of the procession, probing the potentially diverse engagement with, and experiences of, the social places created. She demonstrates how places may be constructed or adapted by means other than buildings, streets or other permanent architectural features. Finally, Sekedat's discussion of Hittite and Roman rock-art and sculpture in central Anatolia presents a view of how an isolated monument can be understood in the wider landscape context. He shows that a monumental Bronze Age Hittite rock-carving in the Fasıllar valley and its connections with a Roman rock-cut relief, the so-called Lucianus Monument, and a Roman-period sarcophagus quarry were not simply natural landscape features but also much older cultural remains drawn upon in the construction of places.

Together, these case studies demonstrate the double meaning of the terms 'to construct' and 'construction', and they underscore that 'place-making' involves both the physical (or rather material) transformation and the social appropriation of space. Thus, they serve as a reminder that both dimensions are part of the same process of place-making as two sides of the same coin.

Contact zones and places of remembrance

Because place-making is a very broad and generic process that always occurs under specific circumstances, it is never neutral and always intertwined with other dimensions, informing and enriching the meanings constructed and inscribed in space. One recurrent dimension of particular interest to Roman archaeology is contact and interaction, because of its potential to provide a fresh angle on 'Romanisation' processes. The two case studies by Baird and Collins represent this possibility best, since they concern two classic instances of the *limes*. Baird's analysis of the ways in which the Roman garrison was housed at Dura Europos is a particularly clear case, as her analysis of the place-making process confirms her understanding of the Europos river valley not so much as a dividing barrier but rather as a connecting area.

An appropriate label for situations like these is 'contact zones'. This term was coined by the geographer M. L. Pratt, who defined it as "the space in which peoples geographically and historically separated come into contact with each other and establish ongoing relations, usually involving conditions of coercion, radical inequality, and intractable conflict".[8] The relevance of this concept here is its explicitly spatial connotations, emphasising the concrete co-presence in a single area of all groups who encounter one another, whether they were in the region as permanent settlers or as temporary officials, soldiers or traders. Although the contributors to this discussion did not use Pratt's term themselves, it may serve to conceptualise the connections between case studies that are otherwise quite different. The imperial villas studied by Booms and the Roman finds in the houses of Dura Europos studied by Baird might seem to be situations that have little in common beyond their generic association with the Roman world, but both places were constructed in physical and social terms to function as contact zones, where very different social groups could meet. It is in this sense that their juxtaposition in this volume is relevant.[9]

Another significant dimension of place-making is memory, as its flexibility and association with material culture facilitate the incorporation of existing traditions and objects with new ones. Memory plays a particularly critical part in the place-making processes discussed by Sekedat and Feldman Weiss, because the gaps in, or fluidity of, the material presences in those situations are bound together by memory: it is indeed only as places of remembrance that the juxtaposition of and references between the Hittite and Roman monuments in the Fasıllar valley of central Anatolia can be understood as more than mere coincidence. As these studies show, memory represents an inevitable feature of place-making, because pristine spaces are very rare, if not non-existent. These studies also underscore the fundamental rôle of memory in the constitution of landscape as a social space, as S. Schama argued in his seminal *Memory and landscape*.[10] Even creating an empty space purposefully — as was not uncommon in Roman colonial practice — cannot remove the memory of what previously occupied the place. A spectacular instance of such an attempt 'to cleanse' local memories is surely the removal of the top and upper slopes of the Byrsa hill in Carthage to make space for the forum and Capitolium of the new Roman *colonia*.[11]

Feldman Weiss' discussion of urban space in Ephesus takes this discussion one step further, as her focus is on the built environment. Her study is to some extent in keeping with conventional approaches to (public) architecture in general, in which monuments act as physical focal points for maintaining memories. In P. Nora's words, they become *lieux de mémoire* or places "where [cultural] memory crystallizes and secretes itself".[12] What is remarkable about Feldman Weiss' paper is that she demonstrates that a *lieu de mémoire* may also be constructed in not-so-monumental ways that depend on embodied practices rather than built monuments.

---

8   Pratt 1992, 6.
9   See also Bradley 2002, 147-61, who points to the significance of boundaries and various ways of marking them.
10   Schama 1995. See also Hirsch and O'Hanlon 1995; Bender 2006. Notable archaeological publications on memory and landscape are: Bradley 2000, Alcock 2002, and Van Dyke and Alcock 2003; on memory and place, see Connerton 2006, 318.
11   Lancel 1995, 149-51.
12   Nora 1989, 9. See also Bradley 1998; id. 2002, 82-111; Knapp 2009.

Together, these case studies testify to the extent to which students of Roman archaeology are engaging with the full complexity of place-making and are actively exploring the Roman archaeological record from fresh perspectives.

Social space, material worlds and Roman archaeology

As may be evident from the papers in this section and from this brief discussion, place-making, or creating meaningful places by drawing boundaries to include and exclude spaces, is a powerful process. Because social interaction always 'takes place' somewhere in the most literal sense of these terms, place-making is inevitably a ubiquitous process, and its significance can therefore hardly be overestimated. It is also a process that, more often than not, involves material culture, which makes it potentially accessible for archaeological analysis and interpretation, and it is this potential that has begun to be tapped by studies like the ones considered here.

What ultimately unites the studies collected in this book, despite the very different settings of their case studies, is their shared focus on the multiple entanglements between people and their material worlds: while all papers take material culture in some shape or form as their starting-point — and these papers cover the entire range, from portable objects and buildings to settlements and landscape —the inhabitants of these landscapes and buildings and the people handling the objects are firmly at the centre of their investigations. As a corollary, all five chapters demonstrate that places are socially and symbolically constructed, regardless of whether they are imperial villas or Anatolian quarries, and that these meanings need constant confirmation through people's activities. In other words, places are continuously in the making, even if they are as solidly constructed as Hadrian's villa at Tivoli.

By way of conclusion, I note that this focus on agency, materiality and the socially constructed nature of meanings underscores that Roman archaeology is making good progress to 'catch up' with theoretical developments in other fields of the discipline. But I also wish to highlight the Roman dimension of these studies, which testifies to the opportunities that the (relatively) abundant Roman archaeological record offers for studies of this type. As the interpretations of these papers demonstrate, it is the combination of the Roman (material) culture and the long-standing traditions of the discipline that creates a fertile basis for probing such complex matters of human and social interaction.

Bibliography

Alcock, S. 2002. *Archaeologies of the Greek past: landscape, monuments and memories* (Cambridge).
Allison, P. M. 2004. *Pompeian households: an analysis of the material culture* (UCLA Monog. 42).
Allison, P. M. 2006. "Mapping for gender: interpreting artefact distribution inside 1st- and 2nd-century A.D. forts in Roman Germany," *Archaeological Dialogues* 13.1, 1-48.
Ashmore, W. 2002. "'Decisions and dispositions': socializing spatial archaeology," *American Anthropologist* 104, 1172-83.
Ashmore, W. and A. B. Knapp 1999. *Archaeologies of landscape: contemporary perspectives* (Malden, MA).
Bender, B. (ed.) 1993 *Landscape: politics and perspectives* (Providence, RI).
Bender, B. 2006. "Place and landscape," in Tilley, Keane, Kuechler *et al.* 2006, 303-14.
Bender, B. and M. Winer (edd.) 2001. *Contested landscapes: movement, exile and place* (Oxford).
Bradley, R. 1998. *The significance of monuments: on the shaping of human experience in Neolithic and Bronze Age Europe* (London).
Bradley, R. 2000. *An archaeology of natural places* (London).
Bradley, R. 2002. *The past in prehistoric societies* (London).

Connerton, P. 2006. "Cultural memory," in Tilley, Keane, Kuechler *et al.* 2006, 315-24.
Dyson, S. 2003. *The Roman countryside* (London).
Grahame, M. 1998. "Material culture and Roman identity: the spatial layout of Pompeian houses and the problem of ethnicity," in J. Berry and R. Laurence (edd.), *Cultural identity in the Roman empire* (London) 156-78.
Grahame, M. 2000. *Reading space: social interaction and identity in the houses of Roman Pompeii* (BAR S886; Oxford).
Hiller, B. and J. Hanson 1984. *The social logic of space* (Cambridge).
Hirsch, E. and M. O'Hanlon (edd.) 1995. *The anthropology of landscape: perspectives on place and space* (Oxford).
Hodder, I. and C. Orton 1976. *Spatial analysis in archaeology* (Cambridge).
Ingold, T. 2000. *The perception of the environment: essays on livelihood, dwelling and skill* (London).
Kent, S. (ed.) 1993. *Domestic architecture and the use of space: an interdisciplinary cross-cultural study* (Cambridge).
Knapp, A. B. 2009. "Monumental architecture, identity and memory," in A. Kyratsoulis (ed.), *Bronze Age architectural traditions in the East Mediterranean: diffusion and diversity* (Weilheim) 47-59.
Lancel, S. 1995. *Carthage: a history* (Oxford).
Laurence, R. 1999. *The Roman roads of Italy: mobility and cultural change* (London).
Nora, P. 1989. "Between memory and history: les lieux de la mémoire," *Representations* 26, 7-25.
Parker Pearson, M. and C. Richards (edd.) 1994. *Architecture and order: approaches to social space* (London).
Pratt, M. L. 1992. *Imperial eyes: travel writing and transculturation* (New York).
Schama, S. 1995. *Landscape and memory* (London).
Tilley, C., W. Keane, S. Kuechler *et al.* (edd.) 2006. *Handbook of material culture* (London).
Van Dyke, R. and S. Alcock (edd.) 2003. *Archaeologies of memory* (Oxford).

PLACE-MAKING THROUGH ROMAN HERITAGE

Making boundaries in modern Cyprus: Roman archaeology as 'touristic archaeology' in politically fractured landscapes
Jody Michael Gordon

A 'snapshot' of Roman archaeology's rôle in place-making in modern Cyprus

The goal of this case-study of how Roman archaeologies are produced for consumption as 'touristic archaeologies' within the context of 'the Cyprus problem' is to contribute to the theme of place-making on the regional and global level.[1] It does so by highlighting how the rival polities of Cyprus have deployed Roman material heritage through tourism in order to produce disparate, bounded 'places' that generate economic and political capital when experienced by tourists/consumers. I also emphasize the social and scholarly repercussions of such practices so that Roman archaeologists may better understand how the archaeologies they produce may be manipulated by third parties, and how this can result in potentially "dangerous and damaging outcomes".[2]

My analysis also presents a 'snapshot' of how places can be made — and constantly remade — using Roman archaeological heritage within tourism media. Through a detailed examination of several forms of digital and print media produced by rival groups embroiled in a longstanding political problem, I illustrate the various ways that Roman archaeology can be purveyed to the tourist/consumer as a politically and economically valuable commodity that contributes to the (re)making of place(s). The media forms analyzed include internet websites, site brochures, and tourist guidebooks. I selected these formats because they arguably represent the key points of contact between the producers who manipulate and consumers who are drawn to Roman archaeological places. However, despite their analytical utility as evidence, websites, brochures and even book editions are ephemeral to various degrees. Like the Roman archaeological places they virtually describe, these media formats "are never completely 'made' but are constantly in a state of re-working and re-visioning" through their use by people across time.[3]

This is especially the case in terms of modern electronic media such as websites, which can be rapidly altered by actors strategically operating within the context of volatile political issues such as 'the Cyprus problem' or the more recent WikiLeaks scandal. For example, in the four years since drafting my original paper the websites originally analyzed have been made, and remade, over and over, while Mehmet Ali Talat, the 'president' of Turkish north Cyprus discussed here, is no longer the leader of the Turkish Cypriot community.[4]

---

1 This study was first presented in the session "Economies of Heritage" at the conference. For a discussion of how "economies of heritage" are defined in this volume, see Lafrenz Samuels and Totten, above, p. 23.
2 Ibid. p. 23.
3 Ibid., above, p. 12.
4 Because internet websites are changed rapidly in accordance with the equally mutable economic and political goals of their producers, some of those cited in my footnotes are either no longer accessible or have changed their content. As argued in the text, this should not detract from my goal of producing a 'snapshot' of Roman archaeology's manipulation as a 'touristic archaeology' aimed at making specific national places during 2008. The actual web content

Thus, in a postmodern, digital world where vast amounts of information are often created, uploaded and destroyed at lightning speed, all that this study can provide is a didactic snapshot of how Roman material heritage has been, and continues to be, strategically marshaled to make places. Nevertheless, this state of flux in the sources of information should not undermine the study's importance, just as an earlier edition of a textbook should not invalidate its scholarly contribution from a specific epistemological viewpoint. Instead, this changeability should underline the contemporary significance of the present volume's attempt to highlight the "dynamism of places" and how Roman archaeology can be often and quickly manipulated and re-manipulated to link "past and present places" with positive and negative outcomes for both archaeologists and society.[5]

The politicization of Roman archaeology within national narratives

Archaeology is a politically charged discipline. This fact becomes most obvious in its entanglements with nationalist ideologies.[6] Although conceptions of nationhood vary, two defining aspects have emerged in nationalist discourse.[7] First, a nation is comprised of a sizeable population with a distinct ethnic or cultural identity. Second, this national group exists within, and has been culturally shaped by, a particular *place* or geographical territory. Thus, nationalist ideologies attempt to establish links between modern groups and local ancient cultures so as to provide a historical precedent that justifies a nation's existence within a particular temporal and spatial dimension.[8]

Frequently, such arguments are conveyed through state-produced, ideologically biased, national historical narratives that are disseminated through economies of heritage aimed at making or remaking modern places.[9] Yet in order to gain political credibility, such narratives must defend their claims with scholarly evidence that has often been drawn from archaeological data. Archaeological data lend effective support to nationalist narratives through their perceived rigorous and reflexive production by scholars and through the very materiality of archaeological objects: each artifact is unearthed from a specific context that can be linked, through place, style and usually time, to a particular culture.[10] Furthermore, archaeological material provides evocative images that spur the national collective memory, synthesizing national identities and their relationships to archaeological landscapes. It is at this point, however, when a modern culture is linked to an ancient one, that archaeological data have often become politicized and new conceptions of place have been constructed.[11]

---

  analyzed below was displayed when the paper was originally presented at the conference.
5 Lafrenz Samuels and Totten, above, pp. 12 and 26.
6 For a brief introduction to this issue and a list of recent studies, see Arnold 2006, 154 and n.1.
7 Banks 1996, 2-3; Stritch 2006, 43.
8 See Lafrenz Samuels and Totten, above, p. 22.
9 My use of the term 'narrative' is based on N. Silberman's (1995, 250-53) understanding of it as a structural mode of conveying archaeological information to a wider populace in ways that can be simply understood, involving "sequences of archetypal story elements, didactically arranged with clear beginnings, middles, and ends". D. Stritch (2006, 51-53) also provides an effective discussion of the creation and use of national narratives in Cyprus.
10 L. Smith (2006, 31) stresses that material heritage has "identifiable boundaries that can be mapped, surveyed, recorded, and placed on national or international site registers".
11 Silberman (1995, 253) has aptly described this politicization by comparing the rôle of the state (within the construction of nationalist narratives to that of the 'discoverer' within the narrative

Aside from its use in Fascist Italy or the British empire, Roman archaeology has been rarely politicized as the objective evidence used to support nationalist narratives, since the Romans were often perceived as invaders who usually disrupted local cultural developments.[12] Such a situation has allowed Roman archaeology to be interpreted by nationalist historians in one of two competing ways. First, one can view the Romans as *Romani capti* or 'preservers' of local culture.[13] This choice characterizes narratives that seek to link modern cultures to local pre-Roman ones. Such 'preservation' narratives can be read archaeologically through Roman remains that preserve the features of the 'hero' cultures of national narratives, which are claimed as the ancestors of modern populations. The second way is to view the Romans as either civilizing or ruthless invaders.[14] This interpretation appeals to expansionist states, which attempt to justify their presence in a conquered region either as a defensive or a civilizing mission.[15] In archaeological terms, Roman remains that obliterate pre-Roman ones can be interpreted as the observable evidence for invasion and a break in the continuity of pre-Roman cultures, which translates into an undermining of the rival 'Romans-as-preservers' narrative. As is shown below, the rival polities engaged in 'the Cyprus problem' have diversely manipulated Roman archaeology along the boundary between 'preserver' and 'invader' narratives in order to make new cultural places.

'Touristic archaeology'

'Touristic archaeology' represents one of the newest nationalist narratives supported by archaeology that has emerged to generate both economic and political capital in politically fractured regions. N. A. Silberman has defined 'touristic archaeology' as both productive yet precarious, considering "attendance figures and revenue expectations are no less important than scholarly insights".[16] Silberman's identification of the tourism industry as a powerful component of economies of heritage has been developed by D. Stritch, who has shown how the tourism industry sometimes plays a central rôle in indirectly augmenting the dissemination of politicized national narratives that once were produced exclusively by the state.[17] This has been possible since the goals of nationalist narratives, and the touristic

---

of the archaeologist-as-hero: "when the discoverer proclaims his or her connection to a modern population that claims descent from the group under study, the archaeological narrative is transformed from mere historical description into something of a political essay".

12 For Italy, see Gilkes 2003, 33-34. For Britain, see Hingley 1996, 135.
13 S. E. Alcock (1993, 1-2), in her analysis of Roman Greece, outlines some common features of 'preservation' narratives: "Not only did Greek culture preserve itself from Roman contamination; what is emphasized is the phenomenon of 'reverse cultural imperialism' (or 'reverse acculturation') with Greece (as Horace said) 'bringing the arts to rustic Latium'".
14 The 20th-c. colonialist enterprises of the British and Italians could both be seen in this manner. Tacitus' *Agricola* provides a literary precedent for both views: civilizing invaders at the end of Book 21, and ruthless invaders at the end of Book 30. See W. Hanson 1997 for an analysis of the Romans as invaders.
15 For example, M. Munzi (2004, 74) argues that such views were key to legitimizing the expansionist agenda of Fascist Italy: "opinions — that Italy could boast a Roman inheritance for the purposes of supporting colonial expansion — were shared by most members of the international colonial elite".
16 Silberman 1995, 261. See also his (1989, 51-67) study of the Nea Paphos archaeological park, which includes a discussion on how the Turkish invasion of Cyprus directly led to the rapid development of 'touristic archaeology' in Cyprus, with positive and negative economic and political effects.
17 See Stritch 2006. Stritch's research is also focused on tourism in the Republic of Cyprus.

allure of exotic regions, can be synthesized into a unified format that functions both as a political statement and an economic advertisement.

The unified format that has proved most applicable has been the marketing of a nation's archaeological heritage. Archaeology has this unifying power because it publicizes the national histories of modern states and makes new places by establishing their links to local archaeological cultures and landscapes. Additionally, archaeological monuments provide images that can be mass-produced for consumption by foreign tourists, enticing them to escape the ordinary and to experience the 'authentic' exotic.[18] Tourism then, although it may seem to use history and archaeology as mere marketing tools aimed at spurring local economies, also provides an outlet for nationalist political ideas, especially in polities in which cultural and territorial unity is threatened.

Roman archaeology and the competing 'touristic archaeologies' of Cyprus

In the following case study of how Roman archaeology has been politicized within the competing national narratives of Cyprus in order to make new places, I investigate how archaeology is produced for consumption as a 'touristic archaeology'. A study of Cyprus is instructive as it ties together many of the issues discussed above. First, due to 'the Cyprus problem', both polities have politicized Roman archaeology in nationalist narratives aimed at linking ancient communities to modern ones.[19] Second, each polity envisions the Romans differently: in the Greek Cypriot south the Romans are portrayed as 'preservers', whereas in the Turkish Cypriot north the Romans are 'invaders'. Third, since the economies of both polities rely on tourism, Roman archaeology has been converted into a 'touristic archaeology' aimed at bolstering political and economic viability.[20]

'The Cyprus problem' involves the attempt to establish a united nation of Cyprus from two cultural groups: a Greek Christian majority and a Turkish Muslim minority. Beginning with the Ottoman conquest in 1571, the 'problem' has dominated the history of Cyprus and remains an issue even today as there is still no solution in sight. Although a historical overview of the conflict is beyond the scope of this article, it is important to note that during the last 37 years the historic cultural divide in Cyprus has expanded into a political and physical one.[21] In 1974, the Turkish army invaded the northern third of Cyprus ostensibly to protect Turkish Cypriot rights from being infringed upon, following a *coup d'état* sponsored by the military *junta* then leading Greece.[22] Because, for the last 37 years, Turkish

---

[18] M. Shanks's (1992, 53 and 58) work on "archaeological erotics" discusses how tourism taps into the "escapist attraction" of archaeology and its "mysterious" ability to take "us away from the common place".

[19] See Constantinou and Papadakis 2002, 81-84, and Reiterer 2003, 28, for discussions on Greek and Turkish Cypriot views of both their own and each other's history. The term 'polity' is used in this study based on its definition in the *Concise OED*, as a "condition of civil order" or an "organized society". I have chosen to use this rather neutral term since both a recognized nation-state and an unrecognized 'non-state' (which is nevertheless a geographically-bounded, organized society) are discussed. The use of other, more specific terms might be misleading.

[20] For the economic importance of tourism to the Republic of Cyprus, see Wilson 1992, 99-115; Christofides 2002, 95; Reiterer 2003, 87. For north Cyprus, see Ugur 2003; Reiterer 2003, 88.

[21] A useful chronological overview of historical events relating to 'the Cyprus problem' is provided by A. B. Knapp and S. Antoniadou (1998, 20).

[22] Turkish Cypriots do not refer to Turkey's intervention in Cyprus as an invasion; instead, it is referred to as the 'Peace Operation'. See Tamkoç 1988, 96.

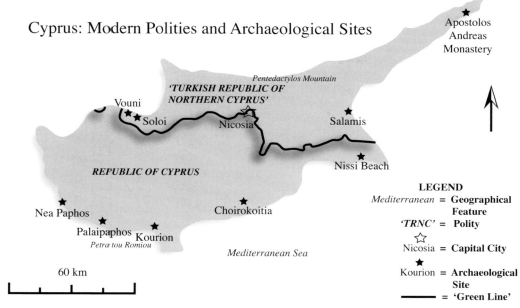

Fig. 1. Cyprus: modern polities and archaeological sites (author).

governments have continued to believe that Turkish Cypriot rights are at risk, the Turkish military occupation of north Cyprus remains in force and has led to the unilateral declaration of a northern polity, 'The Turkish Republic of Northern Cyprus' ('TRNC').[23] Today, the island remains *de facto* divided between two cultural groups inhabiting separate places — the Republic of Cyprus in the south and the 'TRNC' in the north — which hold political agendas with conflicting perceptions of Cypriot history and archaeology (fig. 1).

Because of these physical and perceptional boundaries, the Roman archaeology of Cyprus continues to be produced and circulated by rival tourism industries, governmentally directed by the island's two polities. In this study, by comparing each polity's nationalist narrative as espoused via government websites to the historical narrative of Cyprus generally acceptable to professional historians and archaeologists, I show how both sides have variously interpreted and manipulated the Roman material past.[24] I then examine a series of websites, brochures and guidebooks in order to reveal how Cypriot national narratives have been incorporated into the island's 'touristic archaeology' and have resulted in the circulation of a politicized Roman archaeology. The Republic of Cyprus is discussed first, followed by an analysis of the 'TRNC'.

---

23 Both the Turkish occupation of north Cyprus and the unilateral declaration of the 'TRNC' have been condemned by the United Nations. See UN Security Council Resolution 353 (1974) and UN Security Council Resolution 541 (1983) (for Resolution 353: United Nations 2010, http://www.un.org/documents/sc/res/1974/scres74.htm; for Resolution 541: United Nations 2010, http://www.un.org/Docs/scres/1983/scres83.htm). Since the 'TRNC' remains unrecognized by the UN, the polity, its officers and administrative units are typically referred to in quotation marks.

24 My description of nationalist narratives and their use in Cyprus is related to Smith's (2006, 29) analysis of heritage discourse. For a basic archaeological timeline of Cypriot history, see Hunt 1990, 295-300.

Cypriot tourism advertisements are easy to encounter and acquire both within Cyprus and without.[25] Yet, although tourism documents may appear as simple advertisements, they also can prove to be powerful billboards for political messages that can be consumed uncritically.[26] In general, most tourists are not scholars armed with academically critiqued archaeologies of Cyprus. As a result, the media produced by national tourism industries assume a primary link between tourists and the countries they visit, taking on the rôle of the 'authoritative' guide. It is these types of media that are most effective in widely disseminating politically-charged narratives that politicize tourists and exacerbate internecine conflict by reflecting themes similar to those presented in nationalist histories.

It is also through such governmentally-regulated representations of archaeological data that the public can misperceive how such data are produced and by whom. Most tourists, and especially those from politically stable regions, probably do not ponder how the historical narratives presented by tourism organizations are also political narratives. Instead, as non-expert interpreters, tourists may tend to assume that such organizations are purveying authentic narratives originally produced by archaeologists, because, aside from the obvious motivation for economic gain, tourism organizations may seem to lack overt political motives. Perhaps not all, but many, tourists thus begin to formulate perceptions of national histories, which are not only politicized, but are also believed to be based on verifiable archaeological data.[27]

This situation highlights one of the key reasons why studies of place-making are important for Roman archaeologists. As Lafrenz Samuels and Totten have stated, "the object of study for archaeologists shifts from a focus on the past to an interdisciplinary consideration of broader social contexts" so that archaeology becomes "equipped to inform and contribute to a wide range of contemporary issues".[28] I argue, however, that when data produced by archaeologists are deployed by third parties, this ability to "inform and contribute" — in short, archaeology's social power — can be undermined if archaeologists are implicated as the primary producers of biased or nationalist narratives. In order to preserve their

---

[25] For example, in its annual report for 2006 (Cyprus Tourism Organisation 2006a), the Republic of Cyprus' tourism organization outlined the various ways that the industry aggressively promotes itself to tourism consumers. While various multilingual forms of advertising are discussed, print media and films, the internet, and promotion through local information offices are highlighted as key ways of getting the Cyprus message across to tourists. According to the CTO (2006a, 63), in 2006 over one million people accessed their website, while 307,072 people visited their local information offices.

[26] Smith (2006, 31-32) identifies how heritage discourses developed by 'experts' actually work to encourage uncritical consumption through the construction of heritage as "something that is engaged with passively". She also points out that this passivity has been encouraged by the mass tourism industry and that "the Disneyfication of marketing and interpretation is a feature of real concern". It is certainly incorrect to label all tourists as passive and non-engaged as they visit sites, yet it is likely that a large number of tourists are less engaged than others.

[27] Fagan 2006a, 364-65. I. Russell (2006a, 11) hints at this situation when he recognizes that "Given the growing trend of marketing national heritage ... through tourism industries for economic development, archaeology is not generally the first point of contact for many people wishing to experience the past". As a result, people often experience the past through other media (e.g., tourism advertisements), which are, more often than not, produced by non-archaeologists. Nevertheless, much of the information purveyed through popular media channels may be perceived as based on academic sources by non-academic consumers.

[28] Lafrenz Samuels and Totten, above, pp. 20-21.

social power and relevancy, archaeologists must constantly investigate and mediate how their data is used. Place-making studies of how Roman archaeology is deployed by different groups to make places in economically and politically advantageous ways can thus play a key rôle in informing archaeologists about how their data can be misused and how they, as academic practitioners, might effectively work within such scenarios in ways that positively influence society.

Romans as 'preservers': Greek Cypriot national narratives

The 'Aspects of Cyprus' website

The Greek Cypriot national narrative is lavishly laid out in the on-line presentation 'Aspects of Cyprus', produced by the Press and Information Office of the Republic of Cyprus.[29] Through both text and archaeological images, the Cypriot government presents a history focused on the continuity of Hellenic culture. In the 'History: Introduction' section, the Cypriot narrative really begins in 1200 B.C. when "a process began that was to stamp the island with an identity that it still has today; the arrival of Mycenaean-Achaean Greeks as permanent settlers, who brought with them their language and culture".[30] Through this narrative, a link is established between the present and the past: modern Greek Cypriots share the same language and 'spirit of place' as the original Mycenaean settlers.[31] The introduction then stresses the survival of Greek culture despite frequent invasions, and that Turkish Cypriots "came much later".[32] Finally, the Christianization of Cyprus is highlighted.

The archaeological images accompanying this narrative seem to tell a similar story.[33] One image is of a female cruciform figurine from the Chalcolithic period, often linked to fertility cults preceding that of Aphrodite.[34] This image hints at the blending of indigenous Cypriot and Greek cultures. Then an image of the Aphrodite of Soloi, an iconic Hellenistic sculpture of the island's patron Greek deity, is presented. Lastly, two Roman images are included: the Theater of Kourion, and the remains of the Sanctuary of Apollo Hylates. Such images speak to the idea that the Romans rebuilt Greek structures and preserved Greek religious traditions.

---

29 Press and Information Office of the Republic of Cyprus 2006.
30 Ibid. See A. Reiterer's (2003, 18) description of the first page of a participant narrative of the National Organization of Cypriot Fighters (*EOKA*) revolt against British colonial rule during the late 1950s. The nationalist rhetoric about the 'Achaeans' is almost identical.
31 In postcolonial national narratives of Cypriot history, mentions or omissions of the Mycenaeans play a pivotal rôle. From the Greek Cypriot point of view, if one believes in the 'Achaean Colonization hypothesis', then one can claim that the island has been inhabited by Greeks since the Late Bronze Age. If one omits the Mycenaean presence, such a claim is downplayed. Throughout this paper, therefore, I have regularly highlighted when the Mycenaeans are mentioned, as this serves as a good indicator of the political goals of a narrative within the context of 'the Cyprus problem'.
32 Press and Information Office of the Republic of Cyprus 2006.
33 All of these images are located at the bottom of the 'History' section of 'Aspects of Cyprus' (Press and Information Office of the Republic of Cyprus 2006).
34 This figurine type is also prominently displayed on the new 1 Euro and 2 Euro coins of the Republic of Cyprus, which gives a clear indication of the symbol's national importance to the government of the Republic.

In the 'History: Introduction' section of the 'Aspects of Cyprus' website, the key features of a 'Greek Cypriot Civilization Discourse' become apparent.[35] One aspect is a stress on the archaeological fact that Greek culture can be attested on Cyprus at a very early stage. A second is that the narrative de-emphasizes the archaeological evidence for an 'oriental' contribution to Cypriot culture in favor of the Hellenic/Western roots of Cyprus. In this section, the website again mentions that the Turks "came much later".[36] A third feature emphasizes the contribution of non-Greeks only when they supported Greek cultural continuity or central aspects of Hellenic culture, such as the Greek language or Greek art. The 'History: Brief Historical Survey' section on the Roman period merely states that Paul and Barnabas converted the proconsul to Christianity.[37] In 'Aspects of Cyprus', then, especially if one considers the accompanying Roman archaeological images emphasizing Greek cultural continuity, the Roman era is presented as a bridge of preservation between pagan Greek and Christian Byzantine Cyprus.

If the Romans are understood to be cultural 'preservers', the political benefits for the Greek side of the 'Cyprus problem' are numerous. This national narrative allows modern Greek Cypriots to claim a continuous connection with Cyprus stretching back 3000 years, as well as a connection to Europe by reference to the discourse of Hellenism, which posits that the European *Geist* derives from ancient Greek culture.[38] Furthermore, 'latecomer' civilizations (especially Turkish Cypriots), if they are not 'preservers' of Greek culture, are then 'invaders' with a weak historical link to the land: this view has particular implications when connected to the Ottoman era and the Turkish invasion of 1974. Finally, by emphasizing the preservation of Greek culture through Roman archaeology, the tourism industry can market Roman monuments as symbols of Hellenism that appeal to Western tourists whose vacation expenditures provide significant national economic benefits. Thus the promotion of Cypriot Hellenism through national narratives strengthens the Greek Cypriot claim to Cyprus and reinforces the Republic's political and economic position within the European Union.

Websites and brochures of the Cyprus Tourism Organisation

A similar interpretation of Roman archaeology is offered by the Cyprus Tourism Organisation's (CTO) website.[39] The CTO is a statutory body of the Government of Cyprus and so its website provides dozens of pages full of images and information about the island.

---

[35] I have constructed the term 'Greek Cypriot Civilization Discourse' based on A. Gür's (2007, 48-49) discussion of a Turkish "Anatolian Civilizations Discourse". Gür defines this concept of 'civilization discourse' as the combination of various narratives about a culture's or a nation's history, which together comprise a dynamic discourse that is negotiated, debated, and developed by particular groups over time, often in pursuit of political or economic advantages. In this article I employ the concept of 'civilization discourse' to describe the attempts of both Greek and Turkish Cypriot groups to engage in constructing their respective discourses comprising linked national, historical narratives based on cultural or territorial grounds and focused on the promotion of either the Greek or Turkish roots of Cyprus.

[36] Press and Information Office of the Republic of Cyprus 2006.

[37] Ibid.

[38] Morris 1994, 15-20; Shaw 2003, 62-66.

[39] Cyprus Tourism Organisation 2008. This website is the portal to dozens of secondary and tertiary pages that discuss the Roman monuments of Cyprus. Since the access paths for these websites are too large and unwieldy to quote here, in the following footnotes I will describe how to access them from the main website, http://www.visitcyprus.com/wps/portal. For the governmental status of the CTO, see Stritch 2006, 48.

Roman archaeology as 'touristic archaeology' in politically fractured landscapes

Fig. 2. The theater at Kourion (author).

Since archaeological monuments are one of Cyprus' main features and represent a primary lure for enticing tourists, archaeology, and especially Roman archaeology, plays a vital rôle in the Republic's touristic representation on the internet.

In the presentation of Cyprus' Roman sites, the common nationalist theme of 'Romans as preservers' of Greek culture is again frequently referenced. This begins on the 'Culture' webpage where aspects of Greek civilization are attached to Roman archaeological remains:

> Enjoy an ancient Greek play performed in a Roman amphitheatre (sic) with the most spectacular view on a cliff overlooking the sea.[40]

Here the CTO uses Kourion's Roman theater to create a touristic image that evokes a continuous Greco-Roman culture situated within a romantic scenic landscape (fig. 2).[41] This type of narrative continues in the CTO's description of other Roman sites. For Kourion, it states that the 'House of Achilles' "takes its name from the mosaic of the legendary Greek hero",[42] whereas for Nea Paphos it is stressed that the Roman mosaics are "depicting mainly scenes from Greek mythology" (fig. 3).[43] At the famous Sanctuary of Aphrodite at Palaipaphos, "the glorious days of the sanctuary lasted until the 3rd to the 4th centuries"

---

40 Accessed by clicking on 'Enjoy' and then choosing 'Culture'.
41 This is not an amphitheater; however, it was remodeled to accommodate gladiatorial spectacles and beast hunts in the Severan period. See Stillwell 1961, 78.
42 Accessed by searching 'Kourion Mosaics' in the search box.
43 Accessed by searching 'Pafos Mosaics' in the search box.

Fig. 3. The "Triumph of Dionysos" mosaic from Nea Paphos (author).

Fig. 4. The temple of Apollo Hylates at Kourion (author).

while at Kourion's Sanctuary of Apollo Hylates the Classical Temple of Apollo was "rebuilt in the second half of the 1st century A.D." (fig. 4).[44] Visually impressive Roman monuments are used as a medium through which ancient Greek culture is expressed. Moreover, Roman monuments become politically-charged vessels as preservers of Greek culture from antiquity to the present, echoing a national narrative that stresses Greek cultural continuity.

Roman monuments also serve as stand-ins for Greek monuments in the CTO's brochure, *Cyprus: 10,000 Years of History and Civilization*, where Cypriot antiquities constitute the island's main touristic selling point.[45] The brochure's cover features three images, of which two are Roman mosaics: Leda and the Swan from Palaipaphos (here conflated with Aphrodite, Cyprus' patron

---

44 These pages can be accessed by searching 'Sanctuary of Aphrodite' and 'Apollo Hylates' in the search box.
45 Cyprus Tourism Organisation 2006b.

Greek goddess) and the contest between Apollo and Marsyas from Nea Paphos. Out of the 6 color images featured from the inner cover to page 3, three images are views of the basilicas and theater at Kourion.

Accompanying these images is an 'Introduction', which politicizes archaeology in such a way that it gives Greek Cypriots a moral advantage in the eyes of tourists unfamiliar with 'the Cyprus problem'. The text on page 3 discusses the preservation of Nea Paphos and Choirokoitia as UNESCO World Heritage Sites.[46] This is followed by a mention of how Cyprus' cultural "heritage has been subjected to severe damage" because of the Turkish occupation.[47] Since it has been documented that the Turkish 'authorities' have allowed for the destruction of Cyprus' archaeological heritage, it is important to publicize this problem,[48] but for present purposes I will only point out how a touristic archaeological advertisement can be subtly converted into a political billboard that forces tourists to consider 'the Cyprus problem'. In this instance, the CTO argues that the Republic preserves world heritage while the Turkish occupied north only destroys it.

Following the introduction, the CTO offers a historical narrative which begins by stating that through a nation's heritage "its identity can be expressed and an awareness of its historical continuity through time can be created".[49] The Mycenaeans are described as responsible for "permanently instilling the island's Greek roots".[50] The Romans are again presented as an unobtrusive people who presided over a prosperous era, though an attempt has been made also to discuss some Roman innovations, such as the development of the Cypriot sigillata industry.[51] Through the CTO brochure, tourists may subconsciously begin to form an image of Cyprus that combines a textual narrative dominated by Greek culture with a visual narrative that uses Roman images to represent Greek cultural continuity.

"The Rough Guide to Cyprus"

Mainstream tourist guidebooks about Cyprus written in English by non-Cypriot authors often present a less politicized view of Roman archaeology. This is perhaps because the writers are more physically, emotionally and psychologically removed from 'the Cyprus problem' than are native Cypriots. As foreigners writing mainly for foreigners, many feel they can (or at least should) try to cover the island's two polities in an impartial fashion. Nevertheless, sometimes a Greek Cypriot national narrative can be detected. This is particularly evident in *The Rough Guide to Cyprus* by M. Dubin. In his 'History' chapter, Dubin seems to follow a Greek Cypriot national narrative with an entire section on 'The Mycenaeans' followed by a discussion of 'Myceno-Cypriots' in the Ionian Revolt.[52] The Romans again appear as unobtrusive preservers of Greek culture:

---

[46] Ibid. 3.
[47] Ibid.
[48] See Knapp and Antoniadou 1998; Committee for the Protection of the Cultural Heritage of Cyprus 2000.
[49] Cyprus Tourism Organisation 2006b, 4. See also Smith 2006, 30-31.
[50] Cyprus Tourism Organisation 2006b, 4.
[51] Ibid. 7.
[52] Dubin 2005, 418 and 422. "Myceno-Cypriots" is not a recognized archaeological term for Cypriots of the Archaic period. It seems that here M. Dubin is treating the Achaean colonization of Cyprus as an unchallenged historical fact, and that he seems to think that by the time of the Ionian revolt (499-498 B.C.) these colonists had fused with local populations, creating a Greco-Cypriot ethnic group. Such a theory may not be supported by the archaeological evidence.

not much effort was expended to Latinize the island — Greek, for example, continued to be used as the official language.[53]

Roman monuments also dominate the guidebook's imagery. In Dubin's '25 Things Not to Miss' section, the four ancient monuments shown are all Roman: the Paphos mosaics, the Cyprus Museum's bronze statue of Septimius Severus, the Gymnasium of Salamis, and an Early Christian mosaic from Soloi.[54] A textual narrative highlighting the Greek past is once again combined with Roman-era archaeological remains, creating a touristic vision that politicizes the Roman past by stressing Greek continuity.

The Romans as 'invaders': Turkish Cypriot national narratives

Mehmet Ali Talat's website

In contrast to the Republic's view of the Romans as 'preservers', Turkish Cypriots purvey a different view of history, seeing the Romans as 'invaders'.[55] This viewpoint can be discerned in 'Cyprus History in Brief' on the website of the former 'President' of north Cyprus, Mehmet Ali Talat.[56] The goal of the narrative seems to be the removal of a Greek cultural contribution to Cypriot history in favor of a version that emphasizes Turkish Cypriot links to previous invaders and non-Greek Cypriot cultural groups. The narrative begins by arguing that the first Neolithic settlers came from Asia. It is then stressed that "many civilizations ruled the island in the early ages", including the Hittites and Egyptians.[57] Next, "in 58 B.C. the island came under the rule of the Romans". Then the narrative touches on the coming of Christianity and Byzantine rule, before jumping to the Ottoman period and the Turkish Cypriot view of 'the Cyprus problem'.[58]

A chronology of historical cultures is also presented, yet at points the information is archaeologically questionable or seems to have been exaggerated. For instance, it is claimed that the Hittites and Egyptians ruled Cyprus during the Bronze Age, but there is no archaeological evidence for either of these claims.[59] Tellingly, the Mycenaean 'migra-

---

53 Dubin 2005, 424.
54 Dubin (ibid. 15-21) ranks Salamis no. 1, Septimius Severus no. 5, the Paphos mosaics no. 10, and Soloi no. 14.
55 It must be stressed, however, that since the Turkish Cypriot polity of north Cyprus remains an unrecognized political entity with no legal status in the eyes of the United Nations, the political 'documents' and information it produces are internationally unrecognized too. Nevertheless, I choose to include this information here because it is typical of what can be encountered by tourists on the internet, at a tourist kiosk, or in a bookstore in north Cyprus.
56 As mentioned in the introduction, since this study was presented at the conference in 2008, Mehmet Ali Talat is no longer the 'president' of the 'TRNC', having lost the 'elections' of April 2010 to Derviş Eroğlu. Talat's website was operational until he was politically defeated: 'Turkish Republic of Northern Cyprus Presidency' 2009, http://www.kktcb.eu/index.php?men=246&submen=226. I stress again that the goal of this study is to offer a snapshot of how Roman archaeology has been used to make places in Cyprus in recent years.
57 Ibid.
58 Ibid.
59 There is no record of the Anatolian Hittites ruling Cyprus. As for Egyptian rule, this would make sense for later periods if one considered the Macedonian dynasty of the Ptolemies to be 'Egyptian' in the cultural and ethnic sense that is expressed here, yet this is pushing the nature of the evidence. The only other time when ethnic Egyptians could have ruled Cyprus would have been during the 6th c. B.C. under king Amasis. However, this claim is mainly based on a specific interpretation of Herodotus, which has more recently been viewed skeptically,

tions' are not discussed. It is then stated that the Iron Age was marked by a "Phoenician led renaissance" followed by the rule of "a succession of foreign countries".[60] In truth, many scholars would accept a Phoenician presence and an intervention by Assyria or Persia, yet to call it a "renaissance" may push the point. The year 58 B.C. heralds the "Roman empire ruling Cyprus".[61] Thus in both sections of the webpage the Romans are included in a list of foreign cultures that ruled Cyprus, culminating in the Ottoman takeover and the founding of the 'Turkish Republic of Northern Cyprus'.

An analysis of the Turkish Cypriot national narrative, one which draws on Ottoman and Turkish Republican formulations of history, reveals certain features that seem to politicize Roman archaeology. First, Greek culture is completely omitted from the narrative, the focus shifting to non-Greek groups like the Romans. Obviously, the eradication of Greek culture is politically useful since it disrupts Greek Cypriot claims to land in north Cyprus archaeologically linked to their ancient Greek 'ancestors'. Yet, simultaneously, this omission is politically detrimental because it nullifies a connection to Europe that can be fostered through the *possession* of Greek artifacts, as the Ottomans of the *Tanzimât* era discovered.[62] Based on the above narrative, the solution to this contradiction is to highlight the possession of and identification with Roman culture, a culture that arguably is as European as the Greek.

An identification with the Romans is further maintained by presenting them as one of a string of 'invader' cultures, which, like the Turks, have invaded and occupied Cyprus.[63] Thus a second aspect of the national narrative appears: the linking of modern Turkish Cypriots to previous invaders, and especially non-Greek ones like the Assyrians or Persians. Through this argument, the politically-important historical precedent for the right of a non-Greek culture to exist on Cyprus is established. Such a link has additional resonance since it corresponds to anthropologically documented conceptions of Turkish Cypriot national identities, which indicate a connection to the Cypriot landscape through the 'spilled blood' of invading martyrs.[64]

---

    especially by A. T. Reyes (1994, 70).
[60] 'Turkish Republic of Northern Cyprus Presidency' 2009 http://www.kktcb.eu/index.php?men=246&submen=226.
[61] Ibid.
[62] The *Tanzimât* (Turkish for 'reorganization') is the name given to a period of 19th-c. Ottoman history when the state attempted to reform its institutions along the lines of contemporary European states in order to hinder the empire's continued political and social decline. These reforms also led to the deployment of Greco-Roman monuments indigenous to Turkish territory within new historical narratives, which linked modern Turks to the previous local cultures with the goal of strengthening Ottoman connections to both Europe and the territories possessed by the empire. For more on this phenomenon, see Shaw 2003, 68-70. For an analysis of the relationship between north Cyprus and the EU, see Güven-Lisaniler and Rodríguez 2002.
[63] Connections with Rome are not new to Turkish national narratives. As W. Shaw (2003, 13) illustrates, following the conquest of Constantinople, Ottoman sultans such as Süleyman the Magnificent often styled themselves as inheritors of the Roman empire. In addition, because Turkey referred to the 1974 invasion of Cyprus as the 'Attila Plan' (Panteli 1990, 250: no doubt a reference to the barbarian invader of Rome), one may assume that, despite the use of the term 'Peace Operation', the Turkish intervention was viewed as an invasion in at least some Turkish military circles.
[64] Bryant 2004, 156.

A final feature of the national narrative that politicizes the Romans is their inclusion within a discourse that draws on a Turkish Republican conception of history, which sought to incorporate the history of Turkish lands into a Turkish identity.[65] In this projection, Turkish Cypriot national identity is based on 'the peoples of Cyprus', which, to paraphrase Gür, can be viewed as "an imagined community across ages which shares a common identity" of 'Cypriotness'.[66] This view posits that all groups that share the same landscape produce essentially similar cultures; thus, according to Gür, the nation is essentialized, not through biological continuity, but through territorial *place*: "an essentialism based on a homogenized and territorially defined culture".[67] If one views the Turkish Cypriot national narrative according to this rationale, Roman culture is politicized through its metaphysical link to the national identity of Turkish Cypriots living in the same Cypriot landscapes. Consequently, through a link to the Romans, Turkish Cypriots justify their historical right to occupy Cyprus, strengthen their politically important relationship with Europe, and are able to market 'touristic Roman archaeology' as a feature of the national heritage.

'TRNC Economy and Tourism Ministry' website and brochures

The webpage 'North Cyprus: Pure Mediterranean' produced by a branch of the 'TRNC Economy and Tourism Ministry', presents a parade of images that evoke the essentialist view of Turkish Cypriot national history, culminating with a Roman statue overlooking the Gymnasium at Salamis.[68] The columns of the Salamis Gymnasium's Roman *palaestra* have in fact become *the* signature image for marketing archaeology in north Cyprus since they evoke the grandeur of ancient Cyprus in the tourist's imagination (fig. 5). Nearly every website, brochure or guidebook about north Cyprus will include an image of the Gymnasium. Thus the visualization of antiquity that is produced for tourists who visit north Cyprus is an image that is Roman, not Greek. This is possible since, according to the national narrative reiterated on the 'History' page of this website, the Greeks contributed little to Cypriot history, whereas the Romans took over the island and created impressive monuments like the Salamis Gymnasium.[69] In this narrative, no mention is made of the Mycenaean migrations to Cyprus; instead, Anatolians and Phoenicians brought "Levantine architecture, ceramics and metal working to the island".[70] The history goes on to relate

---

65   Gür 2007, 49; Cagaptay 2006, 48-54. R. Bryant (2004, 152) discusses the rapidity with which the Turkish Republican reforms of Atatürk were taken up by Turkish Cypriots during the 1920s and 1930s. Such a Kemalist view seems to have been continued by the *leaders* of the Turkish Cypriot régime, who consider that "the Turkish Cypriot people is an inseparable part of the great Turkish nation" (Reiterer 2003, 97; Navaro-Yashin 2006, 85). Yet other studies, focused on the Turkish Cypriot *people,* may tell a different story. For example, Navaro-Yashin (2006, 95-96) emphasizes that the Turkish Cypriot people possess a national identity that is different from the mainland Turkish identity espoused by settlers who have immigrated to north Cyprus from Anatolia since 1974.
66   Gür 2007, 49; Cagaptay 2006, 51. Here I am reformulating and paraphrasing for the Turkish Cypriot context a concept discussed by Gür with reference to Turkey.
67   Gür 2007, 49; Cagaptay 2006, 51. On the 'Tourism' page of Talat's website (2008, http://www.kktcb.eu/print.php?men=247&submen=226&ln=en), such an essentialist view is suggested and combined with an exotic panorama of tourist sites: "from Soli and Vouni in the West to the Arabahmet Mosque in Nicosia, from Salamis in Famagusta to the Apostolos Andreas Monastery in the East, it is possible to see the traces of a civilization of 9,000 years".
68   'North Cyprus Tourism Centre' 2008.
69   'North Cyprus Tourism Centre' 2008, http://northcyprus.cc/index.php/front/history.
70   Ibid.

Fig. 5. The gymnasium at Salamis (author).

how the island was used as a Persian base against Greece until it was taken over by the "Ptolemies of Egypt" who presided over a glorious period "punctuated by Rome's invasion of the island in 48 B.C. (sic)".[71] The Romans are thus depicted as an invading force and, in the context of what is a historical narrative of competing civilizations, become metaphysical forebearers of the Turkish forces that invaded the island in 1974. From this website it appears that the Turkish Cypriots also use Roman monuments as a billboard to convey political messages to tourists. Nevertheless, it is telling how, unlike the Greek Cypriot websites and brochures, no mention is made of the plundering of archaeological sites, nor that the north is occupied by a military force.

Tourism brochures produced by the 'TRNC Department of Antiquities and Museums', like the site brochure for the 'Salamis Ruins', also purvey a politicized view of Roman archaeology.[72] The cover of the brochure features the iconic image of the Salamis Gymnasium, with its columns and statues framed at the top by the flag of the 'TRNC' — an attempt to link the image of the Salamis ruins to the fact that they are possessed by the 'TRNC'.[73] In one sense, the possession of these *monuments* by the 'TRNC' can serve as a

---

71   Ibid. Note the stress on the geographic location of the Ptolemaic kingdom, *Egypt*, currently a Muslim region like north Cyprus. The island was actually taken over by Rome in 58 B.C. In 48 B.C., Cyprus was restored to Cleopatra VII by Julius Caesar. The island remained Ptolemaic until Augustus' victory at Actium in 31 B.C. For more on the chronology of these years, see Mitford 1980, 1290-91.
72   'Turkish Republic of Northern Cyprus Department of Antiquities and Museums' (no date).
73   The flag of the Cyprus Republic often appears on the Republic's tourist literature as well. Moreover, entrance tickets to archaeological sites are stamped with flags by *both* sides of the conflict,

subconscious reminder to the tourist that the 'TRNC' possesses the *territory* of Salamis. In a subliminal way, Roman monuments are politicized as a symbol of territorial possession and make manifest the reality of the Turkish occupation of north Cyprus.

"The Bradt travel guide"

Finally, the 'Romans-as-invaders' motif common to national narratives can also be perceived in popular tourist guidebooks. In the 'Historical Summary' in *North Cyprus: The Bradt travel guide* by D. Darke, many aspects of the Turkish Cypriot national narrative are expressed.[74] Following an overview of the usual 'invader' narrative, including a mention of the Mycenaeans, under Roman rule "prosperity [is] enjoyed" while "under Hadrian" the "climax of Roman monumental art" occurs.[75] To support this, Roman archaeological remains are presented through images of the statues and mosaics of Salamis.[76] The Roman period begins when the "Romans make Cyprus part of the province of Cilicia (southern Turkey)".[77] Darke further states that the Romans construct "roads, harbours, bridges and aqueducts", while the Roman proconsul is "converted to Christianity".[78] Yet amidst this prosperity the Jews of Cyprus massacre "240,000 Cypriots" and the "Romans expel all Jews from Cyprus".[79] The narrative ends with the triumph of Constantine and the conversion of the Cypriots to Christianity.

An analysis of Darke's 'touristic history' of Roman Cyprus shows how Roman archaeology can be used to reflect Turkish Cypriot national goals. Darke's history is very similar to the 'invasions' narratives, where the Greeks are neglected and the Romans are presented as simply one of the many cultures to occupy Cyprus. Indeed here modern Turkish actions in Cyprus may be projected onto the actions of ancient groups. Such a projection can be witnessed when Darke describes the Romans joining Cyprus to Turkey, which is similar to what has happened in the north since 1974. Although it is true that Cyprus was at first administered from the Roman province of Cilicia, that political relationship did not endure. Thus, such a metaphorical, ancient link between Turkey and Cyprus is difficult to maintain.[80] Again, Darke's description of the Roman expulsion of the Jews from Cyprus, despite its basis in historical fact, may provide a precedent for the expulsion of the Greeks from the north.[81] The guidebook emphasizes yet another way that Roman history, and the archaeology that underpins it, can be politicized as it is transmitted to the tourist/consumer.

---

respectively. I focus on the 'TRNC' flag here because its use may reformulate a politically-charged Ottoman view of history. This Ottoman perspective stressed that the mere possession of pre-Turkish, Greco-Roman monuments provided the empire with a politically valuable link to these ancient cultural groups and the regions they once inhabited. See Shaw 2003, 68-70.

74 Darke 2006, 5-11.
75 Ibid. 6.
76 Ibid. title page, the 'Don't miss' section, pages 2, 5, 6 and the back cover.
77 Ibid. 6. Note the stress on defining Cilicia as 'southern Turkey'.
78 Ibid.
79 Ibid.
80 For an overview of the Roman annexation of Cyprus and its administration as part of the province of Cilicia, see Mitford 1980, 1289-90.
81 As Knapp and Antoniadou (1998, 23) state, "The invasion and subsequent occupation of the northern part of Cyprus by Turkish troops eventually led to demographic upheavals which produced 200,000 refugees". The historical reference to the expulsion of the Jews is in Cassius Dio (68.32.1-3). See Wallace and Orphanides 1990, 244.

Conclusion

Cyprus, as an *île carrefour* near the eastern end of the Mediterranean Sea, has sat for centuries at the fulcrum of civilizations.[82] Its profound history and archaeology reflect a sequence of cultural settlements, invasions, and integrations variously influenced by the peoples of Europe, Asia and Africa. When one visits Cyprus, this 'spirit of *place*' seems omnipresent, even when one is confronted with all the trappings of modern tourism.[83] One can swim in the foam where Aphrodite was born, view a mountain molded by a giant, and stay at a 'Roman' hotel where the rooms are anachronistically painted like ancient Greek pots.[84] For Cypriots, tourists and archaeologists alike, the material residue of ancient and modern place-making may be experienced both as a physical reality at archaeological sites and in the media of tourism, as well as on a more symbolic level through Cyprus' mythologized landscapes and cultural traditions. This omnipresence gives Cypriot archaeology a true social power, bolstering Cypriot national pride, enticing tourists to buy Aphrodite souvenirs, and luring archaeologists to study an island famous for its cross-cultural interaction.[85]

Given archaeology's social power within the context of 'the Cyprus problem', the foregoing analysis of how 'touristic archaeologies' are produced, circulate, and make places as well as boundaries, aptly shows how 'touristic *Roman* archaeologies' can furnish rival polities with economic and political benefits in ways that other archaeologies cannot. I suggest that an attempt at mediating the political nature of 'touristic Roman archaeologies' is both important and necessary. It is socially important since it moves towards defusing preconceptions about national groups involved in political issues like the 'Cyprus problem'. It is necessary for archaeologists to become involved in such mediations so that they can better understand how the data they produce may be manipulated, and so that their ability to contribute to society in positive ways is not undermined by third parties. Since both Cypriot polities are presently engaged in seeking a just solution to 'the Cyprus problem', the time seems ripe to suggest that an official, reflexive review of how Roman archaeology is both marketed and politicized should be initiated on *both* sides of the Cypriot divide.[86]

---

[82] P. van Dommelen (1998, 11) defines Febvre's term *île carrefour* as an island where "historical currents meet and give rise to new developments". In the case of Cyprus, such a definition seems more than apt.

[83] For more on the concept of 'spirit of place', see Durrell 1969, 156-63.

[84] Here I am referring to the famous *Petra tou Romiou* or the *Rock of Aphrodite*, where Aphrodite was born near Palaipaphos. The mountain molded by a giant is the so-called *Pentadactylos* (five-finger) mountain visible from Nicosia in the Kyrenia mountain range. The mountain's five-pointed top purportedly received its shape when it was gripped by the mythic protector of Byzantine Cyprus, Digenis Akritas. For information on the "'Roman' Hotel", see Roman Hotel 2009.

[85] Arnold (2006, 155) effectively points out that nationalism, although often criticized, can also be a *positive* force in the way it instills local pride. See also Shanks 1992, 53-84.

[86] As this article goes to press in 2012, the leaders of the respective Greek Cypriot and Turkish Cypriot communities, Demetris Christofias and Derviş Eroğlu, have engaged for nearly a year in bicommunal negotiations aimed at seeking a just solution to 'the Cyprus problem'. Although no major breakthroughs have occurred, there is arguably cause for hope as it seems that both leaders recognize the need to negotiate peacefully. According to Christofias (2009, 6), "The profits of lasting peace will be beneficial for the people of Cyprus, of Turkey and for the peoples of our region as a whole. Real political leaders are not the ones who think of the next

Acknowledgements

I wish to thank the organizers of the Critical Roman Archaeology Conference held at Stanford University in 2008 (Corisande Fenwick, Kathryn Lafrenz Samuels, and Darian Totten) both for inviting me to explore the concept of 'touristic Roman archaeologies' and for providing me with excellent editorial insights on the contents of this study. Thanks are further due to Eleni Kalapoda for providing me with the Cyprus Tourism Organisation's brochure, *Cyprus: 10,000 Years of History and Civilization,* and with *Salamis Ruins, Famagusta,* of the 'Turkish Republic of Northern Cyprus Department of Antiquities and Museums'. In addition, I wish to recognize the Department of Classics at the University of Cincinnati, and the Crake Doctoral Fellowship Committee at Mount Allison University, Sackville (NB), for granting me the financial support to undertake this research. I also wish to acknowledge the following colleagues who provided perceptive critiques of earlier drafts: David Arnason, Annemarie Weyl Carr, Jack Davis, Tom Davis, Steven Ellis, LeeAnn Barnes Gordon, Kathleen Lynch, Mhari Mackintosh, Hüseyin Çinar Öztürk, Giorgos Papantoniou, Michael Toumazou, and Gisela Walberg. Finally, I am grateful to an anonymous reviewer for suggestions on improving this article. All remaining opinions and errors are my own.

Bibliography

Alcock, S. E. 1993. *Graecia capta: the landscapes of Roman Greece* (Cambridge).

Arnold, B. 2006. "Pseudoarchaeology and nationalism: essentializing difference," in Fagan 2006b, 154-79.

Atkinson, J., I. Banks and J. O'Sullivan (edd.) 1996. *Nationalism and archaeology: Scottish Archaeological Forum* (Glasgow).

Banks, I. 1996. "Archaeology, nationalism and ethnicity," in Atkinson, Banks and O'Sullivan 1996, 1-11.

Bryant, R. 2004. *Imagining the modern: the cultures of nationalism in Cyprus* (London).

Cagaptay, S. 2006. *Islam, secularism, and nationalism in modern Turkey: who is a Turk?* (Routledge Studies in Middle Eastern History 4).

Christofias, D. 2009. *Statement by H. E. Mr. Demetris Christofias President of the Republic of Cyprus at the general debate of the 64th session of the General Assembly of the United Nations* (http://www.un.org/ga/64/generaldebate/CY.shtml, viewed Dec. 7, 2011).

Christofides, G. 2002. "The development of the Cyprus economy since independence," in J. Charalambous *et al.* (edd.), *Cyprus: 40 years on from independence* (Mannheim) 94-97.

Committee for the Protection of the Cultural Heritage of Cyprus 2000. *Cyprus: a civilization plundered* (Athens).

Constantinou, C. and Y. Papadakis 2002. "The Cypriot state(s) in situ: cross-ethnic contact and the discourse of recognition," in Diez 2002, 75-97.

Cyprus Tourism Organisation 2006a. *Annual report 2006* (Nicosia).

Cyprus Tourism Organisation 2006b. *Cyprus: 10,000 years of history and civilization* (Nicosia).

Cyprus Tourism Organisation 2008. *The official portal of the Cyprus Tourism Organisation* (http://www.visitcyprus.com/wps/portal [viewed 12 February 2008]).

Cyprus Tourism Organisation (no date). *Strategic plan for tourism 2000-2010* (Nicosia).

Darke, D. 2006. *North Cyprus: the Bradt travel guide* (5th edn. rev. by N. Wallis; Chalfont St. Peter).

Diez, T. (ed.) 2002. *The European Union and the Cyprus conflict: modern conflict, postmodern union* (Manchester).

Dubin, M. 2005. *The Rough Guide to Cyprus* (London).

Durrell, L. 1969. *Spirit of place: letters and essays on travel* (New York).

Fagan, G. 2006a. "Concluding observations," in id. 2006b, 362-67.

Fagan, G. (ed.) 2006b. *Archaeological fantasies: how pseudoarchaeology misrepresents the past and misleads the public* (London).

Gilkes, O. 2003. "The voyage of Aeneas: myth, archaeology, and identity in interwar Albania," in S. Kane (ed.), *The politics of archaeology and identity in a global context* (Boston, MA) 31-49.

Gür, A. 2007. "Stories in three dimensions: narratives of nation and the Anatolian Civilizations Museum," in E. Özyürek (ed.), *The politics of public memory in Turkey* (Syracuse, NY) 40-69.

---

election but of the next generation. We have the responsibility to work together to achieve a lasting peace in our region".

Güven-Lisaniler, F. and L. Rodríguez 2002. "The social and economic impact of EU membership on northern Cyprus," in Diez 2002, 181-202.
Hanson, W. 1997. "Forces of change and methods of control," in D. J. Mattingly (ed.), *Dialogues in Roman imperialism* (JRA Suppl. 23) 68-79.
Hingley, R. 1996. "The shared moral purposes of two empires and the origin of Romano-British archaeology," in Atkinson, Banks and O'Sullivan 1996, 135-42.
Hunt, D. (ed.) 1990. *Footprints in Cyprus* (London).
Knapp, A. B. and S. Antoniadou. 1998. "Archaeology, politics and the cultural heritage of Cyprus," in L. Meskell (ed.), *Archaeology under fire: nationalism, politics and heritage in the Eastern Mediterranean and Middle East* (London) 13-43.
Mitford, T. 1980. "Roman Cyprus," *ANRW* II.7.2, 1275-382.
Morris, I. 1994. "Archaeologies of Greece," in id. (ed.), *Classical Greece: ancient histories and modern archaeologies* (Cambridge) 8-47.
Munzi, M. 2004. "Italian archaeology in Libya: from colonial *Romanita* to decolonization of the past," in M. Galaty and C. Watkinson (edd.), *Archaeology under dictatorship* (New York) 73-107.
Navaro-Yashin, Y. 2006. "De-ethnicizing the ethnography of Cyprus: political and social conflict between Turkish Cypriots and settlers from Turkey," in Y. Papadakis, N. Peristianis and G. Welz (edd.), *Divided Cyprus: modernity, history and an island in conflict* (Bloomington, IL) 84-97.
'North Cyprus Tourism Centre' 2008. *North Cyprus pure Mediterranean* (http://www.northcyprus.cc/ [viewed 12 February 2008]).
Panteli, S. 1990. *The making of modern Cyprus* (New Barnet).
Press and Information Office of the Republic of Cyprus 2006. *Aspects of Cyprus* (http://www.aspectsofcyprus.com/aoc/aoc.html [viewed 12 February 2008]).
Reiterer, A. 2003. *Cyprus: a case study about a failure of ethno-national understanding* (Minderheiten und Minderheitenpolitik in Europa 3).
Reyes, A. T. 1994. *Archaic Cyprus: a study of the textual and archaeological evidence* (Oxford).
Roman Hotel 2009 = *Roman Hotel Paphos (Pafos) Cyprus* (http://www.romanhotel.com.cy [viewed 28 October 2009]).
Russell, I. 2006a. "Introductions: images of the past, archaeologies, modernities, crises, and poetics," in id. 2006b, 1-38.
Russell, I. (ed.) 2006b. *Images, representations and heritage: moving beyond modern approaches to archaeology* (New York).
Shanks, M. 1992. *Experiencing the past: on the character of archaeology* (London).
Shaw, W. 2003. *Possessors and possessed: museums, archaeology and the visualization of history in the Late Ottoman empire* (Berkeley, CA).
Silberman, N. 1989. *Between past and present: archaeology, ideology, nationalism in the modern Middle East* (New York).
Silberman, N. 1995. "Promised lands and chosen peoples: the politics and poetics of archaeological narrative," in P. Kohl and C. Fawcett (edd.), *Nationalism, politics and the practice of archaeology* (Cambridge) 249-52.
Smith, L. 2006. *Uses of heritage* (London).
Stillwell, R. 1961. "Kourion: the theater," *ProcAmPhilosSoc* 105, 37-78.
Stritch, D. 2006. "Archaeological tourism as a signpost to national identity: raising Aphrodite in Cyprus," in Russell 2006b, 43-60.
Tamkoç, M. 1988. *The Turkish Cypriot state: the embodiment of the right of self-determination* (London).
'Turkish Republic of Northern Cyprus Department of Antiquities and Museums' (no date). *Salamis ruins, Famagusta* [Tourism brochure].
'Turkish Republic of Northern Cyprus Presidency' 2009. *Turkish Republic of Northern Cyprus Presidency Official Website* (http://www.trncpresidency.org/ [viewed 27 October 2009, site no longer active]).
Ugur, M. 2003. "EU membership and the north-south development gap in Cyprus: a proposal," in V. Fourskas and H. Richter (edd.), *Cyprus and Europe: the long way back* (Mannheim) 121-32.
United Nations 2010 *United Nations Security Council* (http://www.un.org/Docs/sc/ [viewed 25 January 2010]).
van Dommelen, P. 1998. *On colonial grounds: a comparative study of colonialism and rural settlement in first millennium BC west central Sardinia* (Leiden).
Wallace, P. and A. Orphanides (edd.) 1990. *Greek and Latin texts to the third century A.D.* (Sources for the History of Cyprus 1).
Wilson, R. 1992. *Cyprus and the international economy* (New York).

Tarquinia and Cerveteri, the best of Etruria: Etruscan heritage and place-making in contemporary Italy

Darian Marie Totten

Introduction

In 2004, two Etruscan sites north of Rome were inscribed together on UNESCO's World Heritage List. The nomination dossier describes the sites of Tarquinia and Cerveteri as "the two best Etruscan cemeteries in their quality, size and representativity of this type of Etruscan heritage".[1] The inscription of these sites finds itself at the nexus of cultural and political discourses informed by historical and contemporary Italian *localismo*, Italy's rôle in the European Union, and the use of heritage both in the nation-state and internationally. In this paper, I connect the nomination of these sites to other contemporary uses of Etruscan heritage, represented primarily by museum exhibits in Bologna and the debate over the Euphronios krater. The Italian nation-state stands to gain by the inclusion of these sites on the World Heritage List, not only by increasing their international prestige, but also by integrating the Etruscan past as part of the broader landscape of Italian heritage. The material remains of the Etruscans are valuable because they help to advance Italy's claims as the foremost preserver of heritage in an international context. This counters the uses of the Etruscan past at local and regional levels which look beyond the Italian nation-state to the special links that local Italian places have to the wider European community. Therefore, in these national and local/regional contexts, places made as 'Etruscan' communicate conflicting meanings: one that works towards building a national identity, and one that overlooks it.

Etruscan places and European place-making

The rôle of Etruscan heritage in building identities and defining places, primarily in Tuscany and northern Latium, has a long history. I will investigate the case of Etruscan heritage in Bologna to untangle how heritage is used in place-making practices at the local level and to demonstrate in part the diversity of local traditions of heritage in Italy today. *Localismo*, "the political and economic tendency to privilege certain geographic areas at the expense of general interests",[2] refers to the close connections that the citizens of Italy have to their local institutions and identities. It has been viewed by some scholars and politicians as detrimental to the health of the nation-state.[3] The inclination to identify with local instead of national communities has been at issue since the unification of the Italian nation-state in 1861. The picture of *mille Italie* painted by the cultural historian E. Galli della Loggia makes evident how urban identities in the north trumped feelings of national 'belonging', while also making the differences between north and south more evident.[4] For

---

1   Based on the Italian state-party nomination dossier (ICOMOS 2004, 105).
2   The definition is translated from 'Lo Zingarelli minore' (1994), the Italian language dictionary.
3   See Patriarca 2001 for an account of debates surrounding *localismo* in the 1990s; also Guidi 1996 for an archaeological perspective.
4   E. Galli della Loggia (1998, 66) argues that this tendency toward localism must be overcome before Italy can ever really become a modern nation.

many centuries the sentiments of *localismo* have been bolstered by archaeological sites that give legitimacy to claims of local differences. This is relevant for the Etruscan case, where local distinctiveness has been closely connected to archaeological heritage in the form of the sites and objects uncovered by excavations.[5]

Etruscan material remains have been integral to studies of the Etruscan past which, unlike the Roman, could not also be accessed by an ample textual record.[6] The discovery of Etruscan civilization in the 17th c. led to the development of the intellectual moment termed *Etruscheria* (the study of and fascination with all things Etruscan) that persisted into the 18th c. Research and writings by local intellectuals searching for a pre-Roman past, one free from Roman domination, made the Etruscans intriguing.[7] The traces of this civilization were visible and tangible through the material remains that permeated local landscapes. Towns like Tarquinia and Cerveteri had a long history, dating from the 17th to 19th c., of 'excavation' in the necropoleis surrounding them. The material remains from the tombs fascinated local collectors and stirred interest in the Etruscans. By the late 19th c., municipal authorities began to build local identity through engagements with Etruscan material culture. Excavations in Tarquinia were organized by the town's first mayor to enrich the collection of the local museum.[8] In Bologna's wave of Etruscan fervor in the 19th c., the collection of the civic museum was transformed to reflect the emerging prehistoric and Etruscan past, and the carnival of 1874 hosted a parade displaying the costumes, customs and dress of the Etruscans as part of a celebration of this identity.[9] By cultivating this Etruscan past through objects, research and spectacles, local authorities crafted distinct heritages for their cities that remained relevant even after the birth of the nation-state.

Localismo is still present today.[10] This has been a trend since after World War II, when the unifying nationalistic archaeology of the Fascist state was rejected.[11] Today, *localismo* has a new political force, as cities and towns in N Italy increasingly claim legitimacy through

---

5   N. Terrenato (2001) argues that this pre-Roman interest mirrored the diversity of Italian communities in the 17th and 18th c.
6   Momigliano 1950; Cristofani 1978, 603. Books such as *De Etruria regali* by T. Dempster (written in the 17th c., published in the early 18th) and *Explicationes* by G. Buonarotti (18th c.) fit into a historical moment in Italy when the pre-Roman past was used to counter the Roman one. Cf. A. Momigliano (1950, 305): "Thomas Dempster made a hit because Italian scholars were looking for a new focus for the patriotic feelings and cultural interests. Deeply rooted in their regional traditions and suspicious of Rome for various reasons, they found what they wanted in the Etruscans, Pelasgians, and other pre-Roman tribes. Local patriotism was gratified by the high antiquity of pre-Roman civilizations".
7   F. Mascioli (1942, 368) has argued that these men fashioned parallels between the Roman conquest of Etruria and their own experiences of domination under French rule.
8   Leighton 2004, 25. S. Settis (2002) notes the importance of local museums in creating local identities in Italy. While B. Anderson (1983) argued for the importance of museums in the building of national identities, recent work has demonstrated how museums are integral in bringing awareness of the past to local communities (Herreman 2006, 421-23).
9   For a picture of Etruscan fervor at Bologna, see Mansuelli 1984, 43. See Vitali 1984 for discussions of the museum collection and Sassatelli 1984 for an analysis of the festival.
10 N. Terrenato (2001) and A. Guidi (1996) have argued that sentiments of *localismo* were diminished after unification and during the Fascist period. However, as noted here, "Etruscan places", such as Tarquinia and Bologna, never really stopped exploring their pre-Roman past archaeologically, so one should examine such claims on a case-by-case basis.
11 Quartermaine 1995; Guidi 1996; Stone 1999; Terrenato 2001.

the European Union or political parties like the *Lega Nord* (Northern League).[12] Since the early 1990s, the *Lega Nord* has argued for greater autonomy for the north, first with a plan to secede from the Italian state,[13] but more recently with calls for a federalist state organization for the whole of Italy. Party rhetoric claims that an inherent difference — linguistic, social and cultural — is to be found among the provinces and regions of Italy, and that this difference should be employed to form a federalist state. This discourse is further complicated by the expanding rôle of the European Union, which influences how Italians now conceive of their own identities. While there are many northern Italians who do not support the *Lega Nord* party, they do strongly support the European Union, which calls into question how they conceive of their place in the Italian nation-state.[14]

The use of the Etruscan past by the city of Bologna during the *Culture 2000* festival provides a provocative example of the cultivation of *localismo* and the support of supranational institutions. The organizing committee used this as a forum by which to orient the city further towards the European Union. In recent years, the European Union has asked for narratives that underscore connections and interactions between European member-states through cultural initiatives.[15] The 'European Capitals of Culture' is one such initiative, described by the ministers of the European Union as

> a golden opportunity to show off Europe's cultural richness and diversity, and all the ties which link us together as Europeans. The event is so attractive that Europe's cities vie with each other fiercely for the honour of bearing the title.[16]

It offers cities a place on the European stage and brings them many benefits, such as increased revenues from tourism.[17]

Bologna's dossier for the program gives a glimpse into the goals for that "culture year" and the target audiences for its events.[18] The European audience was listed as the top priority, national audiences were second, and local audiences only third; they were also the last group consulted on programming for the "culture year".[19] While the organizing committee had 5 local representatives (the mayor, a member of the chamber of commerce, an at-large local representative, a provincial representative, and a university representative),

---

12 I reference the *Lega Nord* here, not because it advances any particular use of Etruscan heritage in its discourse, but rather as an example of how political parties in Italy can ally strongly to local, provincial or regional interests.
13 Patriarca 2001, 21.
14 Tossutti 2001, 77 discusses how members of the *Lega Nord* are more open to the European Union. J. Stacul's (2006) ethnographic work in the Tyrol has demonstrated how local identities increasingly bypass a connection to the Italian state and turn directly to the European Union. For a general analysis of these trends in Italy, see Tossutti 2002.
15 See Shore and Black 1992, 10; Shore 1996; Meskell 2002, 566; Stacul, Moutsou, and Kopnina 2006a.
16 EU Culture website (http://ec.europa.eu/culture/our-programmes-and-actions/doc413_en.htm [viewed April 2009]). The updated webpage for the Capitals of Culture can be found at http://ec.europa.eu/culture/our-programmes-and-actions/capitals/european-capitals-of-culture_en.htm [accessed March 2012].
17 Other cities of culture for 2000 were Bergen, Brussels, Cracow, Helsinki, Prague, Reykjavik and Santiago da Compostela.
18 Applications to be a *Capital of Culture* should state an organizing principle for the year's events, a budget, and the intended audience(s). The following information on Bologna was taken from the Palmer/RAE Associates Report, a record of the culture year: http://ec.europa.eu/culture/pdf/doc656_en.pdf
19 Other capitals of culture in 2000 noted that local groups were the highest priority.

the local community was not their top priority.[20] The low priority of local interests reflects the organizing board's main goals for the culture program: to increase international prestige for the city, to develop tourism and build cultural programs, and to shape Bologna's image as a European city.[21] Why did Bologna single out the national audience as more important than the local? It stemmed in part from the desire to draw in tourists, both European and Italian. The cultural program above all offered a prime opportunity to communicate to national audiences that Bologna was a cosmopolitan, connected, and *European* place.

The archaeological remains of the Etruscan civilization were invoked to communicate this message.[22] The Etruscans formed the centerpiece of the exhibit hosted and organized by the Museo Civico entitled *Principi Etruschi: tra il Mediterraneo e Europa*. In this way Bologna (Etruscan *Felsina*) advanced this local past on a regional European stage. The exhibit needed to show how Bologna was a center of connection and interaction, in line with the theme 'communication';[23] only then could the Etruscans be used to contribute to European-sponsored discourses of a shared past forged through interconnection and peaceful contact. To make Bologna such a place, the exhibit first needed to demonstrate that the Etruscans of Bologna were just as 'Etruscan' as those of Tuscany and northern Latium (in scholarship, the settlements of the Po valley are often characterized as colonies or off-shoots of those in what is now Tuscany, and thus secondary in importance).[24] The exhibit was organized to showcase the Orientalizing period in general, and the city of Bologna in particular. This period (the 8th to the mid-6th c. B.C.) saw the rule of aristocratic classes who increasingly advertised their power and wealth through goods imported from the East, the Greeks, and the Phoenicians. Major tomb groups, like Cerveteri's 'Tomb of the Seats and Shields' and 'Tomb of the Five Seats', along with evidence from the settlements at Murlo (Poggio Civitate) and Acquarossa, give an impression of the Orientalizing period in Tuscany and Latium. Throughout the exhibit, objects from Bolognese contexts, such as *fibulae* and *tintinnabulae* (a type of object found exclusively in the Po valley), were scattered among other objects from 'Etruria proper'. The final two sections of the exhibit emphasized Etruscan culture from Bologna and its hinterland, displaying beautiful objects such as wicker and bronze helmets, high-backed wooden chairs, and bronze *situlae* made in the area. The juxtaposition communicated that the Etruscans of the Po valley were on par with those found in Etruria proper and contributed much to the advancement of Etruscan civilization. The final part of the exhibition, the 'princely Celtic tombs', emphasized that Bologna was a

---

20 Palmer/RAE Associates Report 2004, 130. There were 7 places on the board; a regional and national representative were also members.
21 Palmer/RAE Associates Report (supra n.18) 2004, II, 129. The Bologna committee notes in its dossier that the city is known mainly as a conference center, and not for its culture.
22 Bologna was the only city in 2000 to use archaeological heritage as part of its cultural program.
23 In a history of Bologna published in 1978 (A. Ferri and G. Roversi 1978, 30-31), the Etruscans of Bologna are noted as a group that fostered connections with other peoples in Europe.
24 G. Camporeale (2001, 3-8) argues that the Etruscan settlements of the Po valley and Campania were "*appendici*" of Etruria (defined as modern Tuscany and N Latium). In this volume, the 'core' of Etruscan civilization is defined by the boundaries of modern Tuscany and northern Latium. In the late 19th c., when the Bolognese archaeologist G. Gozzadini first discovered the Villanovan culture, he argued that the Etruscans developed from this group instead of emigrating from the E Mediterranean. In this way, Bologna was argued to be one of the first Etruscan places (Mansuelli 1984).

prime player in exchange with central Europe.[25] This was shown by the distribution maps of goods connecting Bologna, the Po valley and central Europe. The location and proactive character of Etruscan Bologna made it a fulcrum for European cultural exchange.

By adhering to this Etruscan past, Bologna became a place of mediation and dialogue, as well as being a forerunner amongst Etruscan centers in the peninsula. G. Guazzaloca, mayor of Bologna, advances this history in the opening inscription of the *Principi Etruschi* catalogue:

> [Belonging to this land where the Etruscans lived] susciti anche l'amore e la curiosità che si nutrono per le proprie origini, e l'idea che abbiamo sulla nostra più remota e più attuale identità.

As a city of communication and mediation from its early beginnings, Bologna preserved this character from its Etruscan ancestors. In this way it is intimately invested in the European Union's aims of interconnection and dialogue. Characterizing Bologna as a central actor in European interconnection is a strong statement in the context of Italian politics of the last two decades as local identities, particularly in the north, gravitate away from the Italian nation-state. At the local and regional level, previously Etruscan places were fashioning themselves away from the nation-state both politically and culturally.[26]

To appreciate the context of the Bologna exhibit and how it manifested Bolognese *localismo*, it must be contrasted with earlier and contemporaneous exhibits on the Etruscan past. The exhibit *Gli Etruschi e Europa*, which ran in Paris and then Berlin from 1992 to 1993, was first organized in Florence and presented in other Tuscan cities in the mid-1980s.[27] The organizers argued a similar thesis: the Etruscans were the first to foster European interconnection through trade in the Archaic period. However, the narrative of the Bologna exhibit differed in some crucial aspects. First, at Bologna the main goal was to emphasize the importance of the Etruscans of the Po valley. Second, *Gli Etruschi e Europa* took a close look at the Archaic period, while the Bologna exhibit focused on the Orientalizing period. As a result, Bologna was distinguished as the first place to foster connections with Europe, gaining legitimacy through its primacy. Third, the Paris exhibit noted that Etruscan culture was further disseminated by the conquering Romans, who had adopted many Etruscan ways as they spread through Europe. Referencing Roman conquest can elicit a chilly reception, for narratives of domination and imperialism run counter to current European cultural goals.[28] There were no Romans at the Bologna exhibit, just the inclusive and non-confrontational actions of the Etruscans.

---

25   Bartoloni *et al.* 2000, 381 and 387.
26   It is not insignificant that the northern cities of Umbria, Tuscany and Lombardy were the first to argue for their connection to European institutions: Guidi 1996, 115-16.
27   Pallottino 1992. A *New York Times* (Oct. 7, 1992) reviewer (A. Riding, "Celebrating the Etruscans, Europe's first unifiers") noted of this exhibit: "it falls short of saying that 2,500 years ago Tuscany would have voted 'yes' in a referendum on European Union, but that's the general idea".
28   P. L. Kohl and C. Fawcett (1995a, 17) have advised against the use of archaeological narratives in the construction of European identity that advance abrasive symbols from the past to create meta-national histories. The Romans, whose history of conquest and domination qualifies as abrasive, can be problematic for many nations with Roman remains. See also M. Dietler (1994), who, in his study of French nationalistic discourses on archaeology, argues that the Roman history of conquest and domination is perceived as too negative for national discourses in Europe today.

For *Culture 2000,* Bologna projected its Etruscan past as a way to characterize the city in the present, as a place fostering connection and cultural exchange. In this way, its archaeological heritage was used as a means to make place and emphasize the city's current commitment to furthering the cultural mission of the European Union. While the archaeological remains of this past are not visible in particular archaeological sites or parks, for the modern city rests on top of many of the remains, the objects in the exhibit helped tell the story of the Etruscan legacy. While Bologna also presents the remains of other pasts — the Mediaeval past is the most prominent in the urban fabric today — the archaeological heritage presented in the museum is integral in making Bologna an Etruscan place. The Etruscan story is no longer a strictly Italian one, or even one strictly based in modern Tuscany. Instead, the organizing board of *Culture 2000* drew on the city's particular Etruscan history, while also looking outward to its European connections. In this way, *localismo* cemented links to outside groups and networks beyond the boundaries of the Italian nation-state.

Tarquinia and Cerveteri as national heritage

The inscription of Tarquinia and Cerveteri by the Italian nation-state creates a different set of associations: these places are made to belong to an international heritage landscape as the patrimony of humankind. And it does more than this. While the Bolognese case demonstrates how place-making could occur at the local and regional level, the inscription of Cerveteri and Tarquinia contributes to place-making at the national level.

Tarquinia and Cerveteri — the only two sites in Italy to be nominated exclusively for their Etruscan remains — are argued to be exceptional and unique representations of Etruscan culture. This rhetoric is required in order to convey their universal value, but it also achieves something important for nationalistic claims: these sites come to represent the Etruscan culture for Italy on the world stage. The sites are described thus:

> The two nominated cemeteries including their construction, artistic decoration and objects found in them are some of the best testimonies of the great Etruscan culture ... Each of these cemeteries is different in the characteristics of the tombs and therefore cover together the Etruscan burial culture.[29]

The final phrase makes clear that Tarquinia and Cerveteri give a complete sense of the Etruscan past that is only amplified by nominating the sites under UNESCO's criterion (iii):

> an exceptional testimony of the Etruscan culture, and generally the Italian pre-Roman cultures.[30]

Their significance is compounded by the fact that few pre-Roman sites in Italy are inscribed on the World Heritage List. Only the Sardinian Nuraxi di Barumini and the Sicilian tombs at Pantalica (pre-Greek in construction) have been included on the list to date.[31] One other pre-Roman site, Motya in Sicily, can be found on the tentative list out of 41 sites.[32] Even

---

29 ICOMOS 2004, 103.
30 Ibid. 105.
31 Most of the sites inscribed by Italy are Mediaeval or Renaissance city centers (e.g., Venice, Naples, Verona, Ferrara, Florence and Pisa). Eight properties are exclusively archaeological: the three pre-Roman sites mentioned above, one of the Neolithic period, and four of the Roman.
32 The tentative list is composed of sites that the state wishes to nominate for inscription to the

those sites with Etruscan pasts, such as Orvieto and Volterra, are nominated on the basis of later, primarily mediaeval remains. In making these choices, Italy has amplified the importance of the necropoleis inscribed, by making them the sole Etruscan remains on the list.

These sites are visible and tangible remains of the Etruscans undisturbed by later settlement; as a result, they can be visited on their own terms and experienced at first hand, which gives them a different valence (and perhaps a certain primacy) over Etruscan centers such as Florence and Bologna, whose archaeological remains are concealed by the modern cities and can be experienced only in museums. Unlike Etruscan Bologna, characterized as a dynamic settlement at the intersection of multiple cultures, the interaction between these 'cities of the dead' and wider cultural networks beyond the Etruscans was not presented. The nomination tried to argue that the architecture of the tombs would have influenced other Etruscan cemeteries, such as those at Orvieto and Vulci, still confining their effects to other Etruscan places. Greek artisans might have painted the tombs of Tarquinia but this is mentioned merely to acknowledge their uniqueness, not their rôle in a wider Mediterranean *koinê*. Their only influence on Europe comes later when these sites are said to have inspired Romantic thinkers and poets. While the Etruscans of Bologna are characterized as forging interconnection, those of Cerverteri and Tarquinia are for the most part circumscribed by the limits of the sites.[33]

By being inscribed, Cerveteri and Tarquinia exist both in their local Etruscan contexts and, for national and international audiences, within the network of World Heritage sites. Their designation as World Heritage makes them part of an exclusive group in Italy, set off from the tens of thousands of other heritage sites on the peninsula.[34]

They therefore make up a network of national significance. The use of World Heritage to advance nationalistic claims and identity has been a matter of debate among scholars. A. Omland notes that the World Heritage concept was devised to advance the belief that certain material remains should be preserved for the benefit of all humankind as indicative of a shared human past.[35] While measures have been taken by UNESCO to ensure that nationalist programs are not advanced in an international context, the rôle of signatory states in nominating properties for inclusion makes clear that the nation-state is a central actor in the creation of World Heritage.[36] Just as nationalistic archaeologies have been exposed as steeped in national politics and discourses, so too have been the nationalistic aims of signatory states in this international forum.[37] S. Labadi's analysis of the religious

---

World Heritage List.

[33] These limits are marked out by fences that communicate what does and does not belong to the heritage site. UNESCO requires that these limits be defined, along with an additional buffer zone to protect the site's spatial integrity. In the cases of Tarquinia and Cerveteri, the fenced areas represent only a fraction of the actual extent of the necropoleis: Oleson 1976.

[34] Urbani 2002; Benedikter 2004. M.-C. E. Garden (2006) has argued for a study of the "heritage-scape", comparing and contrasting the experiences of heritage sites to one another in order to understand how they function as places of heritage. A study of this concept at Italian heritage sites would be revealing.

[35] Omland 2006, 243-44.

[36] Omland (ibid. 250-51) quotes a Tunisian official: "World heritage protection is important to sustain national identity, 'but within a worldwide context'".

[37] See Trigger 1995 for archaeology's ever-political stance in the present. S. M. Dingli (2006, 239) argues that global heritage will erase nationalistic tendencies and imperialistic claims.

and industrial heritage nominated by signatory states indicates that such discourse often aims to underline the stability, conformity or unity of the nation.[38] Her conclusions show that nation-states can employ UNESCO World Heritage sites to strengthen nationalistic claims. It is therefore necessary to take into account the particular historical, social and political contexts in which UNESCO World Heritage sites operate.

While the effects of a UNESCO inscription upon local places are debatable and contingent upon context,[39] the importance of World Heritage on the national Italian stage is evident. The Italian media's rhetoric presents World Heritage as a site of competition between Italy and other nation-states. Thus the inscription of Tarquinia and Cerveteri, along with la Val d'Orcia, prompted this headline:

> Ora il nostro paese guida la classifica dei 788 luoghi riconsciuti come patrimonio ambientale. Segue la Spagna. Gioielli dell'umanita, quota 39; Italia prima nella lista Unesco.[40]

Italy strives to remain on top. The Italian commission of UNESCO also feels intense shame when reprimanded for improper care of UNESCO heritage sites.[41] G. Puglisi, president of this commission, states that

> Il marchio dell'Unesco ha una forte valenza culturale e simbolica, e la commissione può decidere di espellere dalla lista i siti non adeguatamente tutelati, ma sugli abusi devono intervenire le Soprintendenze e le Procure della Repubblica, e ci vogliono sanzioni forti.[42]

While he does not explicitly say whether this culture and symbolic importance is for Italy, the whole world, or both, the discourse demonstrates that Italy places great emphasis on the rôle of UNESCO and the inscription of sites within its boundaries. Italy relies on the character and quality of its heritage sites as "authentic" and "of exceptional universal value" to build prestige,[43] while proper care of this heritage is also crucial for Italy's international reputation.

The discourse surrounding World Heritage speaks to larger issues of local diversity and the preservation of heritage in Italy. In this discourse, the values of heritage preservation define Italian cultural identity in many ways. Current debates on whether to privatize selected state-owned heritage properties have elicited heated reaction from Italy's politicians and citizens, and from the international community.[44] For instance, in an interview with G. Urbani, a former head of the Ministry of Culture, one person questioned the ability of outsiders to understand Italian heritage values.[45] In his book *Italia S.p.A* (2002),

---

[38] Labadi 2007, 161.
[39] Bianchi 2002; Breglia 2006; McClanahan 2006.
[40] A. Cianciullo in *La Repubblica,* July 15, 2004. There is a similar example from the inscription of the Mediaeval sites of Mantova and Sabbioneta, and the Rhaetian railway: "Patrimonio dell'umanità: L'Italia dà record: 43 siti" (G. Ziino, *Corriere della Sera,* July 9, 2008).
[41] This occurred in September 2006, when buildings were constructed on inscribed sites in Puglia and Sicily. Berlusconi's government was blamed for allowing development in these areas (de Luca, *La Repubblica,* Sept. 13, 2006).
[42] From de Luca, *La Repubblica,* Sept. 13, 2006.
[43] Translated from G. Ziino, *Corriere della Sera,* July 9, 2008.
[44] R. Benedikter (2004, 383-84), lists the 37 museum directors who voiced concern over the possibility that Italy's system could be privatized. They argued that Italy was the one place where UNESCO's ideal of the museum, "a non-profit organization, [serving] the public benefit", was preserved. For a discussion of privatization of heritage sites in an Italian context, see Zan *et al.* 2008.
[45] Urbani 2002, 59.

S. Settis made a convincing case for why cultural sites and museums should stay legally in the control of the Italian people, as dictated by Italian law.[46] Settis, a foremost cultural commentator, professor and former government official, makes an argument that is nationalistic in character. Unlike previous uses of heritage by the nation-state based on the archaeological remains of one historical group (for instance, the Fascists' advancement of a single national past through Imperial Rome), Settis creates a national narrative around heritage preservation. Heritage preservation itself becomes a patrimony that can unify Italians. The practices of preservation which, he argues, began in the late-Mediaeval pre-unification states define Italy and are the most important contribution that Italy can make to Europe and the world:

> Il contributo italiano alla costruzione dell'identità culturale europea (cioè dell'Europa) è e dev'essere in primo luogo una riflessione sulla *propria* identità, sul *proprio* patrimonio culturale, sulla *propria* cultura della tutela ... L'Italia deve scegliere, e subito, se portare nel concerto europeo la propria tradizione e la propria cultura, civile e giuridica, elaborata nei secoli in questo campo, propendendola agli altri come modello ...[47]

For him, the management of cultural patrimony defines the national character of the Italian people and the state. But is it enough?

Settis never gives preference to a pre-Roman, Roman, Mediaeval or Renaissance past over another: all are important and worthy of preservation. The multiple heritages of the Italian peninsula are embraced, but it is up to Italian citizens to create what he terms the *tessuto connettivo* of heritage in Italy.[48] He emphasizes the rôle of place in constructing these connections to one's local heritage: it is the daily experience of living in these places that fosters this connection, while museum collections also create a sense of belonging and pride in the inhabitants.[49] He believes the *tessuto* is something that all Italians understand.[50] However, this does not mean that all Italian places will relate to their heritage in similar ways. Even if there *is* a shared culture of preservation, heritage can serve to mark out local places as distinct from each other, as the Etruscan case demonstrates. Not all Italians experience this daily connection with the local heritage of others. How, then, can these connections be fostered?

Settis never mentions the rôle of UNESCO in Italy; nonetheless, Italy's eclectic World Heritage List does construct a real heritage landscape marked by diversity, for which he argues: urban centers, rural landscapes, pre-Roman, Roman, Christian, Mediaeval, Renaissance and modern sites are all represented on this list, along with sites of natural heritage, for a current total of 47. The sites are linked by prestige and a shared uniqueness. Pride in

---

46 Settis 2002, 5. He is clear in noting that this is not partisan politics: both the left and right are to blame for the situation that has made some sites and historic properties available for sale.
47 Ibid. 12-13. Of course, there are those who would counter that the model and its implementation are two different things. Italy spends a fraction on the management of its heritage by comparison with other states in Europe: cf. Urbani 2002; Benedikter 2004.
48 Settis 2002, 11.
49 Ibid. 23.
50 Settis is advancing an idea of unity through difference, quite similar to a trend identified by A. Guidi to explain Italian archaeology before 1994. During that period, a diversity of archaeological traditions and remains could be seen as a national characteristic: Guidi 1996, 117. With *localismo* and difference emphasized, however, this ideal of unity through diversity did not achieve the desired result. Guidi gives the example of local archaeologists in places like Sardinia and Sicily who became increasingly suspicious of Italians from outside their provinces digging their sites.

them is broadcast on national and international stages, making them accessible (at least through the media) to all Italians. As a result, they become more authentic representations of particular cultures or periods than others. Settis' *tessuto* thus becomes less than egalitarian: Italy makes particular choices that create a certain heritage landscape on the Italian peninsula, linking sites that form part of World Heritage, and excluding others. Sites considered for inscription are presented to the national *Ministero dei Beni e Attività Culturali*, which decides which will be submitted to UNESCO for nomination. The selection of Tarquinia and Cerveteri was thus a decision approved nationally. With the inscription of the Etruscan sites, Italy is re-orienting the group toward an Italian past located firmly within the borders of the Italian state.

The Etruscans have received more attention, such as those discussed in this paper, from cultural initiatives in the last two decades. Political and social uses of this past by different cities, nation-states and supranational organizations such as the EU have also made Etruscan heritage so dynamic.[51] In addition to the Paris and Bologna exhibits, recent exhibits in Venice and in Spain keep the Etruscans alive on a European stage. An exhibition at the Palazzo degli Esposizioni in Rome highlighted the Etruscan cities of Latium; coupled with latest reworkings of the Villa Giulia's satellite museums at Tuscania, Viterbo and Pyrgi, it demonstrates the investment made in presenting Etruscan culture by the *Soprintendenza dell'Etruria meridionale* and the Italian state.

It is their proximity to Rome, their link to the national capital, that makes the inscriptions of these sites interesting from a national perspective. Rome, as capital city, is the center of the national government's bureaucracy, despite the discomfort many local Romans feel with this status.[52] On the national stage and in the eyes of many modern Italians, Rome is strongly connected with the institutions of the national government. While Tarquinia and Cerveteri were two of the earliest Etruscan sites to come into contact with the expanding Roman city-state, preserving and curating their heritage has also been tied to Rome in the more recent past. The Villa Giulia's collection is well represented by finds from Tarquinia and especially Cerveteri.[53] Some remarkable pieces, such as the sarcophagus of the Bride and Bridegroom, make stark the contrast between the significance of the finds from Cerveteri housed at the Villa Giulia and those still in Cerveteri at the Museo Cerite. The presence of the objects in the Villa Giulia strongly link the sites to Rome, stressing how the capital serves as a central place for the preservation of this material heritage.

Another example of this link has been the debate over the Euphronios krater,[54] the prized work of art looted from the necropolis of Cerveteri and sold illicitly to the Metropolitan Museum of Art in New York for the then-hefty sum of one million dollars. Following an intense public debate between the museum and the Italian state over the provenance

---

[51] Scientific exploration of the Etruscan past has compared the DNA of contemporary Tuscan populations with that of Etruscan skeletons found in tombs in Tuscany, as noted by S. Bule (1996) and N. de Grummond (1996). Through scientific discovery comes legitimacy; just as the Etruscans lived there two millennia ago, so they live there now. A similar study was conducted by Stanford University and the University of Ferrara in 2006.

[52] Herzfeld 2009.

[53] The museum was founded in 1889 to house the pre-Roman, extra-urban antiquities from Latium.

[54] For a discussion of this object and how it was illicitly traded, see Watson and Todeschini 2006. For the trade in illicit antiquities in Italy, see Graepler and Mazzei 1996.

of this artifact, it was returned to Italy in January 2008, to much fanfare. The debate over where to permanently house it underscores how museums are connected to political discourses about heritage.[55] Would Cerveteri and its small, local museum be worthy of this juggernaut of ancient art? R. Buttiglione, a former minister of cultural antiquities, insisted that Cerveteri did not have a museum sufficiently developed for such a great work,[56] but E. Gasbarra, ex-president of the province of Lazio, made it clear that Cerveteri would invest in a state-of-the-art museum, stressing the increased cultural value and significance that this vase would bring to the UNESCO site.[57] Yet A. M. Moretti, then-superintendent of Etruria Meridionale, did not believe this was necessary, stating:

> Cerveteri ha già uno splendido museo che fa parte di un sistema museale al centro del quale ci sono la Rocca di Albornoz a Viterbo e, soprattutto, Villa Giulia.[58]

making it clear that Cerveteri's museum stands on a lower rung in the hierarchy of Etruscan museums in and around Rome.[59] No new museum has yet emerged even though the vase is back in Italy, forming the centerpiece of the *Nostoi* ('homecomings') exhibit at the Quirinal presidential palace. After touring museums and exhibits in Europe, the vase has found its permanent home in the Villa Giulia in Rome. More than any other object, this vase has demonstrated the value of retrieving the stolen objects of the Etruscan civilization and Italy's commitment to its archaeological patrimony. Thus, while Tarquinia and Cerveteri, with their status as World Heritage sites coupled with their unfortunate history of looting, have helped to define these Etruscan places as particularly important for national heritage, the Italian state has decided that this world-renowned vase better serves its own interests in a more accessible, centrally-located museum in the capital. Panels placed beside the Euphronios krater in 2009 in the Villa Giulia emphasize the importance of context for archaeological exploration and proper cultural understanding, underscoring why the piece should be in Italy and not abroad. However, has Italy also denied the piece its proper contextualization by not returning it to Cerveteri? The fate of the krater makes clear how much the national government is invested in fashioning, on its own terms, how Etruscan heritage is presented and viewed through the display of objects and through the marketing of archaeological sites for national and international consumption. It could be no other way: Tarquinia and Cerveteri play a distinctive rôle in how the Italian state defines itself as a foremost preserver of heritage.

Conclusion

Places of heritage, whether archaeological sites, museums, or even whole cities, are political and social spaces that cannot be divorced from present concerns.[60] These Etruscan examples bring to the fore how complex and ambivalent the meanings of heritage can be, based on their context.[61] In Bologna, the *Culture 2000* organizers, working in a northern

---

55 See Price and Price 1995 for the political rôle of museums in Central and South America.
56 P. Broghi in the *Corriere della Sera,* Feb. 6, 2006. His opinion would seem still to hold, as few if any changes have been made to the Museo Cerite in recent years.
57 L. Colonnelli, *Corriere della Sera*, Feb. 5, 2006, p. 15.
58 "Cerveteri already has a splendid museum that is part of a network of museums, at the center of which are the museums of Viterbo and above all the Villa Giulia".
59 C. A. Bucci, *La Repubblica,* Feb. 5, 2006, p. 7.
60 Meskell and Preucell 2004, 315.
61 L. Breglia (2006) uses this term as a way to counteract the idea that the meaning of heritage is univalent.

city with a complex relationship to the nation-state and the European Union, relied on Etruscan heritage to communicate their outward-looking perspective and to characterize the city as a place of cultural and social connection. By making place in such a way, they aided the European Union in characterizing Europe's history as one marked by diversity, but also connection, peaceful interaction, and communication. The use of archaeological heritage thus carries real social and political influence, first in fashioning Bologna as a European city, second in creating a place called the European Union.[62] Narratives such as these serve to give the European Union added legitimacy: the EU is reviving a formative moment in its past for the benefit of the present.

For the Italian heritage landscape, mediated by UNESCO World Heritage, the Etruscans instead become part of a national network of sites linked by their special status. On the world stage, they become representations of Italian heritage, for which the nation is praised. Nearly two-thirds of the World Heritage sites in Italy have been inscribed since 1993, directly subsequent to the emergence of the "Second Republic", a period that was marked by intense political tensions and public disillusionment with the national government. Many Italian politicians and intellectuals believe that the half-century of crafting unity through difference have had grave effects on national unity.[63] While the list represents, in part, the diverse heritage that Italy contains within its borders, it also organizes and advances this heritage for a national and international audience. Through the sites of Tarquinia and Cerveteri, the Italian state has attempted to orient Etruscan heritage toward the interests of the nation.

While archaeologists have long tried to understand how archaeology operates in service of the state,[64] they must now grapple with how this heritage sits within the complex nexus of local, national, supranational and international institutions. The European Union has negotiated, and continuously renegotiates, the rôle of nation-states and national ideologies within in;[65] in a social, cultural and political landscape as diverse as that of Italy, places will continue to be made and remade there too.

Bibliography

Anderson, B. 1983. *Imagined communities* (London).
Bartoloni, G. *et al.* (edd.) 2000. *Principi Etruschi: tra Mediterraneo ed Europa* (Marsilio).
Benedikter, R. 2004. "Privatisation of Italian cultural heritage," *Int. J. Heritage Stud.* 10, 369-89.
Bianchi, R. V. 2002. "The contested landscapes of World Heritage on a tourist island: the case of Garajonay National Park, La Gomera," *Int. J. Heritage Stud.* 8, 81-97.
Breglia, L. 2006. *Monumental ambivalence: the politics of heritage* (Austin, TX).
Bule, S. 1996. "Etruscan echoes in Italian Renaissance art," in Hall 1996, 307-35.
Camporeale, G. (ed.) 2001. *Gli Etruschi fuori d'Etruria* (Verona).
Cristofani, M. 1978. "Sugli inizi dell' 'Etruscheria'," *MEFRA* 90, 577-625.
de Grummond, N. 1996. "Etruscan Italy today," in Hall 1996, 337-65.
Dietler, M. 1994. "'Our ancestors the Gauls': archaeology, ethnic nationalism, and the manipulation of Celtic identity in modern Europe," *American Anthropologist* 96, 584-605.

---

62 In many ways, this aim gives Europeans a common ground, heeding the advice of Herzfeld (2002) that Europeans must forge an identity through the things they share. Valuing communication becomes common ground.
63 Patriarca 2001; Galli della Loggia (1998) takes a pessimistic stance on whether national unity is even possible.
64 A phrase coined by Kohl and Fawcett (1995a).
65 Pagden 2002a.

Dingli, S. M. 2006. "A plea for responsibility towards the common heritage of mankind," in Scarre and Scarre 2006, 219-41.
Ferri, A. and G. Roversi (edd.) 1978. *Storia di Bologna* (Bologna).
Galli della Loggia, E. 1998. *L'identità italiana* (Bologna).
Garden, M.-C. E. 2006. "The heritagescape: looking at landscapes of the past," *Int. J. Heritage Stud.* 12, 394-411.
Graepler, D. and M. Mazzei 1996. *Provenienza: sconosciuta! Tombaroli, mercanti e collezionisti: l'Italia archaeological allo sbaraglio* (Bari).
Guidi, A. 1996. "Nationalism without a nation: the Italian case," in M. Diaz-Andreu and T. Champion (edd.), *Nationalism and archaeology in Europe* (London) 108-18.
Hall, J. (ed.) 1996. *Etruscan Italy: Etruscan influences on the civilizations of Italy from antiquity to the modern era* (Provo, UT).
Herreman, Y. 2006. "The role of museums today: tourism and cultural heritage," in B. T. Hoffman (ed.), *Art and cultural heritage: law, policy and practice* (Cambridge) 419-26.
Herzfeld, M. 2002. "The European self: rethinking an attitude," in Pagden 2002b, 139-70.
Herzfeld, M. 2009. *Evicted from eternity: the restructuring of modern Rome* (Chicago, IL).
International Council on Monuments and Sites (ICOMOS) 2004. *Cerveteri and Tarquinia (Italy): advisory board evaluation* (Paris).
Kohl, P. L. and C. Fawcett 1995a. "Archaeology in the service of the state: theoretical considerations," in iid. 1995b, 3-18.
Kohl, P. L. and C. Fawcett (edd.) 1995b. *Nationalism, politics and the practice of archaeology* (Cambridge).
Labadi, S. 2007. "Representations of the nation and cultural diversity in discourse on World Heritage," *J. Soc. Arch.* 7, 147-70.
Leighton, R. 2004. *Tarquinia: an Etruscan city* (London).
Mansuelli, G. A. 1984. "L'archeologia etrusco-italica a Bologna," in Morigi Govi and Sassatelli 1984, 37-40.
Mascioli, F. 1942. "Anti-Roman and pro-Italic sentiment in Italian historiography," *Romanic Review* 33, 366-84.
McClanahan, A. 2006. "Histories, identity, and ownership: an ethnographic case study in archaeological heritage management in the Orkney Islands," in M. Edgeworth (ed.), *Ethnographies of archaeological practice: cultural encounters, material transformations* (Lanham, MD) 126-36.
Meskell, L. 2002. "Negative heritage and past mastering in archaeology," *Anth. Q* 75, 557-74.
Meskell, L. and R. Preucel 2004. "Politics," in iid. (edd.), *Companion to social archaeology* (London) 315-34.
Momigliano, A. 1950. "Ancient history and the antiquarian," *JWarb* 13, 286-312.
Morigi Govi, C. and G. Sassatelli (edd.) 1984. *Dalla stanza delle antichità al Museo Civico* (Bologna).
Oleson, J. P. 1976. "Regulatory planning and individual site development in Etruscan necropoles," *JSocArchHist* 35, 204-18.
Omland, A. 2006. "The ethics of the World Heritage concept," in Scarre and Scarre 2006, 242-59.
Pagden, A. 2002a. "Introduction," in id. 2002b, 1-32.
Pagden, A. (ed.) 2002b. *The idea of Europe: from antiquity to the European Union* (Cambridge).
Pallottino, M. (ed.) 1992. *Les Etrusques et l'Europe* (Paris).
Palmer/RAE Associates 2004. *European Cities and Capitals of Culture – City Reports*, Part II (Brussels).
Patriarca, S. 2001. "Italian neopatriotism: debating national identity in the 1990s," *Modern Italy* 6.1, 21-34.
Price, R. and S. Price 1995. "Executing culture: musée, museo, museum," *American Anthropologist* 97.1, 97-109.
Quartermaine, L. 1996. "'Slouching towards Rome': Mussolini's imperial vision," in T. Cornell and K. Lomas (edd.), *Urban society in Roman Italy* (New York) 203-15.
Sassatelli, G. 1984. "Il Carnevale del 1874: Balanzoneide ovvero gli Etruschi a Bologna," in Morigi Govi and Sassatelli 1984, 327-46.
Scarre, C. and G. Scarre (edd.) 2006. *The ethics of archaeology: philosophical perspectives on archaeological practice* (Cambridge).
Settis, S. 2002. *Italia S.p.A: l'assalto al patrimonio culturale* (Turin).
Shore, C. 1996. "Imagining the new Europe: identity and heritage in European Community discourse," in P. Graves-Brown, S. Jones and C. S. Gamble (edd.), *Cultural identity and archaeology: the construction of European communities* (London) 96-115.

Shore, C. and A. Black 1992. "The European communities and the construction of Europe," *Anthropology Today* 8.3, 10-11.
Stacul, J. 2006. "Claiming a 'European ethos' at the margins of the Italian nation-state," in Stacul, Moutsou and Kopnina 2006b, 210-28.
Stacul, J., C. Moutsou and H. Kopnina 2006a. "Introduction," in iid. 2006b, 1-19.
Stacul, J., C. Moutsou and H. Kopnina (edd.) 2006b. *Crossing European boundaries: beyond conventional geographic categories* (New York).
Stone, M. 1999. "A flexible Rome: fascism and the cult of *Romanità*," in C. Edwards (ed.), *Roman presences: receptions of Rome in European culture, 1789-1945* (Cambridge) 205-20.
Terrenato, N. 2001. "The perception of Rome in modern Italian culture," in R. Hingley (ed.), *Images of Rome: perceptions of ancient Rome in Europe and the United States in the modern age* (JRA Suppl. 44) 71-89.
Tossutti, L. S. 2001. "Globalization and the 'new localism' in northern Italy," *Mediterranean Politics* 6.1, 64-83.
Tossutti, L. S. 2002. "Between globalism and localism, Italian style," *Western European Politics* 25.3, 51-76.
Trigger, B. G. 1995. "Romanticism, nationalism, and archaeology," in Kohl and Fawcett 1995b, 263-79.
Urbani, G. 2002. *Il tesoro degli Italiani: colloqui sui beni e le attività culturali* (Milan).
Vitali, D. 1984. "La scoperta di Villanova e il Conte Giovanni Gozzadini," in Morigi Govi and Sassatelli 1984, 223-42.
Watson, P. and C. Todeschini 2006. *The Medici conspiracy: the illicit journey of looted antiquities* (New York).
Zan, L., S. Bonini Baraldi and C. Gordon 2008. "Cultural heritage between centralization and decentralization: insights from the Italian context," *Int. J. Cultural Policy* 13, 49-70.

The imperial mirror: Rome as reference for empire
Carsten Paludan-Müller

> The story of its ruin is simple and obvious; and instead of inquiring *why* the Roman Empire was destroyed, we should rather be surprised that it had subsisted so long. Edward Gibbon (2000, 435)

Introduction

The study of empires in general, and the Roman empire in particular, may seem only remotely relevant to our understanding of present international politics and their ideological motivations. However, behind their diverse technologies, institutions and symbolic façades, the empires of the past responded to conditions and situations that on a more general level also unfold in our contemporary world.

Empires aim to establish control over vast tracts of space. Their purpose includes making place by economically, militarily and ideologically controlling their populations and resources. What marks the empire in particular is its scale, and often its heterogeneity. In this sense empire is place-making on the grandest scale. This paper investigates certain aspects of how empires, particularly the Roman, succeeded or failed to expand and uphold the imperial space as an integrated yet diverse hierarchy of places. It is a hierarchy organised in ways that would facilitate the flow of resources into the imperial centre, while also producing and projecting power and policy from the centre towards the periphery, in an effort to uphold the overall system. I will argue that Rome has served as a model for conceiving or analysing later imperial projects, and that this 'imperial mirror' strongly characterizes Roman heritage in the present. The heritage of the Roman empire has contributed to the symbolic repertoire of later imperial projects precisely because its ruins, monuments and history could demonstrate so aptly how imperial power was and is symbolized as place.

Empires defined

In order better to understand the particular rôle of the Roman empire as a point of reference for later imperial projects, we must first look more closely into the definitions of what an empire is supposed to be and to achieve. P. Richardot defines the following key criterions for empires. First, there is a centre of gravity and origin from which the empire springs. Second, an empire has a history of military conquest that furthers its expansion. Third, the régime of empire is authoritarian or has extreme civic inequalities. Fourth, from a logistical standpoint it has a broad spatial scale and high population counts. Finally, it is generally composed of an aggregation of previously segregated territories, polities and ethnicities.[1] M. Hardt and A. Negri define the concept of empire by four criteria. First, no territorial boundaries limit the rule of an empire: its sovereignty encompasses the entire civilized world. Second, the empire presents itself as a regime unbounded by time and history and hence as representing an eternal order. Third, the object of imperial rule is the totality of its subjects' lives. Fourth, in spite of a practice bathed in blood, the discourse of empire is that of peace.[2] Meanwhile, H. Münkler points to the lack of a systematic set of definitions

---

1 Richardot 2003, 8-11.
2 Hardt and Negri 2000, xiv. Against the fourth criterion of Hardt and Negri it can be argued that, like every state, empires must uphold a monopoly on exercising violence. Most states will

to distinguish global realms (*Weltreichen*) from great realms (*Grossreichen*). His approach is based on an established social scientific approach to the general study of empires.[3] He proposes three key elements in the definition of empires as opposed to ordinary states. First, in contrast to states, empires recognize no neighbours as their equals. Their border zones are asymmetrical, with a level of imperial power and control that decreases with the distance from the imperial centre. Conditions for crossing the border are different depending on whether the direction is into or out of the empire. Second, the empire reduces less powerful states to clients or satellites. Third, a definition of empires cannot rely only on the centre/periphery emphasis on 'push' — that is, on a project of domination and expansion initiated from the core; it is also necessary to emphasize processes of 'pull', from the periphery towards the centre.[4]

In her lucid analysis of the Ottoman empire, K. Barkey meets Münkler's request for a more sociological approach. She defines empire as

> a large composite and differentiated polity linked to a central power by a variety of direct and indirect relations, where the center exercises political control through hierarchial and quasi-monopolistic relations over groups ethnically different from itself.[5]

She further emphasises that political, fiscal and military control over the different groups is exercised by the centre and maintained through ongoing negotiations. These negotiations are facilitated by group relations organized in a "hub and spoke structure" — a wheel where the rim is more or less absent, so that the different groups can only or mainly connect through the hub, the imperial centre. In consequence of Barkey's definition, empires are distinct from modern nation-states in their ability and willingness to build on, integrate and maintain a heterogeneous body of ethnic and religious identities. In contrast, the development of modern nation states has been accompanied at times by brutal efforts to homogenise previously distinct population groups into one people sharing a common platform of identity. It is exactly this element of empire that might make it difficult for us today fully to appreciate the dependence of empire on sustained diversity for its own resilience, since most contemporary research into the Roman empire is done within institutions and traditions shaped under the nation-state.

In sum, we may assume a definition of empire, where the constituting features are:
- a spatial hierarchy of places where the central place exercises control over the rest through its ability to project physical and ideological power, backing an asymmetric flow of decisions and resources through networks that privilege vertical connections over horizontal ones;
- an integration of different *ethnies*[6] as components of the empire through specifically adapted relations between the centre and each of the *ethnies*;
- an asymmetrical border where movement into the empire is more restricted than out;
- a zone beyond that border over which control or influence is exercised with an intensity that decreases with distance from the imperial centre.

---

      emphasise their peaceful qualities while at the same time, under certain circumstances, exercising severe violence.
3   Münkler 2005, 15-16.
4   Eckstein (2006, 257-316) argues for an effect of pull as a significant driver behind the Roman intervention in the 3rd-c. Hellenistic wars that destabilized the entire Eastern Mediterranean space.
5   Barkey 2008, 9-15.
6   *Ethnies* is a term adapted from the French by A. D. Smith (1986) that refers to pre-national ethnocultural groups.

Why empires in general, and Rome in particular, remain important references

Even though the nation-state is today's dominant form, it is a very recent one, modelled in the context of the late 18th- and 19th-c. industrialization of Western Europe and N America. The political forms of the city-state and empire have a far longer history, and empire is still with us, even though sometimes it appears in the guise of the nation-state.[7] Here I have chosen a focus on the Roman empire because of its prominent rôle in much of the history of political thinking in the western hemisphere and during a time when the development of the modern world has been heavily influenced by the West. I hope to demonstrate that for the West's idea of power the Roman empire has never been supplanted by any other common point of reference. The evidence for this is embedded both in the symbolic choreography of power and in the political-historical discourse and analysis of power. In practice, it has been important for most of the post-Roman powers in the West to present and understand themselves as heirs to the Roman empire. It also means that Roman history has been, and still is, 'good to think with' in order better to understand the history of geopolitical power and dominance. From this perspective it is important to understand how power is exercised in space. It is manifest both in the symbolic organisation of space (both the built environment and landscapes) and in the military and economic control of space. In short, the study of the Roman empire helps us understand how a vast space can be integrated and transformed into a coherent corpus of places controlled from one centre.

The Roman empire thus remains an archetype of European and western history and the highest point of reference for any later imperial project conceived in the western hemisphere. As indicated by Gibbon in the quotation at the outset of this paper, it is an archetype with at least two opposite readings: one reading heralds the might and longevity of the Roman empire, while the other is preoccupied with its degeneration and downfall.[8] The first has been an inspiration for further imperial projects, the latter for sceptics of them, so that the downfall of the Roman empire remains a *Leitmotiv* in western historical scholarship.[9] However, a preoccupation with the end of a phenomenon is only given full meaning if we consider permanence to be the norm. It is tempting to claim that, in the case of the Roman empire, the reason why we remain so preoccupied with its downfall is because of its success.

Of particular fascination was its ability to persist as an empire for more than 500 years in a more or less continuous pattern of expansion, consolidation and persistence, from the elimination of Carthage, the only remaining rival Mediterranean power, in 146 B.C. to the formal division of the empire in A.D. 395. From then on, we can count another millennium until 1453 when Mehmet II's conquest of Constantinople ended the protracted demise of the Eastern empire.[10] With the end of World War I came the fall of the Ottoman and Austro-Hungarian empires of SE and central Europe, and the revolutionary transformation of the Russian empire. After World War II, the dismantling of the western European colonial empires followed. Subsequently there was then a 'post-imperial' epoch, dominated by the bipolar hegemony of the two superpowers of the U.S.S.R. and U.S.A. With the downfall of the Soviet Union came both a clearer recognition of it as a *de facto* continuation of the

---

7   Osterhammel 2006, 56-57.
8   Assman 1999, 314-22.
9   Kaiser 2004, 65-66; Ward-Perkins 2005, 1-10; Heather 2006, 443-59.
10 The Byzantine empire survived many serious crises, but the sack of Constantinople in 1204 by the Fourth Crusade and the subsequent Latin rule until 1261 was a serious blow from which the empire never recovered.

Czarist empire, and recognition of the unrivalled position of the United States, which some saw as rising to an unprecedented rôle as *the* global imperial power. In this context Rome is no longer merely a point of reference for a retrospective analysis of past empires: it has become an inspiration or a mirror for imperial projects to come.

Translatio imperii,[11] *inspiratio imperii*: crafting claims to the Roman legacy

The Roman empire has been used both to legitimise and reflect upon later imperial projects. This began with the Carolingians and their pervasive use of classical references in administrative and religious architecture, and the frequent references to Greece and Rome in political discourse. A few examples may serve to illustrate the potency and prominence of the Roman symbolic arsenal in the legitimisation of later imperial projects in Europe and N America. I focus first on references formed through concepts, symbols and images. I then analyse the rôle of these in the making of places for the exercise of power claiming heir to the imperial Roman legacy.

Imperial lineages and papal alliances

During the centuries following the defeat and abdication of the last Western emperor, Romulus Augustus in A.D. 476, the Holy See in Rome encouraged, inspired and legitimized several revitalizations of the worldly Roman empire, in recognition of its need to compensate for its lack of an armed force. Protagonists of diverse imperial projects sought the legitimacy that could be obtained from an alliance with the Pontifex Maximus[12] of Rome. In the West the line of *Translatio Imperii* runs from the crowning at Rome of Charlemagne in 800, through the long and complicated alliance between the Pope and the Holy Roman Empire, to its eventual dissolution by Napoleon I in 1806. Napoleon had himself crowned as French emperor two years earlier in a spectacular ceremony with strong choreographic allusions to the crowning of Charlemagne, reducing the Pope to the role of a subordinate bystander.[13] In 1472, Sophia Paleologue, a niece of the last Byzantine *basileus*, Constantin XI (1405-53), married Ivan III, Grand Duke of Moscow. This alliance formed the basis of an eastern line of *Translatio Imperii*, with the Russian empire claiming status as the "Third Rome".

The eagle: appropriating the effigies of empire

Most of the imperial projects that attempted to establish their rule over major parts of the European continent used the eagle, a symbol of the Roman army, as their emblem and mark on places. This goes for the Holy Roman, the Habsburgian, the Czarist Russian, the Napoleonic, the German Kaiser Reich, and the Third Reich, and, of course, the imperial project of Fascist Italy. In the West this was also the case for the United States, where the topography, architecture and terminology of power openly refer to a Roman legacy, with names like the Capitol and Senate in common use, and where not only the eagle but also the *fasces* belong to the symbolic legacy from Rome. The European Union carries no eagle on its coat of arms, but it reckons the signing of the Treaty of *Rome*, in 1957, as its founding moment.[14]

---

11   *Translatio imperii* is a post-antique term for the successive transfer of the power once held by the Roman emperors.
12   The Pontifex Maximus was the highest priest of the Roman Republic; the title later passed to the emperor, and from there to the Bishop of Rome.
13   For a history of the European continental empires, see Tulard 1997.
14   Even if Rome may not have been explicitly chosen for its imperial past as the locus for signing

Fig. 1. The E façade of the Louvre, an example of the classicist French Baroque alienating itself from the contemporary Italian in order to claim allegiance to Imperial Rome.

Making places for imperial ascendance: Louis XIV's France, the United States, and Fascist Italy

One of the most impressive political programs to identify with the Roman empire was that of Louis XIV, King of France from 1643 to 1715. During his reign, France established itself as the dominant European power, despite a fierce geopolitical environment. He sponsored innovations in road construction and military architecture, and employed state-of-the-art three-dimensional modelling of landscapes, fortifications, cities and towns in order to improve the processes of analysis and decision-making for strategic and tactical purposes.[15] Fortifications, naval bases and siege-works were more technologically advanced, the road system radically improved. This was part of a concerted push to improve military and economic control over space. The king employed many of the same military engineers for symbolic place-making. Versailles became an enormous landscaping project, a scenography with ponds, fountains, axes and vistas that projected the idea of total control over an unlimited space.

In architecture, the French baroque style was explicitly developed in opposition to the more opulent style developed by Bernini (1598-1680) for the Papal church and court in Rome. Bernini's plans for the Louvre were passed over and instead a long, stately colonnaded E façade was built (fig. 1), designed by Claude Perrault (1613-1688) with assistance from Louis Le Vau (1612-1670) and Charles Le Brun (1619-1690). The austere classicist architectural language was considered a more appropriate expression of the ambition to foster an imperial Roman legacy, and was further developed as an official style at Versailles. In light of these developments, 17th-c. France provides an illuminating case of the development of functional designs (military and economic) together with the symbolic manifestations of control over space and place.

---

      the treaty, European politicians were well aware of the added symbolic value given to the treaty by the name of Rome.

15   Faucherre, Monsaingeon and de Roux 2007.

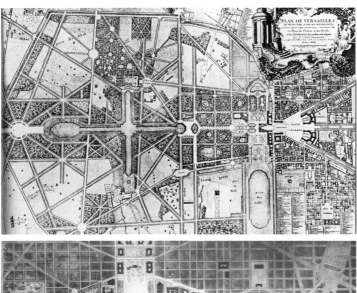
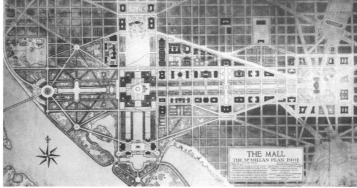

Fig. 2. The 1901 plan for the monumental layout of Washington D.C. around the Mall (below) echoes Le Nôtre's grandiose axial layout of the Versailles garden (above).

Similar references to the Roman empire were frequently employed by those constructing the British empire. However, probably the most impressive symbolic claim on the Roman legacy was made by the founding fathers of the United States of America. In 1785, while minister to France, Thomas Jefferson designed the State Capitol of Virginia in Neo-Roman style, assisted in the process by the French draftsman Charles-Louis Clérisseau. Jefferson's architecture became paradeigmatic for Capitol buildings in many state capitals, and no less so in the federal capital of Washington, D.C. L'Enfant's plan of 1901 shows strong inspirations from the classicistic monumentality of French architecture, seen in Le Nôtre's baroque garden of Versailles or Haussmann's re-ordering of 19th-c. Paris (fig. 2). The idea of military control of space is projected onto the symbolic landscape architecture of the Mall in Washington. This vast promenade not only includes many war memorials but also the Air and Space Museum. The juxtaposition is a statement of the unrivalled supremacy of the United States to survey any threat from any place on the globe and project the power to confront it. In Washington, as in 17th-c. Versailles, the military operational control over space and place is represented symbolically in the spatial organisation of the central place of political power.

Both France and the United States succeeded at different times and on different scales in establishing themselves as great powers that claimed to inherit the legacy of Rome. Fascist Italy provides a particularly fascinating example of an aborted imperial project. Because its epicentre was Rome itself, it had direct access to the physical remains of this Roman legacy. It produced the Fascist architecture of *Romanità*, whose quality cannot be denied. Lastly it offered a stark contrast between the symbolic manifestations of the Fascist imperial project and its actual geopolitical achievements. For Mussolini (1883-1945), Rome was the obvious central stage for symbolic manifestations of the Fascists' claim to be heirs to, and resuscitators of, the Roman empire. "Rome is our point of departure and reference. It is our symbol or, if you wish, our myth" was the declaration of Mussolini on April 22, 1922.[16] For that reason he enhanced existing initiatives to 'cleanse' later urban structures from the antique imperial ones. This included the destruction of some 5000 housing units of mediaeval and later periods in the path of the Via dell'Impero, a military parade street to connect Mussolini's governmental seat at Palazzo Venezia with the Colosseum. Around the Forum Romanum, Circus Maximus and Mausoleum of Augustus extensive re-editing of the urban fabric liberated the remains of the imperial past from the perceived contamination by mediaeval and later periods of urban development. The Fascist régime engaged in large-scale archaeological projects but primarily with the aim of arranging and editing an image of Rome that could support the establishment of a strong visual and physical connection between the empire of the past and the Fascist empire under construction.[17] Along with staging archaeological heritage projects, the Fascists undertook the development of a contemporary architecture, a stripped-down version of classicism known as *Novecento*. This was most famously embodied in the construction of the EUR, a new neighborhood built south of the historic centre for the planned 1942 World Exhibition. EUR was conceived as a 'fourth Rome', following on from the Republican, Imperial and Papal Romes, with classical forms and materials re-interpreted in projects in accordance with the ideas of *Romanità* and *Novecento*. Not finished in accordance with the original plans (nor until after the war), it nonetheless presents the most complete modern architectural re-interpretation of a perceived Roman imperial legacy, with huge vistas and modern versions of the Colosseum and Pantheon, as instruments for the Fascist project of resurrecting a Roman empire.[18]

These examples provide insights into the conscious use of the Roman repertoire of symbols and the awareness of its legitimising potential. Ever since its ascendancy the Roman empire has remained the sublime point of reference for western geopolitics and political culture. It makes sense to think that the reason is that the Roman empire, encompassing no less than one-sixth of the estimated global population of its day,[19] should be considered the most successful organization of European and Mediterranean space and populations to this day. It is no wonder then that rulers with imperial ambitions have attempted to establish symbolic links between themselves and the Roman empire.

Empires of our time: the U.S.A. and the E.U.

The renewed interest in the history of empires is a consequence of the recent collapse of the bipolar global order. The concomitant question is what kind of power structure can guarantee global order and stability. The 20th c. has been labelled 'The American Century', and there is little doubt that, if dominated by a single actor, world history in this period has been dominated by the U.S.A. However, during much of this time shifting constellations of big players were present as partners, competitors, and adversaries to be reckoned with,

---

16 Quoted in Painter 2005, 3.
17 Painter 2005, 1-38; Tung 2001, 61-64.
18 Astarita 1994, 355-56, Ustárroz 1997, 241-46; Painter 2005, 125-31.
19 Hopkins 2004, 108.

and it was only after the collapse of the Soviet empire in 1989 that the question arose about the potential for the world's last superpower to establish itself as the unrivalled empire of a global age.

Much of the analysis of recent American foreign policy has been conducted from that perspective. Both inside and outside American circles of power, *Pax Americana* has long been used as a term echoing the Augustan *Pax Romana*, just as *Pax Britannica* did before it. No other single power has the same military strength as the United States[20] but, as history demonstrates, military power in itself is hardly sufficient to build a new Rome — or, to be more precise, the military power of an empire needs support from a sufficient economic base as well as from a determined political will.

The U.S.A.: an empire of a different kind?

Gibbon had already foreseen the potential of America:

> Should the victorious Barbarians carry slavery and desolation as far as the Atlantic Ocean, ten thousand vessels would transport beyond their pursuit the remains of civilised society; and Europe would revive and flourish in the American world, which is already filled with her colonies and institutions.[21]

The Roman empire was a vast, contiguous territorial empire. The American empire, on the other hand, started as the overseas imperial territory of another empire, the British. After the American declaration of independence in 1776, a long period of continental expansion towards the north, south and, most dramatically, towards the west followed. Already the founding fathers openly referred to the United States as a nascent empire, different from the one they had just seceded from and having more in common with the (early) Roman one through its Republican nature and ability to include new people in its citizenship.[22] However, this inclusiveness was bestowed on Europeans, not on the original inhabitants or on African slaves. Already from 1817, and by law from 1825, the Native American tribes were removed from territories east of the 95th longitude.[23] This process of ethnic cleansing continued during most of the century in what one might call the culmination of the American empire's predatory phase.[24] The United States achieved its continental scale through a breathtaking territorial expansion that lasted less than 100 years. With extended access to navigable seas and a comfortable distance from any potential rival, the United States was in a uniquely privileged position to build itself up as a global player (fig. 3). It could, so to speak, assume the rôle of an insular seaborne empire, like Britain, combining that with the resources of massive territories on a scale surpassed only by the landlocked Russian empire.

The American geopolitical situation is comparable to that of Rome in the sense that the Roman empire established itself from a tiny nucleus, the city-state, and expanded dramatically over the Italian peninsula. From that territorial platform, Rome developed its maritime potential and took control over territories all around the Mediterranean. The difference, however, is that the United States never incorporated vast overseas territories into its empire. Once it had filled the space between the Atlantic and the Pacific, and had pushed its border south to the Rio Grande, it changed from a Roman territorial model of expansion to a Venetian model of expansion, by extending its empire in the form of networks

---

20   Lacoste 2008, 42-54.
21   Gibbon 2000, 440.
22   Ferguson 2005, 34.
23   Ibid. 36.
24   Hayes 2007, 140-49 and 200-3.

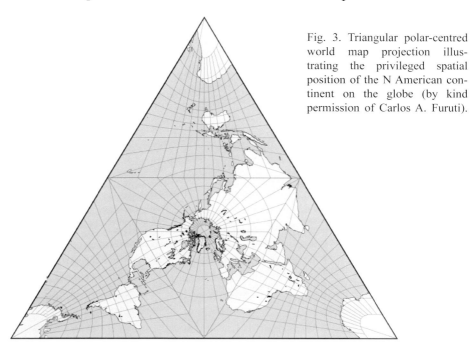

Fig. 3. Triangular polar-centred world map projection illustrating the privileged spatial position of the N American continent on the globe (by kind permission of Carlos A. Furuti).

and nodes that facilitate commercial flow and military control. Like Rome and the Italian mainland, the United States has moved from self-sufficiency in the production of its basic needs to a position of dependence on overseas import of vital supplies. In the case of Rome, there was an absolute reliance on grain from Sicily, Africa and Egypt in order to feed the imperial capital. In the case of the United States, the import of oil is needed to uphold its political and economic viability. For Rome, the network of sea routes linking Rome with Sicily, North Africa and Egypt was vital, and so was control over the grain-producing territories. For similar reasons the United States has sought to establish and maintain access to, and control over, some of the world's major oil fields and supply lines in the Middle East.[25] Unlike Rome, the United States has not imposed taxation throughout the space under its imperial control, but with the dollar installed as the universal currency and bonds issued in floating dollars, it has been able to compensate for a declining production of commodities and continue to support a disproportionately high level of public and private consumption through the cheap import of capital. In much the same way as Rome,[26] it has been able to finance its military expenditures at the same time as it has upheld standards of living for a significant majority of the population in the imperial centre.[27]

The reliance on import of capital to uphold consumption entails obvious vulnerabilities. Rome lost tax money by weak control over the tax base or through shipments of tax money being attacked as they moved through unsecure areas. In the case of the United States, vulnerability in the import of capital stems from the more mysterious mechanisms of the global financial market, but it can also be affected by factors such as military security:

---

25 As a democratic and a liberal market economy, the American empire is, of course, very different from the Roman: it is much more complex in the way it interacts with the world inside and outside its sphere of dominance. There is much more to the economic maintenance of the U.S.A.'s global position than the supply of oil and capital: for fuller analyses of the nature of the American empire, see, e.g., Schmidt 2004; Todd 2004; Ferguson 2005; James 2006; and Khanna 2008.
26 Ward-Perkins 2005, 41-45.
27 James 2006, 77-85; Bergsten 2009, 20-38.

the United States must appear to be a safe place for long-term investment. Militarily, the United States employs a strategy similar to that of the Roman empire: training and arming local tribes and warlords to take the burden off their own citizens.[28] As in the case of Rome, building up a strong military capacity in areas beyond the firm control of the empire comes at a cost, as can be seen in the conflicts in and around Afghanistan and Pakistan during recent decades.

Rome also grew as an empire through its ability to spread cultural norms and attractive goods to a growing number of citizens and territories, while absorbing and integrating diversity. Its polytheistic religious policy was able to accommodate an increasing diversity of deities and cults, including eventually Christianity. When Christianity took over and the empire was recast as monotheistic, this less tolerant religion did away with the integrative potential that had long supported Rome's survival. Today, multiculturalism is the equivalent to Roman polytheism. It permits (at least in principle) continuous expansion of the global market, which generates the wealth of the United States in a way analogous to that of the Roman state. Here, according to H. James,[29] resides the real dilemma of Rome and the United States (and other liberal democracies): polytheism and multiculturalism are both unable to deal with intolerance without violating their own principles. One must choose between disintegration resulting from the proliferation of incommensurable values and disintegration resulting from violent reactions to the forceful imposition of a single set of values.

The European Union

The Treaty of Rome and the European Union are seen by some as an imperial project of an entirely new kind,[30] while others see it as a manifest non-empire.[31] Economic, social and political-ideological benefits, with diversity rather than military strength, are supposed to guarantee cohesion and expansion.[32] Gibbon saw Europe's subdivision into a number of independent nations as the best guarantee against bad government and the corruption that often results when power is concentrated in the hands of a single ruler. Whether the European Union represents a possible competitor or successor to the United States is disputed.[33] If Europe manages to coordinate its priorities into a coherent set of policies and re-establish a prominent global position, it will probably be because of its ongoing experiment with what has been labelled a post-modern form of power and decision-making.[34]

---

28   Münkler (2006, 352-54) concludes his analysis by discussing the concept of the "post heroic society", which he sees as a determining characteristic of both late imperial Rome and the West of today. Citizens, no longer willing to bear the sacrifices that empire requires, cannot defend against enemies willing to sacrifice themselves in an effort to destroy the empire. This argument echoes that of Gibbon.
29   James 2006, 142.
30   Khanna 2008, 6.
31   Burbank and Cooper 2010, 414.
32   Slotterdijk 1994, 42-60; Le Goff 1994, 62-65; Münkler 2005, 245-54.
33   See, e.g., Assheuer 2008.
34   The need for speed of decision and for pointed action lay behind the concentration of power in the hands of Augustus. Capacity for swift decision-making is advantageous so long as the decisions are good, but disastrous when they are bad. The complex European process of decision-making, balancing many interests and considerations, may provide a certain control not found in authoritarian systems or even within a single democratic state, but its weakness may be a reluctance to act when swift action is needed.

Discussion: Imperial formations, the articulation and rôle of place

The main question must be whether global integration has moved beyond a point where unifocal imperial domination is at all possible within a closely interconnected geopolitical space, such as those areas once dominated by Rome or China.[35] Even though the Roman and Chinese empires existed at the same time, were aware of and traded indirectly with each other, they were not competitors or political actors within one another's space.[36] They were separated by vast territories that throughout history have proven difficult to bring under lasting political and military control. Any attempt to expand either empire deep into those lands would have carried the risk of fatal overstretching.[37]

The close economic integration of the world (or what we now call globalization) developed later, initiated from Europe in the late 15th c. A.D., and proceeded slowly with the gradual subordination of other empires under European colonial powers, particularly those of Western Europe.[38] There is an ongoing discussion (known as the divergence debate) about the reasons behind the European and, later, the American domination of those processes. Why initially Europe and not China? And to what extent does the answer have implications for understanding the geopolitical developments of today? Much of the debate has revolved around the differences between China and Europe in constraints and incitements to economic, technological and scientific growth. A recurring theme in this context is the significance of the overseas resources available to Europe from its colonial possessions. Another is the differing potential for further intensification of food production in China *versus* Europe in the 18th c. A third theme is the significance of the introduction of fossil fuels (coal) as a primary source of energy for production and transport in Europe. Finally, there is the intangible question of the rôle of culture in general and political systems in particular.[39]

None of the theories seems to provide a deeper explanation for the great divide. Many of the causes pointed to seem to be either insufficient in themselves or part of what has to be explained, rather than the explanation itself. A different approach has been suggested by David Cosandey,[40] who points to the rôle of the physical layout of Europe compared to that of the other continents. His argument is interesting in the context of empire. He points out that the western part of Europe is spatially fragmented by coastlines, mountains and

---

35 Westerners are often baffled by the perceived temporal continuity of the Chinese empire, which we tend to contrast with the volatility, shifts and cataclysms of western imperial constructions. In fact, China has indeed seen many political breakdowns and periods of fragmentation, while the West has retained a certain measure of continuity from a global perspective. The foundation of China as one empire took place under the Chin dynasty (221-206 B.C.). Following this there arose a complex sequence of shifting imperial dynasties, interrupted by several warring realms but more frequently division into a northern and a southern one. Several dynasties succumbed to conquerors from the north, some of which created their own dynasties. The last one, the Ch'ing, lasted from 1644 to 1911. Between 1840 and 1949 China was internally fragmented and under severe pressure from Russia, the Western colonial powers, and Japan, which competed and fought for control over Chinese territories and markets.
36 Curtin 1984, 94-96; Wood 2002, 42-47; Lewis 2007, 141-43.
37 Under the Han dynasty (202 B.C.–A.D. 202) the Chinese managed for a time to push their control as far west as Kashgar in Xinjiang
38 For a critical discussion of the quality of today's globalizations see Chauprade 2007, 888-98.
39 For a short summary of the debate, see O'Brien 2006.
40 Cosandey 2007.

rivers, in a way that, on the one hand, favours internal communication by navigation, and, on the other, also allows for the development of politically discrete entities of considerable size, each within fairly stable boundaries, since many of them are coastal. In Cosandey's perspective, the Roman empire was a European anomaly. By contrast, the physical geography of China lacks the same internal fragmentation, and is thus more favourable to the construction of a long-lasting unified political system (an empire). A central element in his explanation is that the existence in Europe of a stable (though not peaceful) fragmentation into competing territorial states has long promoted competition in technological innovation and economic development. This competition was focused within Europe itself, in order for the states to develop the strength of their respective power bases beyond that of their neighbours. In a comparatively less fragmented and thus more stable China, there were not the same competitive incentives to drive technological and economic development forward, but a greater emphasis on centralised political control and upholding the *status quo*. This is a line of thought related to that of Edward Gibbon, who also saw Europe's contemporary political fragmentation as beneficial compared to a monolithic empire, serving as a guarantee against political and cultural degeneration.[41]

With today's communication and transport technologies, the physical layout of continents has diminished in importance. What still matters is the ability for political systems to stimulate and accommodate innovation. In this respect, a geopolitical system that strikes a peaceful balance between the dynamics of violent competition and monolithic inertia may offer the best prospect for future chapters of global history.

The empire of our time may be coming to rely on control over shifting networks, flows and nodes, rather than on contiguous or vast bounded territories. The accelerating global urbanization reveals a new nested hierarchy of cities and a social segregation of urban spaces and networks.[42] A patchwork configuration of First- and Third-World places, or of dominating and dominated, is emerging. The 'empire' and the 'barbarians' are still separated, but no longer by a clearly defined *limes*, controlled by a single coordinated power.[43] Therefore the struggle between dominating and dominated assumes new forms, since a partly aterritorial empire by implication has fewer territories that can be conquered or liberated by those who oppose it. In that respect, empire is invulnerable to territorial warfare but not to attacks on its networks, nodes and morale.[44] This is the logic behind the rise of al-Qaida, at a moment when territorial warfare has lost its meaning as a threat to the dominant powers of our day.

---

41   After this manuscript was completed, discussion has intensified around convergence and divergence in the long-term political development within the Chinese and Euro-Mediterranean spaces, starting with the rise, respectively, of the Qin and the Roman empires. Scheidel (2009), for instance, discusses this in a macroscopic perspective. He underlines the long period of converging development in the two imperial state formations. This convergence lasted until the collapse of the Western Roman Empire. While China subsequently went through cycles of alternating unity and fragmentation, Europe and the Mediterranean shifted into a lasting fragmentation with competing states, none of which was capable of establishing a new hegemony.
42   For an analytical discussion, see Koolhaas and Mau 1995, 1252-55; Hardt and Negri 2000, xiv-xvi; and Graham and Marvin 2001.
43   The nature of the *limes* and other early boundaries has come under renewed discussion during recent years: see, e.g., Curta 2005.
44   Münkler 2006, 291-309.

Conclusion

This may be the lesson to be learned from Rome: as long as the empire was able to function as a set of integrated places with the capacity to offer substantial benefits (e.g., prosperity, peace, justice, even the prospect of inclusion), it stood in a strong position in both its internal and its external relations. However, with the concentration of political power and the dismantling of the political and military responsibility of its citizens, the empire not only did away with the menace of civil war, characteristic of the Late Republic; it also lost the resilience of the Early Republic towards external threats. With the abandonment of the cultural tolerance of the polytheistic system, the Roman empire lost its ability to accommodate the diversity and uphold the dignity of its citizens. With increasing demographic pressure on the imperial borders from dislocated Germanic tribes, militarily trained and equipped through their interactions with Rome, the empire lost its ability to guarantee peace and safety both externally and internally. With the absolute dependence of the imperial centre on long supply lines from the provinces came vulnerability and, in the end, the collapse of the empire's ability to uphold its level of governance and guarantee the safety and material needs of its citizens.

Yet this does not signify that place has become insignificant: empire is as much about place today as it has been throughout history. While not necessarily about direct and permanent control over vast territories, empires, now as before, rely on the ability to access territorially bounded resources and to control and eliminate eventual threats to their 'vital interests' emanating from within those territories. Equally, empire and its place-making is about the ability to convince people, through narratives and symbols, of the imperial capacity to marshall sufficient power to counter any threat.

The long-term success of an empire depends on its ability to offer benefits such as prosperity, peace and justice to populations and territories within its field of gravity. But it is not only that. Today, as always, the willingness of people to sustain an empire requires an idea, a set of perceived universal values that relate to human dignity, the meaning of civilization and citizenship, and their hopes and fears. To achieve that consensus of values on a global scale will require the ability to develop corresponding mechanisms for accommodating a diversity of deep-rooted value systems into a coherent platform for political action. Until that happens, we are more likely to see the co-existence of competing empires and constellations of great powers founded on different historical traditions and perceived interests.

For both good and bad, the Roman empire has left us with places, images and ideas that nourish a memory of an imperial archetype in the western mind. It continues to inspire and warn us with images of civilization, achievement, integrative strength, ruthless oppression and cataclysmic collapse. It is a mirror to which we shall keep returning.

Bibliography

Assheuer, T. 2008. "Der Aufstieg der Anderen: Wie wird die Welt am Ende der US-Vorherrschaft assehen? Amerikas Intellektuelle streiten über die Machtpole der Zukunft," *Die Zeit* 37(4), 51.
Assman, A. 1999. *Erinnerungsräume, Formen und Wandlungen des kulturellen Gedächtnisses* (München).
Astarita, R. 1994. "EUR exposition universelle de Rome," in J. Dethier and A. Guiheux (edd.), *La ville, art et architecture en Europe 1870-1993* (Paris).
Barkey, K. 2008. *Empire of difference: The Ottomans in comparative perspective* (Cambridge).
Bergsten, C. F. 2009 "The dollar and the deficits: how Washington can prevent the next crisis," *Foreign Affairs* Nov./Dec. 2009, 20-38.

Budde, G., S. Conrad and O. Janz (edd.) 2006. *Transnationale Geschichte, Themen, Tendenzen und Theorien* (Göttingen).
Burbank, J. and F. Cooper 2010. *Empires in world history: power and the politics of difference* (Princeton, NJ).
Chauprade, A. 2007. *Géopolitique, constantes et changements dans l'histoire* (3rd edn., Paris).
Cosandey, D. 2007. *Le secret de l'Occident: vers une théorie générale du progrès scientifique* (rev. edn., Paris).
Curta, F. (ed.) 2005. *Borders, barriers, and ethnogenesis: frontiers in late antiquity and the Middle Ages* (Studies in the Early Middle Ages 12, Turnhout).
Curtin, P. D. 1984. *Cross-cultual trade in world history* (Cambridge).
Eckstein, A. M. 2006. *Mediterranean anarchy, interstate war and the rise of Rome* (Los Angeles, CA).
Faucherre, N., G. Monsaingeon and A. de Roux 2007. *Les plans en relief des places du Roy* (Paris).
Ferguson, N. 2005. *Colossus: the rise and fall of the American empire* (London).
Gibbon, E. 2000. *The history of the decline and fall of the Roman empire* (London).
Graham, S. and S. Marvin. 2001. *Splintering urbanism, networked infrastructures, technological mobilities and the urban condition* (London).
Hardt, M. and A. Negri 2000. *Empire* (Cambridge, MA).
Hayes, D. 2007. *Historical atlas of the United States* (Berkeley, CA).
Heather, P. J. 2006. *The fall of the Roman empire: a new history of Rome and the barbarians* (London).
Hopkins, K. 2004. "Conquerors and slaves: the impact of conquering and empire on the political economy of Italy," in C. B. Champion (ed.), *Roman imperialism: readings and sources* (Oxford) 108-28.
James, H. 2006. *The Roman predicament: how the rules of international order create the politics of empire* (Princeton, NJ).
Kaiser, R. 2004. *Das Römische Erbe und das Merowingerreich* (München).
Khanna, P. 2008. *The second world: empires and influence in the new global order* (New York).
Koolhaas, R. and B. Mau 1995. *S, M, L, XL* (Rotterdam).
Lacoste, Y. 2008. *Geopolitique: la longue histoire d'aujourd'hui* (Paris).
Le Goff, J. 1994. *La Vieille Europe et la Nôtre* (Paris).
Lewis, M. E. 2007. *The early Chinese empires, Qin and Han* (Cambridge, MA).
Münkler, H. 2005. *Imperien, Die Logik der Weltherrschaft — vom Alten Rom bis zu den Vereignetne Staaten* (Berlin).
Münkler, H. 2006. *Der Wandel des Krieges: Von der Symmetrie zur Asymmetrie* (Göttingen).
O'Brien, P. K. 2006. "The divergence debate: Europe and China 1368-1846," in Budde, Conrad and Janz 2006, 68-82.
Osterhammel, J. 2006. "Imperien," in Budde, Conrad and Janz 2006, 56-67.
Painter, B. W., Jr. 2005. *Mussolini's Rome: rebuilding the eternal city* (New York).
Richardot, P. 2003. *Les grands empires, histoire et géopolitique* (Paris).
Scheidel, W. 2009. "From the 'Great Convergence' to the 'First Great Divergence'. Roman and Qin-Han state formation and its aftermath," in id. (ed.), *Rome and China. Comparative perspectives on ancient world empires* (New York).
Schmidt, H. 2004. *Die Mächte der Zukunft: Gewinner und Verlierer der Zukunft* (München).
Slotterdijk, P. 1994. *Falls Europa erwacht* (Frankfurt).
Smith, A. D. 1986. *The ethnic origins of nations* (Oxford).
Todd, E. 2004. *Après l'empire. Essai sur la décomposition du système américain* (Paris).
Tulard, J. (ed.) 1997. "Les empires occidentaux de Rome à Berlin," in M. Duverger and J.-F. Sirinelli (edd.), *Histoire générale des systèmes politiques* (Paris).
Tung, A. M. 2001. *Preserving the world's great cities: the destruction and renewal of the historic metropolis* (New York).
Ustárroz, A. 1997. *La lección de las ruinas* (Barcelona).
Ward-Perkins, B. 2005. *The fall of Rome and the end of civilization* (Oxford).
Wood, F. 2002. *The Silk Road: two thousand years in the heart of Asia* (Berkeley, CA).

Roman archaeology and the making of heritage citizens in Tunisia

Kathryn Lafrenz Samuels

Introduction

"We have more mosaics than Rome", a museum official tells me of Tunisia. A smile of pride accompanies the remark. We are discussing the museum's collections one sweltering August afternoon in the Bardo Museum. Roman sites in North Africa are treated as an important resource, being well-preserved and the focus of national initiatives to increase the kind of high-value tourism that cultural tourism entails. Like any important resource, Roman material heritage plays into numerous cultural, political and economic relationships. The official's pride for Tunisia's mosaics indicates some of those relationships: countering colonial legacies and predatory trade agreements, but also claiming the Roman empire as part of Tunisia's heritage, linking the country ever closer with western heritage and its contemporary political alignments.

As an archaeologist committed to understanding the use of the past in present-day North Africa for transnational concerns, I study the heritage management practices of a global range of actors for archaeological sites and material in the region. Studying the intersections of these diverse management strategies demonstrates how Roman heritage is used to mediate global relations. The actors involved typically include international organizations, national heritage agencies, and various community and civil society groups. Drawing on my training as an archaeologist and an ethnographer, I characterize my approach as an 'archaeological ethnography', to examine how the past is 'put to work' and implicated in a diversity of social, political and economic projects in the present-day.[1] This paper draws on fieldwork and archival research, conducted from 2004 to 2009, to focus on one facet of contemporary Roman heritage: citizenship. Specifically, Roman archaeological sites in Tunisia are produced and managed as places for fashioning individuals into responsible, tolerant citizens of the world. Two intertwined transnational aims — economic development and political change — combine to form political subjects through recourse to the archaeological past. The result I call a 'heritage citizen'.

A host of international actors — foreign governments, international organizations, non-governmental organizations (NGOs), multinational corporations and funding agencies — seek economic development in North Africa in order to enact political change. The global community strives to 'open up' the region: transitioning Morocco, Algeria, and Tunisia from authoritarian régimes to democratic states, through such democratization measures as encouraging free speech and association, a plurality of political parties, regular elections, and the enforcement of human rights and the rule of law more generally.[2]

---

1   Archaeological ethnography is a rapidly developing field with a number of different approaches, diverse in their articulations of ethnographic and archaeological aims and methods, from ethnographies of archaeological excavations to community-based collaborative approaches as well as multi-sited research. See Herzfeld 1991, 2009 and 2010; Handler and Gable 1997; Meskell 2005 and 2007; Breglia 2006; Edgeworth 2006; Castañeda and Matthews 2008; Hamilakis and Anagnostopoulos 2009; and Mortensen and Hollowell 2009. I review a number of these works elsewhere (Lafrenz Samuels 2011).
2   I use 'democratization' to refer to foreign or internationally-driven efforts to produce political

Importantly, democratization measures encouraged by the international community extend beyond the confines of the state as well, seeking to instill democracy as the model of global governance. To achieve the shared goals of democratization and economic growth, the global citizen is moulded in this specifically western form of advanced liberal ('neoliberal') democracy, which mimics self-regulating market mechanisms. These political and economic ideals are internalized by individuals to form responsible, self-monitoring global citizens.

Ironically, however, economic development in the region reinforced rather than undermined authoritarianism. The United States and Europe have tacitly gone along with this state of affairs because of their own interests in security for the War on Terror and Europe's lucrative trade with the region.[3] Pre-Revolution Tunisia, likewise, publicly met international recommendations for opening up to global political and economic networks, with heritage tourism being one of the key sectors where Ben Ali's government performed Tunisia's 'façade democracy'.[4] Roman archaeological sites, with their monumental, western-style remains, were developed as symbols of Tunisia's own western heritage and as places where foreign tourists could experience this heritage and form perceptions of Tunisia as an open, democratic society, integrated into global economic flows, sharing both similar values and friendly relations with the West.[5]

Tourists and Tunisians (and Tunisian tourists) alike at Roman sites engage with this vision of Tunisian society and its connection to an imagined global community.[6] In doing so, they are themselves formed as citizens of the world. In this respect, archaeological sites are fashioning individuals' political selves, just as people are constructing and developing the Roman remains as a 'site'. However, the place-making implications of this study extend beyond the making of heritage citizens and the making of Roman archaeological sites, since I am also concerned with addressing why Roman archaeologists might involve themselves with studying the present contexts and uses of the Roman past.

Recent discussions on the ethics and responsibilities involved in archaeological practice advocate an embedded approach, situated within the contexts of one's work and eschewing

---

change, along the lines of S. Huntington's (1991) exposition of Third Wave democracy. The present book was in proofs before the revolution of early 2011 that demonstrated and inspired emergent forms of democratic practice to the world. On democracy and democratization in N Africa, see Anderson 1995; Entelis 1997 and 2005; Angrist 1999a and 1999b; Willis 2002; Grindle 2007. For the Middle East or Arab countries more generally, see Hudson 1996; Schlumberger 2000; and Harik 2006.

[3] Indeed, democratization efforts in N Africa call into question democracy's own potential for repression. The paradoxes of democratization measures and economic development fueling authoritarianism are laid out in Sadiki 2002a and 2002b; King 2003; Keenan 2006; Blin 2009; Durac and Cavatorta 2009; Harrigan and El-Said 2009; Holden 2009; and Powel 2009.

[4] My dissertation (Lafrenz Samuels 2010) discusses these dynamics between Tunisia and the international community at greater length in the context of developing the Roman site of Uthina for tourism.

[5] Importantly, the 'West' (and its western heritage) to which I refer is not some assumed totality but rather a project, a political goal (Asad 2003, 13).

[6] B. Anderson's (1983, 6) foundational study argued that the nation was an "imagined community" because community members will "never know most of their fellow-members, meet them, or even hear of them, yet in the minds of each lives the image of their communion". His insights have since been picked up and extended to communities beyond or alongside the nation-state: e.g., by Appadurai 1991 and Taylor 2004, among many others.

the universalizing ambition of normative ethical codes, charters and rules of conduct.[7] In negotiating an ethical engagement for archaeological practice and its products, we face the important issue of how to define the context of our work. What are the parameters of definition? Where does this context reside — at the boundaries of an archaeological site, or with the local community, region, nation-state or global community? Moreover, does our ethical engagement as archaeologists end with publications, written for an academic audience, or should we be concerned with the broader implications and uses of our work? In this respect ethics may be understood as an issue of 'place-making' in the present, in articulating the importance of defining or contouring a specific orientation between oneself and the world and between one's practices and their consequences (whether intended or not).

We have yet to fully problematize 'context' as an ethical and spatial construction, despite archaeology's focus on contextually-based interpretations of the past. The work of Roman archaeologists, which must deal with the extent and diversity of the Roman empire, responds well to many different scales of analysis. Thus our work is also situated within many present-day ethical contexts. Here I am interested in demonstrating one specific orientation: that the material heritage of the Roman empire is mobilized within global discourses on development, democracy and the making of particular kinds of citizens for this global stage. The ethical context in question concerns how Roman archaeology works at the transnational scale, shaping relationships between global and national interests.

The rise of a global heritage community: Carthage must be saved

One of the most influential international organizations working on archaeological and heritage matters is the United Nations Educational, Scientific and Cultural Organization (UNESCO), based in Paris. Through its World Heritage Centre, UNESCO manages the World Heritage List of over 900 sites whose protection concerns the whole of humanity, as both a common heritage and a common responsibility. The root of the idea for a common heritage of humankind arose from UNESCO's involvement in the Aswan High Dam.[8] Beginning in 1959, UNESCO provided financial and technical assistance to the Egyptian and Sudanese governments in order to mitigate the effects of the dam's floodwaters on the archaeological heritage of the impacted areas. The Aswan High Dam launched UNESCO's reputation as global conservator.

Prior to the Nubian campaign, UNESCO had been involved in various small-scale projects advising governments on the conservation of heritage sites, and UNESCO's work in Tunisia began shortly after the country's independence in 1956. Further, Tunisia itself was instrumental in drafting the 1972 *Convention Concerning the Protection of the World Cultural and Natural Heritage*. Tunisia's delegate, Rafik Saïd, played a pivotal rôle during the drafting process, hammering out compromise positions during the final debates over defining appropriate development, and the balance between national rights and international responsibilities.[9] The Roman legal heritage of international law was also invoked by Gérard Bola, UNESCO's Assistant Director of Culture and Communication and one

---

7   Colwell-Chanthaphonh and Ferguson 2004; Meskell and Pels 2005; Vitelli and Colwell-Chanthaphonh 2006.
8   See UNESCO 1990 and 2004.
9   Batisse and Bola 2003, 84-90. For the 1972 Convention, see UNESCO 1972.

of the main architects of the convention, who summed up his feelings on the debates and compromises reached:

> Et pour ce qu'il en étaient de mes doutes concernant certains points de détail de la Convention, je me suis dit, comme le sage jurisconsulte romain qui m'avait tant influencé au début de mes études, '*De minimis non curat praetor*'.[10]

Following the Aswan High Dam campaign, the Punic and Roman site of Carthage was UNESCO's next large international salvage project. The area covered by the ancient site of Carthage was rapidly being developed into a trendy upscale suburb of Tunis in proximity to the presidential palace. Just 6 months before the adoption of the 1972 Convention, the Director-General of UNESCO, René Maheu, addressed an audience in Carthage. His speech highlighted the campaign to save Carthage from the encroaching suburban sprawl:

> Even if nothing important or spectacular were to be discovered, it is a fine and fitting thing that the great brotherhood of those for whom there is no nobler and no more rewarding search than for the truth about Man should come together from the four corners of the earth to meet here ... Let us answer the harsh voice which, from the beginning of time, has tirelessly re-echoed its message of hate in every nation and which once said: "Carthage must be destroyed", with the call of the future which, too, is as old as mankind, which it has guided out of the shadows. This is the voice of concord, that concord which presided over the construction of the new city raised by Augustus on the ruins made by Scipio. And it is indeed with our thoughts turned more to our future, that future which we ourselves so gravely threaten, than to the past, that we say today: "Carthage must be saved". Together we shall save it.[11]

Maheu ended his speech with a heightened pitch that pits the concord of humanity, enacted through preservation, against hate and its accomplice, the destruction of material heritage. He emphasized the geographical spread — "from the four corners of the earth" and "in every nation" — of those concerned for the fate of Carthage, jointly recognizing the universality of the global community but also that the world is organized into nations. The object of concord, Carthage, is a "new city raised by Augustus on the ruins made by Scipio", encapsulating how preservation efforts will undo past neglect.[12] In this respect, the speech constructed around Cato's famous line "*Carthago delenda est*" provides a neat contrast to UNESCO's work, whose redemptive purpose involves not simply conservation but also the building of a 'new city', of presidential import, in the suburbs of Tunis. This balancing of conservation and development was necessary for the specific dynamics of Carthage, an ancient site rapidly being excavated by bulldozers to make way for new wealthy residences, but also an ancient site in which the Tunisian state saw value for developing tourism.

From these early projects at Aswan and Carthage, the concept of World Heritage was formed. Maheu's speech illustrates the comfortable position of World Heritage within

---

10 "Whatever were my doubts about some details of the Convention, I told myself, as the wise Roman lawyer who influenced me so early in my studies 'De minimis non curat praetor'" (Batisse and Bola 2003, 89). On the connections between Roman law and international law, see Maine 1861.
11 Maheu 1972, 4.
12 Note that Maheu speaks about Carthage with reference to its Roman rather than Punic heritage. This is typical of the international focus on the Roman past of Tunisia. Carthage's Punic past, on the other hand, had been mobilized by nationalist elements of the Tunisian government in support of former President Ben Ali, in political clubs called "Hannibal clubs", books (e.g., Chaâbane 2005, Haddad 2002), comic books (Belkhodja 1998, 2003), and traveling museum exhibits, among many other activities (Hazbun 2007; Saidi 2008). For a discussion comparing the Punic heritage in Sardinia and Tunisia, see van Dommelen (forthcoming).

the political philosophy of 'cosmopolitanism'. Cosmopolitanism imagines the whole of humanity as belonging to a single global community that shares an appreciation for diversity. However, cosmopolitanism is far from a unified political philosophy; it has inspired a broad literature and a number of different approaches with competing aims. Cosmopolitanism holds great potential for social justice. Yet invoking a shared global community can also be used to undermine the very concerns cosmopolitanism sought to address, particularly when it is yoked to neoliberal politics, global markets and universalizing ambitions.[13]

Making Roman archaeological sites

Western management of Roman material in North Africa bears a long legacy. The French and Italians drew on Roman material as the physical evidence of civilization and its material endurance. Their management of this heritage justified their own imperial aspirations.[14] B. Goff likens the colonial scramble for reclaiming the former territory and material heritage of the Roman empire with the "scramble for Africa", whereby "possession of the classical heritage is almost effortlessly transformed into a metonym for other kinds of possession".[15] On the eve of independence, during the 1955 Franco-Tunisian agreements, the Tunisian Department of Antiquities and the French Archaeological Mission agreed to divide up Tunisian history: the French were to be in charge of ancient history, and the Tunisians were responsible for all Islamic and later material. Meanwhile care was taken to clear major Roman sites, such as Dougga, of any material dated after the Roman period; thus a great deal of the Islamic material past was swept aside.[16] Today the region of North Africa is promoted by the World Bank as a leading example of the development of material heritage for economic growth,[17] particularly through the promotion of western tourism to sites of 'World Heritage'.[18]

The case of Dougga is instructive for understanding the place-making involved in Roman archaeological sites. Dougga is one of the most visited sites in the country due to its size and excellent preservation. The site is also important because it points beyond its local geographic particularities. Western tourists flock to Dougga not only for its global appeal as a World Heritage site but also to witness the expansive territorializing ambitions of the Roman empire, and to connect with a heritage that transcends local and national boundaries. Tourist itineraries reflect this point as well, with most tourists passing through on package tours that contribute little revenue to the local communities of New Dougga and Tebersouk.

Although relatively small in antiquity, the town was well-known for its euergetism and dual constitution: two communities living together under two municipal governments. Before the Romans arrived, Dougga was a center of power under the Numidian kingdom ruled by Massinissa (202-148 B.C.). His successors patterned their municipal

---

13   On political cosmopolitanism, see Appadurai 1991; Ivison 2002 and 2006; Nussbaum 2002; Sen 2002; and Appiah 2006. L. Meskell (2009) discusses the potential of cosmopolitanism for transformative archaeologies.
14   Shaw 1980; Mattingly 1996; Terrenato 2001; Hingley 2001, 2002 and 2005; Altekamp 2004; Begg 2004; and Munzi 2004.
15   Goff 2005, 7.
16   Mahjoubi 1997.
17   Cernea 2001a and 2001b.
18   Feilden and Jokilehto 1998; ICOMOS 2005; UNESCO 2005a.

administration on Punic models. The community was governed by *suffetes*, while the Roman colonists were governed as a *pagus*. Dougga's civic pride and dual communities have become an interpretative focal point for demonstrating historical examples of prosperity as flowing from co-existence and tolerance in the face of political plurality.[19] In this respect Dougga fits in well with the rationale of World Heritage and with the kinds of collaborative projects ongoing at the site between Tunisia, the French government, and international organizations.

Further, to make this site required archaeological work, clearance, and the delineation of site boundaries. The clearing of Dougga's undesirable levels and structures began in the 1890s with the first scientific interest in the Roman ruins. It included the clearing of modern structures as well; the town of New Dougga was created when the community residing amidst the ruins was relocated to the valley below. The process of relocation remains contested down to the present, as community members continue to use the land to keep and tend flocks, orchards and olive groves. They also use the site as a supplementary source of income by acting as guides, thereby undermining the official guides and prices. Yet recent planning for development of the site, co-ordinated bilaterally between the Tunisian and French governments, are especially eager to define the physical boundaries of the site. Previous site boundaries had been drawn up, but were not respected as UNESCO and site developers wished them to be.

Development plans envision that 'sites' are made by cordoning off the archaeological remains from the local community, to gain tighter control of site operations and create a physical boundary demarcating a specific space for World Heritage. The development partnership between Tunisia and France, and the recommendations of UNESCO, effectively ask the local community living on and near the site to reconfigure their rights of property and access into the rights of humankind, and to expand their citizenship from being rooted in a specific locality to include membership in a world community. The "common heritage of mankind" legal principle so instrumental for World Heritage sites had its genesis in theorizing property rights over oceans, Antarctica, and outer space,[20] but has now been refigured as a human right decoupled from place.[21] Of particular interest, and consequence, for the process of place-making is the community's disenfranchisement from property rights, which are being usurped by international organizations and governments espousing an allegiance to the global good. Acts of place-making simultaneously displace through their powers of enclosure. The result is an enclosure of the commons[22] for the sake of the "common heritage of humankind".

This predicament is not unique to Dougga. Similar concerns with site boundaries and what is perceived as undesirable and unaesthetic encroachments by local communities are also found at the Roman sites of Volubilis (Morocco), Timgad and Tipasa (Algeria). At Tipasa, the undesirable activities of the community are contrasted to the presence of tourists, who are regarded as breathing life into the site.[23] UNESCO's recommendations for site

---

19 Poinssot 1983; Khanoussi 1992 and 2008; Warmington and Wilson 2003; Aounallah 2005.
20 Joyner 1986; Merryman 1986; Herber 1991; and Strati 1991.
21 Jokilehto *et al.* 2005; Labadi 2007.
22 Marx 1867/1995; Chippindale 2000; and Polanyi 2001.
23 ICOMOS 1982.

boundaries are regularly ignored or superficially appeased by some segments of the local communities and by regional authorities. In the 2004 periodic report on World Heritage in Arab countries, numerous managers' reports cited urban pressure, illegal construction, illegal settlements, threats to the site's "visual integrity", garbage, and livestock grazing.[24]

Making heritage citizens

Twenty-three years after Maheu's speech at Carthage, another Director-General of UNESCO, Federico Mayor, would deliver another speech at Carthage extolling the city as a symbol of tolerance. Mayor again highlighted Carthage as a site bearing universal value, and an object lesson for simultaneously teaching universal values while "not imposing our own models, beliefs or points of view" or presuming "to lay down rules or norms for those remote from ourselves".[25] He also highlighted the importance of education in combating intolerance and becoming a "complete citizen".[26] Humanity, or becoming human, is equated to becoming a citizen of the world. This citizen is invested with responsibilities to all fellow human beings. In the context of Carthage, these responsibilities include the continuing preservation of a symbol of tolerance: a site of World Heritage.[27]

Education continues to be central to UNESCO's mission to form global citizens. Several recent publications from UNESCO are geared toward educating the youth about the responsible stewardship of the material past, particularly World Heritage.[28] For older children, a UNESCO guide for secondary school teachers in Arab countries includes lesson plans and activities on monitoring and preserving material heritage, as well as assessing tourist satisfaction.[29] For younger children UNESCO created a cartoon character named 'Patrimonito'. In each episode, Patrimonito confronts a particular threat to archaeological sites and mitigates the threat through responsible stewardship practices (e.g., Norwegian wooden churches are saved from careless disposal of cigarettes, the Plaza San Francisco de Havana is cleared of litter from thoughtless tourists, and the rock-hewn churches of Lalibela in Ethiopia are protected from weathering by erecting scaffolding). Further, many of the Patrimonito episodes include fantastic forms of technology which serve to protect and teach about the material heritage; for example, an artifact is placed in a blinking box that pops forth a visual display giving an identification of the artifact. Technology is viewed as key to building a connected global society rich in knowledge. In these cartoon strips, children are presented with a version of archaeology heavily built around various forms of technology. Archaeology is not presented as a practice of human interpretation.

At Dougga, pedagogy was joined with technology as a place-making technique. During 'Heritage Month' in May 2006, students were introduced to the site through not one but two tours: one virtual, on a bus at the entrance to the park; the other 'real', walking

---

24 UNESCO 2004, 41-42.
25 Mayor 1995, 2-3.
26 Ibid. 2.
27 Such obligations of each person to every other person, inherent to cosmopolitan philosophies, are present in archaeology's foregrounding of an ethical engagement for the discipline. As L. Meskell (2009, 6) argues, archaeology has always been cosmopolitan in outlook, working in both multi-scalar and contextual registers.
28 UNESCO 2002a, 2002b and 2005b; Aslan and Ardemagni 2006.
29 Aslan and Ardemagni 2006.

through the site with a guide. The bus at the entrance was equipped with a number of computers on which the students took turns viewing animated 3D reconstructions of the site.[30] Positioning the bus at the entrance located the physical boundary of the site while also using virtual tour technology to present a deterritorialized representation of the site before the walking tour began. Precedence is granted to the virtual tour, which feeds into globalization narratives that portray modern life as increasingly de-linked from place. However, we can also read the placement of the bus as a liminal zone that demonstrates the impossibility of a complete de-linking from place, so that heritage citizenship involves place-making that is a *re*territorialization — a novel reconfiguration of place — rather than a *de*territorialization.[31]

Didactic tools for forming heritage citizens extend to adults as well. A sign displayed behind the desk at the welcome center of the Roman site of *Sufetula* (Sbeitla) exemplifies how 'heritage citizens' are formed within the market logic of a service industry like tourism. The sign provides detailed instruction for the behavior and comportment of responsible heritage employees in welcoming tourists to the site, encouraging internal modes of self-monitoring in the employee:

Welcome in Ten Commitments
1. I shall facilitate the benefit of my services
2. I shall provide an excellent and customized welcome
3. I shall inform and advise
4. I shall be a good listener, to better serve
5. I shall evaluate the quality of the welcome to improve it
6. I shall ensure the cleanness of the surrounding environment and participate in its embellishment
7. I shall never let my sincere smile desert me
8. I shall address myself to interlocutors with politeness and kindness
9. I shall grant all cares to my appearance
10. I shall make the customer's satisfaction my first objective.

The sign is translated into 5 languages so that the tourist knows what to expect in terms of service. The employees are primarily college-age or recent graduates who have studied and are eager to talk about archaeology. Yet their expertise and knowledge is to be channeled into a service economy that promotes the experience of the visitor, with an emphasis on the right welcome, appearance and smile. Employees at Roman sites are also formed as heritage citizens through the on-going negotiation between Tunisia's 'façade democracy' and international efforts in democratizing Tunisia and the region more broadly. As the sign demonstrates, this negotiation fits into the international community's dual purposes of economic development and democratization. In the wake of the Tunisian revolution in early 2011, a well-grounded analysis awaits on the character of Tunisia's home-grown democracy and its articulation with international democratic models.[32]

---

30   Article in *La Presse* for May 8, 2006: "Dougga, ou l'initiation des jeunes à l'archéologie".
31   Deleuze and Guattari 1983; Craig and Porter 2006.
32   The revolution will likely foster new heritage management conditions in the country and region. Just how different national management practices are from previous strategies will speak to whether Tunisians' inspiring struggles for self-determination and social justice do indeed result in hard-won 'revolutionary' transformation.

Conclusion

Through the above examples I offer one perspective on the broader contexts of Roman archaeology today and how our discipline is used — through the intersections of economic development, democracy movements, and Roman material heritage — to fashion what I call 'heritage citizens'. Global relations are structured through the various bonds of obligation and rights that citizenship entails. The above examples also offer a particular orientation for understanding the contexts of Rome's material heritage in North Africa, both as a material presence that shapes specific relationships to those pasts, and a vehicle for drawing on the heritage of the western tradition to extend, justify or obscure contemporary inequalities wrought by that same tradition.

Central to any investigation of how Roman archaeology works in contemporary social, political and economic ambits is the question of how we might position ourselves within these broader contexts so as to develop a more ethically informed and responsible practice. If we consider ethical engagements to be best approached by situating our work within its many contexts, we need to pay close attention to the formation of these contexts, who defines them, and to what benefit and loss. Casting a wide net for the ethical contexts of Roman archaeology is crucial because it directs attention outward to the broader settings of Roman material heritage, the often uneasy or ambivalent relationships toward the material heritage adopted by 'the West', and its connection with empire and repression. As 'the past' is increasingly framed as a source of power and acts as a locus for authority in negotiating social relationships, we should question how this authority is made effective through the discourses and material practices of archaeology, and how the heritage of the western tradition is complicit in this process.

North Africa offers a frame of reference for interrogating the products of archaeological practice and the relationship between the West and 'the rest'. This is not simply a juxtaposition of the region's rich Roman material heritage within modern Islamic nations and indigenous Berber communities, a setting sometimes in conflict with western influences and interventions. Rather, the region also throws into stark relief the continuing legacy of colonial and imperial strategies for domination, now taking the form of economic development and international democratization efforts.

Ethical practice in Roman archaeology requires a more sharply-attuned inward optic than anything archaeology has encountered before, in questioning the discipline's place in the world and the work that it does. Yet Roman archaeology holds great promise for introspection; in studying the western tradition itself, it delves into the roots and animating spirit of the discipline of archaeology to examine deeply embedded assumptions about what archaeology is (how it is defined, studied and managed), its articulation with empire, colonialism and western hegemony, and the relationships it produces and authorizes.

Bibliography

Altekamp, S. 2004. "Italian colonial archaeology in Libya 1912-1942," in Galaty and Watkinson 2004, 55-72.

Anderson, B. 1983. *Imagined communities: reflections on the origin and spread of nationalism* (London).

Anderson, L. 1995. "North Africa: the limits of liberalization," *Current History* 94.4, 167-71.

Angrist, M. P. 1999a. "Parties, parliament and political dissent in Tunisia," *J. North African Studies* 4.4, 89-104.

Angrist, M. P. 1999b. "The expression of political dissent in the Middle East: Turkish democratization and authoritarian continuity in Tunisia," *Comparative Studies in Society and History* 41, 730-57.

Aounallah, S. 2005. "Notes sur la société et les institutions de Thugga et d'Uchi Maius (Dougga, Henchir Douemistunisie du Nord-Ouest)," *Africa n.s.* 3, 113-33.

Appadurai, A. 1991. "Global ethnoscapes: notes and queries for a transnational anthropology," in R. G. Fox (ed.), *Recapturing anthropology: working in the present* (Santa Fe, NM) 191-210.

Appiah, K. A. 2006. *Cosmopolitanism: ethics in a world of strangers* (New York).

Asad, T. 2003. *Formations of the secular: Christianity, Islam, modernity* (Stanford, CA).

Aslan, Z. and M. Ardemagni 2006. *Introducing young people to heritage site management and protection: a practical guide for secondary school teachers in the Arab region* (Rome).

Batisse, M. and G. Bolla 2003. *L'invention du 'Patrimoine Mondial'* (Paris).

Begg, D. J. I. 2004. "Fascism in the desert: a microcosmic view of archaeological politics," in Galaty and Watkinson 2004, 19-32.

Belkhodja, A. 1998. *Hannibal: the challenge of Carthage* (transl. S. Bey; Tunis).

Belkhodja, A. 2003. *Le retour de l'éléphant* (Tunis).

Blin, M. 2009. "Structural reform and the political economy of poverty reduction in Tunisia: what role for civil society?," in Harrigan and El-Said 2009, 145-75.

Breglia, L. 2006. *Monumental ambivalence: the politics of heritage* (Austin, TX).

Castañeda, Q. E. and C. N. Matthews (edd.) 2008. *Ethnographic archaeologies: reflections on stakeholders and archaeological practice* (Lanham, MA).

Cernea, M. M. 2001a. "At the cutting edge: cultural patrimony protection through development projects," in I. Serageldin, E. Shluger and J. Martin-Brown (edd.), *Historic cities and sacred sites: cultural roots for urban futures* (Washington, D.C.) 67-88.

Cernea, M. M. 2001b. *Cultural heritage and development: a framework for action in the Middle East and North Africa* (Washington, D.C.).

Chaâbane, S. 2005. *Le retour d'Hannibal ou la résurgence d'une époque* (Tunis).

Chippindale, C. 2000. "The concept of the commons," in M. J. Lynott and A. Wylie (edd.), *Ethics in American archaeology* (Washington, D.C.) 91-92.

Cohen, J. (ed.) 2002. *For love of country?* (Boston, MA).

Colwell-Chanthaphonh, C. and T. J. Ferguson 2004. "Virtue ethics and the practice of history," *J. Social Archaeology* 4, 5-27.

Craig, D. and D. Porter 2006. *Development beyond neoliberalism: governance. poverty reduction and political economy* (New York).

Deleuze, G. and F. Guattari 1983. *Anti-Oedipus: capitalism and schizophrenia* (Minneapolis, MN).

Durac, V. and F. Cavatorta 2009. "Strengthening authoritarian rule through democracy promotion? Examining the paradox of the US and EU security strategies: the case of Bin Ali's Tunisia," *Brit. J. Middle Eastern Studies* 36.1, 3-19.

Edgeworth, M. (ed.) 2006. *Ethnographies of archaeological practice: cultural encounters, material transformations* (Lanham, MA).

Entelis, J. P. (ed.) 1997. *Islam, democracy, and the state in North Africa* (Bloomington, IN).

Entelis, J. P. 2005. "The democratic imperative vs. the authoritarian impulse: the Maghrib state between transition and terrorism," *The Middle East Journal* 59.4, 537-58.

Feilden, B. M. and J. Jokilehto 1998. *Management guidelines for world cultural heritage sites* (Rome).

Galaty, M. and C. Watkinson (edd.) 2004. *Archaeology under dictatorship* (New York).

Goff, B. 2005. "Introduction," in id. (ed.), *Classics and colonialism* (London) 1-24.

Grindle, M. S. 2007. *Going local: decentralization, democratization, and the promise of good governance* (Princeton, NJ).

Haddad, M. 2002. Non delenda Carthago: *Carthage ne sera pas détruite. Autopsie de la campagne anti-tunisienne* (Paris).

Hamilakis, Y. and A. Anagnostopoulos (edd.) 2009. *Archaeological ethnographies: special issue* = *Public Archaeology* 8.2-3.

Handler, R. and E. Gable 1997. *The new history in an old museum: creating the past at Colonial Williamsburg* (Durham, NC).

Harik, I. 2006. "Democracy, 'Arab exceptionalism', and social science," *The Middle East Journal* 60.4, 664-84.

Harrigan, J. and H. El-Said 2009. *Economic liberalisation, social capital and Islamic welfare provision* (New York).

Hazbun, W. 2007. "Images of openness, spaces of control: the politics of tourism development in Tunisia," *Arab Studies Journal* 15-16, 10-35.

Herber, B. P. 1991. "The common heritage principle: Antarctica and the developing nations," *Am. J. Economics and Sociology* 50, 391-406.

Herzfeld, M. 1991. *A place in history: social and monumental time in a Cretan town* (Princeton, NJ).
Herzfeld, M. 2009. *Evicted from eternity: the restructuring of modern Rome* (Chicago, IL).
Herzfeld, M. 2010. "Engagement, gentrification, and the neoliberal hijacking of history," in L. Aiello (ed.), *Engaged anthropology: diversity and dilemmas* (= *CurrAnthr* 51, no. S.2) S259-S267.
Hingley, R. (ed.) 2001. *Images of Rome: perceptions of ancient Rome in Europe and the United States in the modern age* (JRA Suppl. 44).
Hingley, R. 2002. *Roman officers and English gentlemen: the imperial origins of Roman archaeology* (London).
Hingley, R. 2005. *Globalizing Roman culture: unity, diversity and empire* (London).
Holden, P. 2009. "Security, power or profit? The economic diplomacy of the US and the EU in North Africa," *J. North African Studies* 14.1, 11-32.
Hudson, M. 1996. "Obstacles to democratization in the Middle East," *Contention* 5.2, 81-105.
Huntington, S. 1991. *The Third Wave: democratization in the late twentieth century* (Norman, OK).
International Council on Monuments and Sites (ICOMOS) 1982. *Tipasa: advisory board evaluation* (Paris).
International Council on Monuments and Sites (ICOMOS) 2005. *Background paper: special expert meeting of the World Heritage convention on the concept of outstanding universal value, Kazan, 2005* (Paris).
Ivison, D. 2002. *Postcolonial liberalism* (Cambridge).
Ivison, D. 2006. "Emergent cosmopolitanism: indigenous peoples and international law," in R. Tinnevelt and G. Verschraegen (edd.), *Between cosmopolitan ideals and state sovereignty* (New York) 120-34.
Jokilehto, J. et al. 2005. *The World Heritage List: filling the gaps — an action plan for the future, monuments and sites* (Paris).
Joyner, C. C. 1986. "Legal implications of the concept of the common heritage of mankind," *The International and Comparative Law Quarterly* 35, 190-99.
Keenan, J. H. 2006. "Security and insecurity in North Africa," *Review of African Political Economy* 108, 269-96.
Khanoussi, M. 1992. "Thugga (Dougga) sous le Haut-empire: une ville double?," *L'Africa Romana* 10, 597-602.
Khanoussi, M. 2008. *Dougga* (2nd edn.; Tunis).
King, S. J. 2003. *Liberalization against democracy: the local politics of economic reform in Tunisia* (Bloomington, IN).
Labadi, S. 2007. "Representations of the nation and cultural diversity in discourse on World Heritage," *J. Social Archaeology* 7, 147-70.
Lafrenz Samuels, K. 2010. *Mobilizing heritage in the Maghrib: rights, development, and transnational archaeologies* (Ph D. diss., Stanford Univ.).
Lafrenz Samuels, K. 2011. "Field work: constructing archaeological and ethnographic intersections," *Camb. Arch. J.* 21.1, 152-56.
Maheu, R. 1972. *Saving Carthage* (Paris).
Mahjoubi, A. 1997. "Reflections on the historiography of the ancient Maghrib," in M. Le Gall and K. J. Perkins (edd.), *The Maghrib in question: essays in history and historiography* (Austin, TX) 17-34.
Maine, H. J. S. 1861. *Ancient law: its connection with the early history of society and its relation to modern ideas* (London).
Marx, K. 1867/1995. *Capital* (Oxford).
Mattingly, D. 1996. "From one colonialism to another: imperialism in the Maghreb," in J. Webster and N. Cooper (edd.), *Roman imperialism: post-colonial perspectives* (Leicester Archaeology Monog. 3) 49-69.
Mayor, F. 1995. *Introduction: the teaching of tolerance in the Mediterranean area* (Paris).
Merryman, J. H. 1986. "Two ways of thinking about cultural property," *Am. J. Int. Law* 80.4, 831-53.
Meskell, L. 2005. "Archaeological ethnography: conversations around Kruger National Park," *Archaeologies: Journal of the World Archaeological Congress* 1.1, 83-102.
Meskell, L. 2007. "Falling walls and mending fences: archaeological ethnography in the Limpopo," *J. Southern African Studies* 33, 383-400.
Meskell, L. 2009. "Cosmopolitan heritage ethics," in ead (ed.), *Cosmopolitan archaeologies* (Durham, NC) 1-27.
Meskell, L. and P. Pels 2005. "Introduction: embedding ethics," in iid. (edd.), *Embedding ethics* (New York) 1-28.
Mortensen, L. and J. Hollowell (edd.) 2009. *Ethnographies and archaeologies: iterations of the past* (Gainesville, FL).

Munzi, M. 2004. "Italian archaeology in Libya: from colonial Romanità to decolonization of the past," in Galaty and Watkinson 2004, 73-108.

Nussbaum, M. 2002. "Patriotism and cosmopolitanism," in Cohen 2002, 3-17.

Poinssot, C. 1983. *Les ruines de Dougga* (2nd edn.; Tunis).

Polanyi, K. 2001. *The great transformation: the political and economic origins of our time* (2nd edn.; Boston, MA).

Powel, B. T. 2009. "The stability syndrome: US and EU democracy promotion in Tunisia," *J. North African Studies* 14.1, 57-73.

Sadiki, L. 2002a. "Bin Ali's Tunisia: democracy by non-democratic means," *Brit. J. Middle Eastern Studies* 29.1, 57-78.

Sadiki, L. 2002b. "The search for citizenship in Bin Ali's Tunisia: democracy versus unity," *Political Studies* 50, 497-513.

Saidi, H. 2008. "When the past poses beside the present: aestheticising politics and nationalising modernity in a postcolonial time," *J. Tourism and Cultural Change* 6.2, 101-19.

Schlumberger, O. 2000. "The Arab Middle East and the question of democratization: some critical remarks," *Democratization* 7.4, 104-32.

Sen, A. 2002. "Humanity and citizenship," in Cohen 2002, 111-18.

Shaw, B. D. 1980. "Archaeology and knowledge: the history of the African provinces of the Roman empire," *Florilegium* 2, 28-60.

Strati, A. 1991. "Deep seabed cultural property and the common heritage of mankind," *Int. and Comp. Law Quarterly* 40, 859-94.

Taylor, C. 2004. *Modern social imaginaries* (Durham, NC).

Terrenato, N. 2001. "Ancestor cults: the perception of Rome in modern Italian culture," in Hingley 2001, 71-89.

UNESCO 1972. *Convention concerning the protection of the World Cultural and Natural Heritage* (Paris).

UNESCO 1990. "The World Heritage Convention: a new idea takes shape," *The UNESCO Courier* Oct. 1990, 44-45.

UNESCO 2002a. *Mobilizing young people for World Heritage* (Paris).

UNESCO 2002b. *World Heritage in young hands* (Paris).

UNESCO 2004. *Periodic report and regional programme: Arab states 2000-2003* (World Heritage Reports 11).

UNESCO 2005a. *Operational guidelines for the implementation of the World Heritage convention*, WHC-05/2 (Paris).

UNESCO 2005b. *World Heritage: today and tomorrow with young people* (Paris).

van Dommelen, P. forthcoming. "Punic identities and modern perceptions in the west Mediterranean," in J. Quinn and N. Vella (edd.), *Identifying the Punic Mediterranean* (BSR Monog.).

Vitelli, K. D. and C. Colwell-Chanthaphonh (edd.) 2006. *Archaeological ethics* (2nd edn.; Walnut Creek, CA).

Warmington, B. H. and R. J. A. Wilson 2003. "Thugga," in S. Hornblower and A. Spawforth (edd.), *The Oxford classical dictionary* (3rd edn. rev.; Oxford) 1521.

Willis, M. J. 2002. "Political parties in the Maghrib: the illusion of significance?" *J. North African Studies* 7.2, 1-22.

COMMENTARY
Inheriting Roman places
Richard Hingley

The papers presented in the second part of this volume addressed how Roman places — including ruins and landscapes — are inherited and re-worked, and how archaeologists contribute to this active creation of place through their excavations, displays, and interpretations (Lafrenz Samuels and Totten). Many monuments across the Roman empire survive in sufficiently impressive condition that they have been reworked in later times for a variety of reasons.[1] Three of the papers address the re-making of a number of Roman places in the contemporary world, but one (Paludan-Müller) explores how classical concepts of built space influenced past societies. One significant issue that is raised by these papers is how archaeologists can work ethically when contributing to the re-making of Roman places. Many of the past accounts of the reception of Roman culture have built fairly monolithic ideas about the centralizing power of the image of Rome, an idea that is reflected upon in a number of these papers. For Paludan-Müller, the Roman empire has never been supplanted by any other common point of reference in the West. In Lafrenz Samuels' paper, the fundamental rôle played by classical Roman models in the formation of western imperialism provides the context for a critical and self-reflexive appreciation of Roman place-making, emphasizing the particular significance of Roman studies to the contemplation of contemporary archaeological ethics. To ground these ideas, recent accounts have proposed that Rome operated across its empire as a transformative power that served to articulate local, provincial and imperial identities,[2] a perspective that helps to bring further clarity to the power of Rome as a centralizing concept.[3]

The study of nation-making through the manipulation of Roman monuments is not new to archaeology,[4] but the papers in this volume demonstrate that, in the contemporary world, Roman places also play vital rôles in creating and cementing regional identities and in fostering global citizenship through tourism (Lafrenz Samuels; Totten). They explore the variety of ways in which Rome operates to create such connections in a number of places across the central, southern and eastern Mediterranean. They make a considerable contribution to discussions of the values projected by the inheritance and re-use of Roman remains today, particularly because they focus attention on areas that often appear ill-served by recent writings about national uses of the image of Rome. Attention has often been focused upon the reception of Roman images and remains across Western Europe, including Italy and the western Mediterranean,[5] but far less critical attention has been paid to the rôle of Rome as an inherited image across N Africa and the eastern Mediterranean.[6] This makes the contributions here that explore Roman place-making in Tunisia (Lafrenz Samuels) and Greek and Turkish Cyprus (Gordon) particularly welcome. Indeed, all four

---

1 E.g., Hopkins and Beard 2005; Hingley 2010; Witcher *et al.* 2010.
2 Woolf 1998 and 2001; Witcher 2000.
3 See Hingley 2005 and 2009; Morley 2010.
4 E.g., Moatti 1993; Hingley 2000; Struck 2001; Terrenato 2001; Wulff Alonso 2003.
5 For Italy, see Mouritsen 1998; Terrenato 2001; Hopkins and Beard 2005. For Spain, see Wulff Alonso 2003. For Britain, see Hingley 2000 and 2008. For Germany, see Struck 2001.
6 But see Bénabou 1976; Mattingly 1996; Ball 2000.

papers offer new directions that serve to emphasize the range of ways that Rome is drawn upon in the contemporary world.

I will draw out three interrelated themes from these papers to consider how they can contribute to the self-reflexive tradition in Roman archaeology.

Rome as a centralizing image

The ways that Rome has been drawn on in nationalizing discourses in the modern world is a popular topic,[7] but Paludan-Müller's paper raises a number of interesting issues. The ruined monuments of the City of Rome and the other Roman cities provide one significant legacy of the Roman Empire. Paludan-Müller shows that the concepts behind the spatial organization of these structures were drawn upon in the West to cement national unity, for example in the France of Louis XIV and Napoleon I, in Fascist Germany and Italy in the 20th c., and in the United States during the 18th to 20th c. He also argues that the national context of much of the research that is undertaken on the Roman Empire potentially blinds Romanists from fully appreciating "the dependence of empire on sustained diversity for its own resilience" (146). This is because most of this research is undertaken within institutions and traditions "shaped under the nation-state" (146). Nation-states, according to Paludan-Müller, often act to suppress the diversity on which empires are based.

The complexity here is that, although ethnic and cultural diversity usually have been important in attempts to create imperial unity, many empires resorted to alternative means of force and imposition to create order.[8] Nationhood and imperialism appear often to have had a complex interrelationship of mutual dependence, both in the ancient and the modern worlds. N. Shumate's study, *Nation, empire and decline*, explores how Roman colonial discourse stressed the unifying action of Rome; she also addresses the means through which these ideas were taken on board to define national rhetoric from the Renaissance to the 21st c.[9] The mutual inter-dependence of national and imperial discourses through time appears fundamental to the long-term survival of empires.

The unifying image of imperial Rome as a nationalizing discourse has often been countered in particular contexts through a focus on the negative aspects of Roman imperialism. Two of the papers in this volume explore cultural traditions of place-making that draw on a critical reading of the Roman example — in other words, they seek to explore how images of Rome are drawn upon to create anti-Roman forms of unity. Gordon writes of the "politicization of Roman archaeology within national narratives" (112) on either side of the divide between Turkish and Greek Cyprus. Gordon argues that the Turkish view of the Roman occupation of Cyprus is based on the idea of the Romans as cruel invaders, who suppressed local populations, including replacing and supplanting the classical Greek culture in the island (122-24). This is reminiscent of other nationalizing accounts in various countries of Western Europe that have drawn upon the cruelty of imperial Rome.[10]

---

7   For examples of nationalizing discourses, see Mouritsen 1998, Hingley 2000; Struck 2001; Terrenato 2001; Wulff Alonso 2003; Shumate 2006.
8   I am thinking here of the British Empire of the 19th-20th c., which is often felt to have fallen partly because of its failure to integrate ethnic variation across its vast territories.
9   Shumate 2006; cf. Webster 1996, 12.
10 E.g., for Germany, see Struck 2001, 98-99. For Britain, see Hingley 2008, 127-28.

D. Totten argues that in Italy a renewed focus on Italy's individual regions has developed since the end of the Second World War, building on origins in the 17th to 19th c. This re-invention of tradition has occurred as a reaction to the unifying nationalistic Roman archaeology of Mussolini's Fascist Italian state.[11] In this context, Rome is too abrasive an image for many Italian cities today (Totten 135, n.29). The Etruscan identity communicates the aspirations of this region more effectively to an international audience, including the assertion that Rome took on the culture of Etruria, incorporated it into its own repertoire, and then exported it across the Roman world (135). This is an image with a particular regional valence, one that distances the Etruscans from the negative connotations of national and imperial dictatorial domination, but also includes the claim that in the classical past the region made a significant contribution to both European and world civilization, an idea which justifies the global significance of the Etruscan World Heritage sites.

Totten argues that the Etruscan cemeteries of Cerveteri and Tarquinia contribute significantly to place-making at the national and international levels. They are defined as "exceptional and unique representations of Etruscan culture" that justifies their inscription as World Heritage Sites (Totten, 136). It is the readability of these places as monuments that have not been altered by later occupation (except, of course, as a result of their excavation and display) that leads to their international significance as sites that communicate regional connections to international cultural development. These are ideas that, to a degree, counter the idea of Roman imperial centralization and military force, but they are also claims that foster regional unity in a way that is comparable to nationalizing discourses.

Rome as a globalizing image

Paludan-Müller draws on M. Hardt and A. Negri's influential but contested study of globalization, *Empire*, an account that emphasizes the fundamental rôle of diversity in empire.[12] This book has had a significant impact on Roman studies by helping to re-conceptualize ideas about Roman imperialism and culture.[13] For example, N. Morley states:

> Hardt and Negri's monumental *Empire* takes Rome as the model for the all-encompassing world order, generating its own basis of legitimacy by presenting its order as permanent, eternal and necessary.[14]

Hardt and Negri build upon the centralizing nature of Roman models, since they construct an understanding of Roman culture as a tool in the creation of cultural unity, but posit a unity that is itself based on hybrid forms of identity.[15]

A number of papers in this volume provide interesting insights into the contemporary relevance of global images of regional variation in the making of Roman places. The editors draw out this issue in their Introduction, stressing that:

> In many ways the heritage of the Roman empire better suits place-making at the global and regional scale rather than the national, which is one reason why Roman material bears increased relevance in today's globalizing society (Lafrenz Samuels and Totten, 22)

---

11 Terrenato 2001, 82.
12 Hardt and Negri 2000.
13 Including Hingley 2005, 9 and 117-19; id. 2009, 61 and 70; Willis 2007; Morley 2010, 125-27.
14 Morley 2010, 8.
15 See Hingley 2009, 70-71.

In Gordon's study of Cyprus, the Romans have a deeply contrasting significance for communities to either side of the 20th-c. *'limes'* formed by the frontier between the Greek and the Turkish territories. As already remarked, Gordon expresses the Turkish view of the Romans as cruel invaders, but the Greek Cypriot use of the image puts an equally nationalist yet more Eurocentric spin on the former Roman control of the island, expressing the rôle of Rome as cultural preserver. Gordon observes (118) that this national narrative allows modern Greek Cypriots to claim a continuous connection with Cyprus stretching back three millennia. This is a claim that ties the remains of their ancient past into the discourse of Hellenism, which itself is one of the key concepts behind Eurocentric concepts of European origin. Evidently both the contrasting positive and negative images of Rome that are drawn upon in Cyprus project views that ultimately derived from the writings of Latin authors.[16]

Lafrenz Samuels writes of the pride of Tunisians for the mosaics from their impressive Roman ruins as ways in which the current population can counter "colonial legacies and predatory trade agreements" (159). This is accomplished by effectively claiming these remains and, indeed, the Roman Empire, as Tunisia's own, since the well-preserved Roman monuments of Tunisia are built according to a fairly common Mediterranean style of architectural design.[17] The power of this idea is that it links the country more closely with Western heritage while also drawing on influential political alignments focusing on Tunisian democracy and aiming to encourage successful tourism to provide income to local communities and to the government itself (Lafrenz Samuels, 159-60). These are issues that have serious ethical implications that the author draws upon with careful consideration since, as elsewhere in today's world, economic integration can sometimes be seen to be reinforcing authoritarianism rather than helping to undermine it.

Problems with the Roman inheritance

Lafrenz Samuels provides a highly critical take on Roman place-making, expressing how such an attitude to the heritage

> directs attention outward to the broader settings of Roman material heritage, the often uneasy or ambivalent relationships toward the material heritage adopted by 'the West', and its connection with empire and repression (167).

This ties in with Paludan-Müller's observation (145), that the "imperial mirror" strongly characterizes Roman heritage in the present. Lafrenz Samuels shows that, even though they are used to communicate positive messages to support the tourist industry, the Roman remains in Tunisia help to throw into "stark relief" the continuing legacies of colonial and imperial control, issues that still deeply influence Tunisia's relationship with the West. The fundamental rôle played by classical Roman models in the formation of Western imperialism therefore becomes the context for a critical appreciation of Roman place-making. For an author who is writing from a Western perspective, such issues make the study of Roman imperialism deeply relevant today. In a recent volume, Morley has argued that the Roman empire is worth studying as a means to understand and question "modern conceptions of empire and imperialism, and the way they are deployed in contemporary political debates".[18]

---

16   For the complexity and subtlety of Roman imperial discourse, see Shumate 2006, 83-93.
17   This forms an interesting example of "The Empire writes back"; see Ashcroft *et al.* 1989.
18   Morley 2010, 10.

A focus on Roman place-making in N Africa and the eastern Mediterranean gives such a focus a particular economic and political immediacy.

Totten considers that archaeologists have focused considerable interest on understanding how archaeology operates in the "service of the state", but that we also need to grapple with how this heritage sits in "the complex nexus of local, national, supranational and international organizations and institutions" (142). This asks archaeologists and heritage managers to assess the values that Roman places, including World Heritage Sites, communicate. This is vital in order for us to work beyond the nationalistic and globalizing stereotypes that often appear to be promoted.[19] It also requires that we should aim to engage not just the tourists and visitors but also local residents to contribute to, use, and appreciate the complex identities represented by these monuments. Challenging simple and oppositional views by expressing the complexity of the past and its political relationship to the present should form part of the responsibility of heritage managers, creating approaches for what Lafrenz Samuels calls "heritage citizens", a category that includes all types of visitors and the national, regional and local communities in the countries that contain these places. Gordon (127) observes that:

> Since both Cypriot polities are presently engaged in seeking a just solution to the 'Cyprus problem', the time seems right to suggest that an official, reflexive review of how Roman archaeology is both marketed and politicized should be initiated on *both* sides of the Cypriot divide.

An equally critical reflexive approach to Roman places across the whole of Europe, N Africa and the Near East would be valuable, producing accounts that articulate a complex mosaic of regional responses to Rome and also reflecting the different contexts in which its heritage has been received and managed in today's increasing global world.

Summary

In conclusion, these four papers offer stimulating accounts of a number of new ways in which studies of Roman culture are developing. By exploring the re-creation of Roman remains and architectural concepts in recent and contemporary contexts, they work to create a connection between studies of the Roman Empire and works that have been developing post-colonial approaches to classic writings.[20] A focus on contemporary Roman place-making in the southern and eastern parts of the Mediterranean basin brings archaeologists face to face with ethical issues that should be at the core of our discipline in the early 21st c., topics which resonate with the 'post-colonial' writings that have been transforming Roman archaeology for the past two decades.

Bibliography

Ashcroft, B. *et al.* 1989. *The empire writes back: theory and practice in post-colonial literatures* (London).
Ball, W. 2000. *Rome in the East: the transformation of an empire* (London).
Bénabou, M. 1976. *La résistance africaine à la romanisation* (Paris).
Goff, B. (ed.) 2005. *Classics and colonialism* (London).
Hardt, M. and A. Negri 2000. *Empire* (London).
Hardwick, L. and C. Gillespie (edd.) 2007. *Classics in post-colonial worlds* (Oxford).
Hingley, R. 2000. *Roman officers and English gentlemen: the imperial origins of Roman archaeology* (London).

---

19   E.g., Labadi 2007; Witcher *et al.* 2010, 115.
20   See Goff 2005; Shumate 2005; Hardwick and Gillespie 2007; Morley 2010.

Hingley, R. (ed.) 2001. *Images of Rome: perceptions of ancient Rome in Europe and the United States in the modern age* (JRA Suppl. 44).
Hingley, R. 2005. *Globalizing Roman culture: unity, diversity and empire* (London).
Hingley, R. 2008. *The recovery of Roman Britain 1586-1906: 'a colony so fertile'* (London).
Hingley, R. 2009. "Cultural diversity and unity: empire and Rome," in S. Hales and T. Hodos (edd.), *Material culture and social identities in the ancient world* (New York) 54-75.
Hingley, R. 2010. "Tales of the frontier: diasporas on Hadrian's Wall," in H. Eckardt (ed.), *Roman diasporas: archaeological approaches to mobility and diversity* (JRA Suppl. 78) 227-43.
Hopkins, K. and M. Beard 2005. *The Colosseum* (London).
Labadi, S. 2007. "Representations of the nation and cultural diversity in discourses on World Heritage," *J. Social Archaeology* 7.2, 147-70.
Mattingly, D. 1996. "From one colonialism to another: imperialism in the Maghreb," in Webster and Cooper 1996, 49-70.
Moatti, C. 1993. *The search for ancient Rome* (London).
Morley, N. 2010. *The Roman empire: roots of imperialism* (New York).
Mouritsen, H. 1998. *Italian unification: a study in ancient and modern historiography* (London).
Shumate, N. 2006. *Nation, empire, decline: studies in rhetorical continuity from the Romans to the modern era* (London).
Struck, M. 2001. "The Heilige Römische Reich Deutscher Nation and Hermann the German," in Hingley 2001, 91-112.
Terrenato, N. 2001. "Ancestor cults: the perception of ancient Rome in modern Italian culture," in Hingley 2001, 71-90.
Webster, J. 1996. "Roman imperialism and the 'post-imperial age'," in ead. and Cooper 1996, 1-18.
Webster, J. and N. Cooper (edd.) 1996. *Roman imperialism: post-colonial perspectives* (Leicester Archaeology Monog. 3).
Willis, I. 2007. "The empire never ended," in Hardwick and Gillespie 2007, 329-48.
Witcher, R. 2000. "Globalisation and Roman imperialism: perspectives on identities in Roman Italy," in E. Herring and K. Lomas (edd.), *The emergence of state identities in Italy in the first millennium B.C.* (Specialist Studies on Italy 8; London) 213-25.
Witcher, R., D. P. Tolia Kelly and R. Hingley 2010. "Archaeologies of landscape: excavating the materialities of Hadrian's Wall," *J. Material Culture* 15.1, 105-28.
Woolf, G. 1998. *Becoming Roman: the origins of provincial civilization in Gaul* (Cambridge).
Woolf, G. 2001. "The Roman cultural revolution in Gaul," in S. Keay and N. Terrenato (edd.), *Italy and the West: comparative issues in Romanization* (Oxford) 173-86.
Wulff Alonso, F. 2003. *Las esencias patrias* (Barcelona).